Gun**Digest**® PRESENTS

CONCEALED CARRY CLASS

THE ABCs OF SELF-DEFENSE TOOLS AND TACTICS

TOM GIVENS

Gun Digest® Books, an imprint of Caribou Media Group, LLC
Gun Digest Media
5600 W. Grande Market Drive, Suite 100
Appleton, WI 54913
www.gundigest.com

To order books or other products call 920.471.4522 ext. 104
or visit us online at **www.gundigeststore.com**

CAUTION: Technical data presented here, particularly technical data on handloading and on firearms adjustment and alteration, inevitably reflects individual experience with particular equipment and components under specific circumstances the reader cannot duplicate exactly. Such data presentations therefore should be used for guidance only and with caution. Caribou Media accepts no responsibility for results obtained using these data.

ISBN-13: 978-1-946267-95-5

Cover Design by Gene Coo
Interior Design by Dave Hauser
Edited by Chuck Smock
Photos by Yamil Sued (unless otherwise noted)

Printed in the United States of America

10 9 8 7 6 5 4 3 2

contents

Author Tom Givens has more than four decades experience as a firearms instructor and spent 25 years in various aspects of law enforcement and specialized security work, including stints in street patrol and investigations.

Introduction

Why another book on shooting? There are lots of books about guns and shooting, but darn few about fighting with the gun to save your life or that of a loved one. In this book I have tried to go beyond the basics of how a handgun works, and how to shoot it, and get into how to integrate that handgun into your overall personal security program. Skill with a handgun is needed, but that skill is useless without an understanding of the dynamics of fighting, and the commitment to take control of one's own fate.

Why consider my advice on the subject? That's a fair question, since bad advice on personal-defense matters could be very costly. I consider myself a lifelong serious student of defensive weaponcraft, and as a serious student, I continually strive to learn more about my field. I have found teaching a subject is the best way to truly learn it, and I have been teaching weaponcraft for some 44 years, full time for the past 23 years. I have been carrying a gun professionally in one form or another for 49 years at this writing. Before I became a full-time instructor, I spent 25 years in various aspects of law enforcement and specialized security work, including stints in street patrol and investigations, and I have arrested scores of armed and dangerous criminals. I have been involved in armed confrontations both as a police officer and as a private citizen, and I have seen firsthand that decent people, with proper training, can fight back and overcome criminal attacks.

I owned and operated my own firing range and training center for more than 18 years. During that time, I oversaw the firing of about 1.5 million handgun rounds each year, with all types of handguns. During those years I trained about 2,500 students each year, from private citizens to security personnel and police officers to military police, intelligence units and Special Forces detachments. I also teach on the road, all over the United States and in Europe. Over the years, scores of my military students have used the skills we teach successfully in combat, and at this writing we have had more than 65 private-citizen students involved in defensive gunplay in the United States. These are just the ones I know of, who have reported back to me or been reported to me through law-enforcement channels. Thus, we have a lot of feedback on, and validation of, our training techniques.

In addition, I have actively competed with a handgun for many years, allowing me to continually evaluate guns and related gear in simulated armed conflicts. I not only got to see how my gear worked, I got to observe hundreds of other competitors using their guns and accessories in at least somewhat realistic conditions and under a fair bit of stress. I shot on the rifle team in high school, and I shot in Police Pistol Combat early in my law enforcement career. Back in the day, I held a Class A rating in IPSC, when that was the highest rating available. I also won several state and regional championships in the 1970s and 1980s in that game. I was involved in helping set up the International Defensive Pistol Association (IDPA), with a member number A00008. I also spent two years on the board of directors during IDPA's early formative years. I hold a Master rating in three IDPA divisions: CDP, ESP and SSP. I

have won several state and regional championships in IDPA competitions. All of this gives me a pretty broad perspective on the competitive shooting side of the handgun world.

I also hunt with a handgun, having harvested a number of deer and wild hogs while using a service type handgun.

Over the years I have done a fair bit of work as an expert witness in court cases involving firearms and firearms training. I've been accepted as an expert witness in federal courts in Alaska, Kansas, Tennessee and Illinois. I have been accepted as an expert by state courts in Illinois, Alaska, Ohio, Mississippi and Tennessee. My personal reference library contains more than 300 books on firearms and firearms training. This is my fifth published textbook on the subject, and I've written more than 100 magazine articles in SWAT Magazine, Combat Handguns, Handguns, American Handgunner, Soldier of Fortune and other publications.

It has been said that a book like this is 95-percent plagiarism and 5-percent opinion (I stole that line from fellow trainer John Mattera). Very few of us invent anything new in this business. What we do is observe each other's techniques, listen to each other's explanations, take each other's training, and attempt to adopt what works and discard the rest. In this I have been most fortunate, as over the years I have

The author was involved in helping set up the International Defensive Pistol Association (IDPA), with a member number A00008. He also spent two years on the board of directors during IDPA's early formative years. He holds a Master rating in three IDPA divisions and has won several state and regional championships in IDPA competitions.

trained with a virtual Who's Who in the firearms training industry. This has given me exposure to a broad range of training styles, tactical techniques and instructional methods, and I have combined and distilled these into my curriculum. My sincere thanks go out to these dedicated teachers, who have taught me so much of what I'm trying to pass on to you in this book. These instructors include Jeff Cooper, Chuck Taylor, Ken Hackathorn, Jim Higginbotham, Clint Smith, Dennis Tueller, John Farnam, Dave Grossi, Southnarc, Ernest Langdon, Jeff Gonzales, Massad Ayoob, Wayne Dobbs, Todd Green and many others. I attended an advanced 499 course at Gunsite all the way back in 1980. I have attended the NRA's Law Enforcement Firearms Instructor Schools for handgun, shotgun and Tactical Shooting Instructor, and I have been through the FBI police firearms instructor school. Truthfully, I have learned something of value in

every single class I've taken over the past four decades, and I am deeply indebted to all the trainers who have allowed me to get to this point. This book is intended as a sort of conduit for wisdom from all of these assorted sources to you.

I sincerely hope this book will make you think about your personal security and how to achieve it. The mental skills involved in gun fighting are more important than the physical skills, and mental skills require personal effort, just like learning physical skills. The end result of this effort is, of course, peace of mind, which is well worth the time and effort invested.

Finally, I would like to thank Yamil Sued and Tamara Keel, who took the photographs used to illustrate this work. Also, a big thanks to Ken Campbell and the staff at Gunsite, who let us use some of their equipment and one of their ranges for some of the photography.

Author's Note

T his book is divided into two sections. The first half deals specifically with the software issues I alluded to in the introduction. This covers such things as legal issues, controlling stress, learning to be more aware of your environment and making tactical decisions under stress.

The second half deals with the hardware issues, such as gun selection, holster selection, ammunition and shooting technique.

Both of these areas, software and hardware, require attention, time and effort. Far too many people focus solely on the hardware and neglect the software issues. This can be a very costly mistake.

The author has trained with a wide variety of the most well-known firearms instructors in the industry. This training has given him exposure to a broad range of training styles, tactical techniques and instructional methods, and he has combined and distilled these disciplines into his teaching curriculum.

1

WHY CARRY A CONCEALED WEAPON?

"The number-one cause of on-the-job deaths in the United States is homicide."

For many of us, this type of question seems silly, given the current state of affairs in the United States early in the 21st century. Carrying a concealed weapon allows one, regardless of gender, age or physical ability, to control his or her own immediate environment and thereby have options in various emergencies that unarmed people simply do not enjoy. Carrying a gun is simply part of recognizing and accepting responsibility for one's own actions, one's own safety and the security of one's own family. Indeed, with the level of lawlessness evident in today's society, it might be the social duty of decent, intelligent people to arm themselves.

A cursory review of recent statistics is all the justification we need:

• The number-one cause of on-the-job deaths in the United States is homicide.

• One of every six on-the-job deaths is a homicide.

Each year in the U.S., there are about 15,000 reported murders. This figure does not include homicides not reported, including persons who just vanished without a trace. The true figure is thought to be closer to 30,000 to 40,000 persons.

Advances in trauma care mean fewer than one in 10 people who are shot with a firearm actually dies from that injury. In 2017, there were almost 1 million people shot, stabbed or bludgeoned seriously in the U.S.

Although these did not become homicide statistics, thousands of them were left blind, paralyzed or otherwise crippled for life. In Memphis, Tennessee, for instance, in 2013 there were 154 homicides. There were, however, 9,165 incidences in which someone tried to kill someone else; they just were not successful. The main trauma center there, for instance, which is only one hospital out of 20 in the metropolitan area, treated 3,100 people for gunshot wounds that year alone. According to the U.S. Department of Justice, Bureau of Justice Statistics (BJS), almost 6 million people a year in the U.S. are victims of some violent crime each year. Therefore, this is not some arcane, esoteric threat that occasionally happens. Violence and violent crime are an everyday fact of life in modern U.S. cities.

The annual BJS report for 2017 showed the following numbers, for just that one year: total violent crimes, 5,612,670; rapes, female victim, 393,980; robbery, 613,840; aggravated assault, 993,170; serious violent crime involving injury to the victim, 643,760; stranger violence (victim and offender unknown to each other), 2,034,100.

According to the BJS, you have a 1-in-49 chance of being the victim of a violent crime in a single

Throughout most of this past century, as the population became more urbanized and government began playing a larger role in everyone's daily life, more and more cities/states adopted laws against the carrying of weapons in a misguided attempt to prevent violence. It hasn't worked very well, has it? In Chicago (pictured) alone, more than 530 people were murdered in 2018. (File photo)

> **"I do not carry a pistol so that I may impose my will on others. I carry a pistol so that others may not impose their will on me."**

year, not your lifetime. So, the odds are not "one in a million," they are "one in a few dozen." If we only consider aggravated assault and no other violent crimes, there were an average of 2,721 aggravated assaults per day in 2017. The FBI's definition of aggravated assault is "an unlawful attack involving serious bodily injury to the victim, or the use of a deadly weapon or other means likely to cause death or serious injury." In other words, that's almost 3,000 times each day someone tries to injure someone else in the United States. Taking sensible precautions against something that common is not being paranoid, it's being smart.

Each year, fewer than a dozen people die from snake bites in the United States, and around 50 are killed by lightning. Almost everyone takes precautions against snake bites and lightning strikes, although statistically the threat is insignificant. Criminal violence, on the other hand, takes place every day, in every sort of place, all over the nation, and effects one in every 50 people every year. Why then doesn't everyone carry a gun? Everyone likes to think, "Violent crime only happens to someone else." Well, to everyone else on the planet, you are someone else!

Consider this data from the FBI uniform crime report for 2017, a sadly typical year. In that one year, there were 1,247,321 violent, interpersonal crimes reported by police agencies to the FBI. These are murder, forcible rape, robbery, aggravated assault, and assault. Please note that this is a voluntary reporting system, and many police agencies do not report totals to the FBI, so this number is actually much lower than the true total. According to the FBI, aggravated assault accounted for 65 percent of these violent crimes, while robbery accounted for 25.6 percent. These are the crimes that require us to go armed.

Most people are what I call willfully ignorant. Not only do they not know the actual level of crime indicated by these statistics, they don't want to know. If they knew, they might actually have to do something about it.

Throughout most of this past century, as the population became more urbanized and government began playing a larger role in everyone's daily life, more and more cities/states adopted laws against the carrying of weapons in a misguided attempt to prevent violence. It hasn't worked very well, has it? In addition, the populace has been taught for several generations now to depend on the government for everything, including education, social mores and personal security. The problem is, the government cannot and will not guarantee your personal safety. The police, except in extremely rare cases, will only come along after the fact to make a report. Your personal safety is, as it always has been, your responsibility.

Over the past decade or so, a number of states have recognized that a disarmed citizenry is at the nonexistent mercy of sociopathic criminals who often engage in mindless violence even after the victims have submitted. The proliferation of drugs, youth gangs and highly disturbed persons has created a call from citizens that they be allowed the means to protect themselves and their families; and this call has been answered in every state. As of 2014, all 50 states in the U.S. have at least a theoretical system for private citizens to acquire a permit or license to carry a handgun on their person for self-defense. Illinois, the last holdout, was forced to come online in 2014. In fact, states that have enacted reasonable carry permit laws have since seen a decline in the rate of homicide and other violent crimes. It should be obvious that citizens who go to considerable time, paperwork, and expense to legally carry a firearm will not be a problem. The problem is the population of thugs who ignore laws against murder, rape, robbery, drug peddling, etc., and who should not then be expected to obey laws against carrying guns.

One thing I would like you to consider: In our culture there is always a lot of media-generated noise about civil rights and human rights. What do you suppose the most basic human right or civil right is? It is the right to self-defense. Without the right to self-preservation all of the other rights are meaningless. You have a right to be alive, and to live without being killed, crippled or raped in an unlawful, immoral attack by a sociopath. Telling you that you have the right to self-defense, but that you may not possess a weapon is ludicrous. It is just like telling you that you have the right to a free press, but that you may not possess ink or paper. If you have the right to self-defense, you have the right to be armed.

The remainder of this book will be geared toward helping us learn how to exercise that right, and take back control over our own lives.

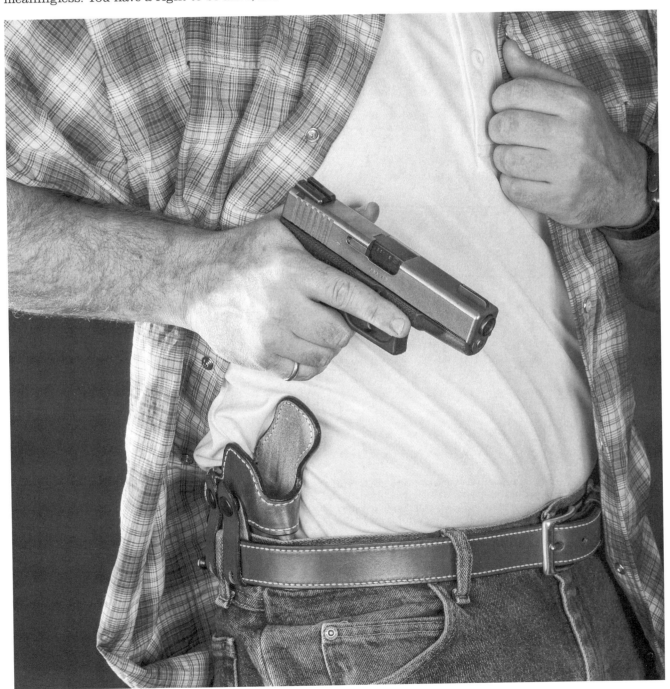

As of 2014, all 50 states in the U.S. have at least a theoretical system for private citizens to acquire a permit or license to carry a handgun on their person for self-defense. (File photo)

Workplace Violence

Violence in America is an everyday issue, and no one is immune. According to the National Association of Security Professionals (NASP), the total number of reported homicides in the U.S. is about 15,500 per year, but adjusted for unreported cases, the total is thought to be about double that figure. The same goes for other crimes, which are often grossly under-reported for a number of reasons.

Violence in the workplace mirrors the situation in the country as a whole. The Occupational Safety and Health Administration (OSHA) reports 1,000 workplace homicides per year, but that does not include a huge number committed at businesses too small to come under OSHA reporting guidelines. OSHA reports 51,000 sexual assaults in the workplace per year, but again those not coming under OSHA are thought to number as high as 500,000 incidents per year.

The author sees nothing wrong with wearing his concealed pistol to church. Anywhere there are people gathered, there is a potential for lethal violence. (File photo)

The Occupational Safety and Health Administration (OSHA) reports 1,000 workplace homicides per year, but that does not include a huge number committed at businesses too small to come under OSHA reporting guidelines. More Americans are murdered at work than die from any other on-the-job cause. (File photo)

More Americans are murdered at work than die from any other on-the-job cause.

Some of the factors that increase the risk of violence in the workplace include: exchanging money with the public; working alone or in isolated areas; providing services and care; and working in retail sales. That pretty well sums up darn near everyone's job.

What can you do to reduce your risks?

1. Accept that violence can occur anywhere, anytime there are people present. You are not "safe" just because you're at work.

2. Take outbursts, erratic behavior or threats by co-workers seriously. Report such activity to security or HR and insist on follow-up.

3. Where allowed, wear your gear. When someone is shooting up your office, the sidearm at home in the sock drawer will not be of much use to you.

Church Security Notes

Every now and then, some astonished Sheeple will ask me, "You mean you'd wear a concealed pistol to church?" Well, duh. Anywhere there are people gathered, there is a potential for lethal violence. Consider these facts, from a recent church-security conference I attended:

There has been a 200-percent increase in reported crimes against churches in the past five years.

From January 1999 through July 2010 there were 473 reported violent incidents in U.S. churches, involving 200 fatalities.

In one study of 335 church incidents, the causes were listed as:

- Domestic violence, 18 percent
- Personal conflicts, 27 percent
- Robbery, 27 percent
- Gang related, 10 percent
- Random, or Other, 18 percent (this includes mental cases)

In these studied incidents, the weapons used were:

- Firearms, 60 percent
- Knives, 16 percent
- Automobiles, 20 percent

In these 335 studied incidents, 596 were people killed or seriously injured. In these cases, 63 percent of the victims were male, and 37 percent were female. In 446 reported incidents, the attacker was male in 92 percent of the incidents.

2

LEGAL ISSUES IN CARRYING A HANDGUN

The decision to carry a concealed handgun for self-protection affords the individual control over his or her own destiny and gives people options they would not otherwise have in the event of unforeseen emergencies. Free citizens, of good character and sound judgment, should have the ability to make decisions and take actions that can literally mean the difference between life and death for themselves and their loved ones. With this privilege, however, comes awesome responsibility. Armed citizens have the power of life and death over all with whom they come in

contact with during the course of daily life, and this responsibility cannot be taken lightly. As a result, the legally armed citizen will be held accountable for his actions by the courts and other authorities. It is vital to understand the law, be aware of the possible consequences of various courses of action you may undertake and take steps to ensure your actions will always be lawful, reasonable, and court defensible.

Of course, the first issue is obtaining a license or permit to carry. At this writing, all 50 states have some provision for the carrying of concealed firearms by civilians. Yes, I know, one should not have to

Free citizens, of good character and sound judgment, should have the ability to make decisions and take actions that can literally mean the difference between life and death for themselves and their loved ones. Civilians who legally obtain a concealed-carry permit take on a huge responsibility for the right to be prepared to survive a potentially violent confrontation.

apply to a bureaucrat for permission to defend one's own life. Since the right to self-defense is the pre-eminent civil right or human right one should not have to ask government permission to exercise that right. That's the theory of life. Please note the theory of life and the practice of life sometimes do not mesh. To avoid complications like going to jail, you are strongly advised to obtain a permit through whatever system you must in order to go legally armed and avoid a number of serious issues. In my state, carrying a pistol without a license is a low-end misdemeanor and will generally get you a fine and a stern look from the judge. However, in some jurisdictions carrying a concealed weapon without a license is a felony, something not to be taken lightly.

Obtain a carry permit and attempt to follow the rules religiously. One common requirement is that the pistol be kept concealed at all

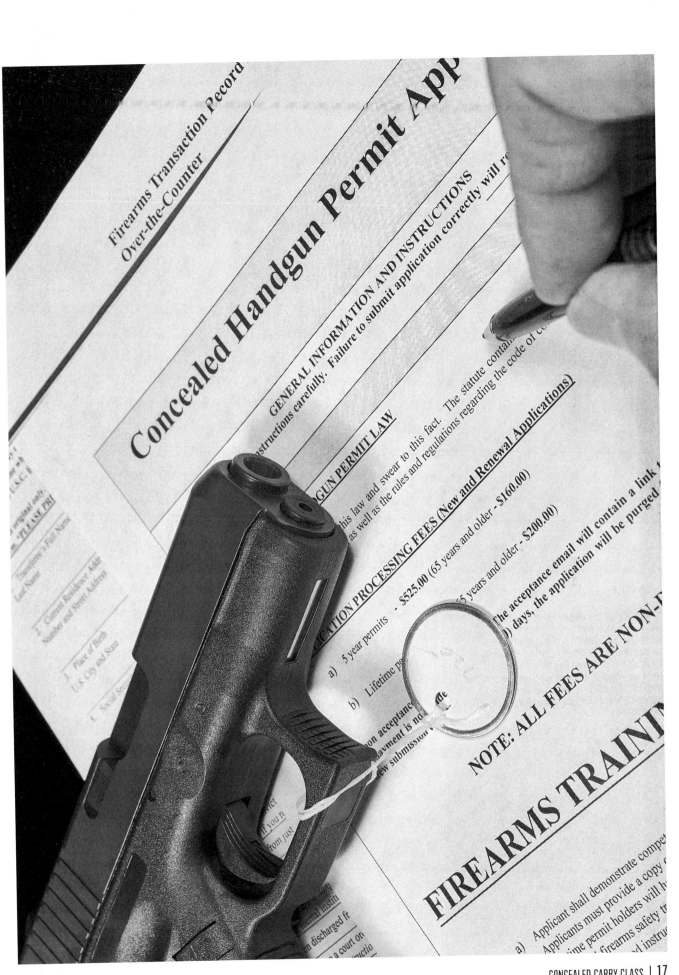

Firearms Transaction Record
Over-the-Counter

Concealed Handgun Permit App

GENERAL INFORMATION AND INSTRUCTIONS
instructions carefully. Failure to submit application correctly will re

GUN PERMIT LAW

his law and swear to this fact. The statute contain
as well as the rules and regulations regarding the code of co

ICATION PROCESSING FEES (New and Renewal Applications)

a) 5 year permits - $525.00 (65 years and older - $160.00)

b) Lifetime pe...........5 years and older - $200.00)

on acceptance........The acceptance email will contain a link t
ayment is no...........) days, the application will be purged
w submission

NOTE: ALL FEES ARE NON-

FIREARMS TRAINI

a) Applicant shall demonstrate compet
Applicants must provide a copy
ime permit holders will h
firearms safety tr
d instru

The author serves on the advisory board of the Armed Citizens' Legal Defense Network, a legal assistance program for lawfully armed citizens that actually pays for attorney fees and other legal expenses and provides top-notch expert witness services to its members in return for a very small annual fee.

times, so as not to alarm the public at the sight of the pistol. Obey this requirement. Keeping your weapon fully concealed until needed gives you a tactical advantage. In addition to preventing unwanted attention from licensing or law enforcement authorities, flashing, half covering, or brandishing your sidearm needlessly are the marks of an insecure, unstable, emotionally immature personality, who has no business with a deadly weapon. Be discreet.

In some jurisdictions, you will be required to post a bond in favor of the licensing authority. Please note that this does nothing to protect you against civil suits brought by the shootee or his family. It only protects the licensing authority from suits brought against them for having licensed you. You can be sued, frivolously or righteously, for any use of your weapon. There are insurance companies that have special liability insurance to cover this sort of thing for legally authorized gun carriers. You might also be able to obtain a personal liability umbrella rider on your homeowner's insurance policy.

You really do need some form of liability coverage, as lawsuits over shootings are quite common in some parts of the country. Even if you absolutely have to shoot some thug who is threatening your life at the time, he (or his survivors) may well sue you later, claiming you violated his rights or wrongfully injured/killed him. Even if you are in the right and win in court, you still will lose, because of heavy lawyer fees and related costs.

I strongly suggest you look into one of the legal assistance programs designed for lawfully armed citizens. These organizations can provide both legal counsel and expert witness services to their members who are involved in either criminal or civil litigation resulting from a self-defense incident. In my opinion, the best of these is the Armed Citizens' Legal Defense Network (ACLDN). The ACLDN actually pays for attorney fees and other legal expenses and provides top-notch expert witness services to its members in return for a very small annual fee. The annual membership dues also get you a number of educational DVDs and other materials, worth the cost of membership by themselves. John Farnam, Massad Ayoob, Dennis Tueller, I and several others serve on the advisory board of this organization, so I am very familiar with its operation. As of this writing, it has helped several members win unmeritorious prosecutions against them in self-defense incidents.

Finally, I want to stress that as a legally armed citizen, you will be held to a higher standard of conduct than an ordinary Joe by the police and courts, both civil and criminal. You are presumed to know better. You will be required to exercise judgment, restraint, and tolerance, far beyond that required of a typical person. Here are some tips:

• Never, ever drink or do drugs and carry a gun! This is a sure one-way ticket to jail.

• Do not wear a pistol to clearly inappropriate locations or events.

• Do not show off your pistol to friends, co-workers, etc. Be low-profile.

• Learn to ignore minor provocations. The guy who cut you off in traffic and gave you the one-finger salute must not be chased down and yelled at. If a confrontation ensues, and it will, and you are armed with a deadly weapon, trouble could follow. Exercise restraint.

"... as a legally armed citizen, you will be held to a higher standard of conduct than an ordinary Joe by the police and courts, both civil and criminal."

• Always have your official identification (permit or license) on your person and handy in case your weapon is spotted, or you have to draw it.

• Most of us get into enough trouble in life unintentionally. Don't go looking for more. Avoid the temptation to intervene in situations that are clearly none of your business. I suggest following John Farnam's famous dictum of the Three S's: "Don't go to stupid places. Don't hang out with stupid people. Don't do stupid things." Making this dictum your standard operating procedure will go a very long way toward keeping you out of trouble.

EXAMPLES

You're in a bank, as a customer, when a robbery occurs. If the thief is only taking money and not shooting at or otherwise directly and immediately threatening anyone's life, stay put, be quiet and be a good witness. If you unwisely precipitate a shootout in a crowded bank, you will be held responsible for all injuries, including innocents hit by the bad guy's fire. Money can be replaced, lives cannot.

On the other hand, if the robber starts executing people and you are capable of engaging him, that's a different issue.

Do not interject yourself into shouting/shoving matches between strangers. Unknown to you, the combatants could be drinking buddies or a habitually violent couple who fight incessantly, but stay together. If you interfere, you might wind up having to fight both (all) of them. Butt out. Call the police if the disturbance warrants their presence.

You see two scruffily dressed, shabby-looking men shooting at a third person as you pull into a parking lot. Back off and call police. If you bail out and fire at the suspects, they could turn out to be two undercover narcotics officers firing at a dope dealer who attacked them when they tried to arrest him. How do you think responding police officers will treat you if you mistakenly shoot two police officers who pose no direct threat to you?

The key is to reserve any use of your firearm to situations in which you or a known innocent third party is under lethal attack. If you have the slightest doubt about a situation, do not fire.

Do not interject yourself into shouting/shoving matches between strangers. Unknown to you, the combatants could be drinking buddies or a habitually violent couple who fight incessantly, but stay together. If you interfere, you might wind up having to fight both (all) of them. Butt out. Call the police if the disturbance warrants their presence.

The Founding Fathers on Guns and Freedom

In the past couple years, there has been a great deal of debate about just what the Second Amendment to the United States Constitution means. I think it is instructive to read exactly what the Founding Fathers had to say on the subject, as they were very clear about their intentions. This is what our Founding Fathers, and others, had to say about gun control and freedom.

"The Constitution of most of our states (and of the United States) assert that all power is inherent in the people; that they may exercise it by themselves; that it is their right and duty to be at all times armed."

— **Thomas Jefferson**

"(The Constitution preserves) the advantage of being armed which Americans possess over the people of almost every other nation ... (where) the governments are afraid to trust the people with arms."

— **James Madison**

"Laws that forbid the carrying of arms ... disarm only those who are neither inclined nor determined to commit crimes ... Such laws make things worse for the assaulted and better for the assailants; they serve rather to encourage than to prevent homicides, for an unarmed man may be attacked with greater confidence than an armed man."

— **Thomas Jefferson, quoting Cesare Beccaria**

"Arms in the hands of citizens (may) be used at individual discretion ... in private self-defense..."

— **John Adams, A defense of the Constitutions of the Government of the USA, 471 (1788).**

"... arms ... discourage and keep the invader and plunderer in awe, and preserve order in the world as well as property. ... Horrid mischief would ensue were the law-abiding deprived the use of them."

— **Thomas Paine**

"To disarm the people (is) the best and most effectual way to enslave them ..."

— **George Mason, 3 Elliot, Debates at 380.**

"The best we can hope for concerning the people at large is that they be properly armed."

— **Alexander Hamilton, The Federalist Papers at 184-8.**

Thomas Jefferson, second from left on Mount Rushmore in South Dakota, and his fellow Founding Fathers of the United States had plenty to say about the rights of U.S. citizens to keep and bear arms. (File photos)

"Guard with jealous attention the public liberty. Suspect everyone who approaches that jewel. Unfortunately, nothing will preserve it but downright force. Whenever you give up that force, you are inevitably ruined ... The great object is that every man be armed. Everyone who is able might have a gun."

— **Patrick Henry**

"To preserve liberty, it is essential that the whole body of the people always possess arms and be taught alike, especially when young, how to use them ..."

— **Richard Henry Lee writing in Letters from the Federal Farmer to the Republic (1787-1788).**

"The Constitution shall never be construed to authorize Congress to prevent the people of the United States, who are peaceable citizens, from keeping their own arms."

— **Samuel Adams, debates & Proceedings in the Convention of the Commonwealth of Massachusetts, 86-87.**

"... the people have a right to keep and bear arms."

— **Patrick Henry and George Mason, Elliot, Debates at 185.**

"The right of the people to keep and bear arms shall not be infringed. A well regulated militia, composed of the people, trained to arms, is the best and most natural defense of a free country ..."

— **James Madison, I Annals of Congress 434 (June 8, 1789).**

"The people are not to be disarmed of their weapons. They are left in full possession of them."

— **Zachariah Johnson, 3 Elliot, Debates at 646.**

"No free man shall ever be debarred the use of arms."

— **Thomas Jefferson, Proposal Virginia Constitution, 1 T. Jefferson Papers, 334 (C.J. Boyd, Ed., 1950).**

3

APPROPRIATE USE OF FORCE

> **"Any force you use in defense has to be minimal: The least amount of force that can get the job done to stop the attack."**

Specific laws vary from state to state, but in general, U.S. law authorizes a citizen to defend himself against an unlawful assault by using a like degree of force. Simply put, you may legally respond with the same level of force that your attacker is using or attempting to use against you. The various degrees of force can be envisioned as a stairway, starting with the minimal force at the bottom step and escalating all the way to the top at deadly force. The stairway concept discussed here consists of several degrees of force, from presence, to verbal commands, to pepper spray, to hard hands, all the way up to deadly force. It might help to imagine two parallel stairways, with you on one and your attacker on the other. If attacked you may respond to the same level (the same step) your attacker is on, but you may not climb higher on your stairway than he is on his.

Any force you use in defense has to be minimal: The least amount of force that can get the job done to stop the attack. And it has to be reasonable, meaning a typical person, under the same circumstances, would do the same thing.

Many people misunderstand this stairway concept, and think it means that one must move up one step at a time trying each available option. No, that is not what it means. It is simply a way to conceptualize that there are lower levels of force, higher levels of force and intermediate levels in between. Wherever on his stairway your attacker is, you may automatically and immediately go to that level without taking any other steps first.

Let's look at two of the keywords in the description above. First, we said your actions had to be "minimal." That simply means the least amount of force that will actually stop the unlawful assault against you. Notice I did not write the least amount of force you could possibly employ, it's the least amount of force that will actually get the job done. An easy way to remember this is you have no right to punish someone. You have no right to punish him for scaring you or even for hurting you. What you do have is the right to make him stop his aggressive behavior against you. Once that aggressive behavior has been successfully stopped you have no right to pile on anymore punishment.

The other word was "reasonable." In any use of force, your actions must be objectively reasonable. That means that a normal, sane, decent, ordinary person, given the same facts and circumstances you had at the moment, would have done essentially the same thing you did. Neither of these concepts is mysterious or hard to understand.

Remember this stairway concept, as it is vital to legally justifying your actions. If a person punches you in the nose, for instance, you probably cannot lawfully shoot him. Why? Because you are going much further up the ladder than he has. Does this mean that if a person shoots at you, you must first go to the steps of persuasion, commands, physical control, etc., before resorting to deadly force? No, it does not. An emergency situation requires you to skip over to the same plane the suspect is on, namely deadly force.

If the assailant's actions move downward on the stairway, you must also de-escalate your response. For example: A man shoots at you and misses. You draw your gun and prepare to fire. Seeing this, he throws down his gun, puts his hands up and shouts that he surrenders. You are no longer legally justified in firing, and must de-escalate, move downward on your stairway.

Before we go any further, we probably ought to define some terms. What exactly do we mean by the term "deadly force?" Deadly force is any type or degree of force that can be reasonably expected to produce death or serious bodily injury. Thus, deadly force can consist of many acts other than firing a gun at a person. Stabbing or cutting a person with a knife or other edged weapon, deliberately hitting a person with a car, striking a person in the head

with a club, whether a nightstick or a fireplace poker or tire iron could all be examples of the use of deadly force. In my state, the legal definition of serious bodily injury includes broken major bones, protracted unconsciousness, a large bleeding wound, or loss of use of a limb or organ. In many states, the definition also includes the forcible rape of either sex.

I do not think one has to be a doctor or lawyer to understand the concept of death. Serious bodily injury includes the sort of injuries we noted above. In really simple terms, it would be life-threatening injuries or the types of injuries that you would expect to have to stay in the hospital and have surgery in order to survive. Please note we are referring to serious injury here, not black eyes or split lips.

There is only one jurisdiction in the entire United States (Texas) that authorizes use of deadly force to protect property. In Texas, one can use deadly force to prevent the theft of property, but only at night. No other state in the U.S. allows this. The law's position is that no property has either intrinsic or extrinsic value greater than that of a human life. If someone is running off with Aunt Tillie's silver service that goes back to the Revolutionary War and you take a shot at him, whether you hit him or not, guess which one of you has committed the more serious offense under the law? You have. I suggest you remember the acronym IDOL, which stands for "Immediate Defense Of Life." That is the only circumstance in which you are legally entitled to use deadly force.

You also may not use deadly force to stop a fleeing criminal. Police officers in this country, ever since the Supreme Court decision Garner versus Tennessee, have had strict limitations on when they can use deadly force to stop a fleeing felon. That applies only to police officers, however. Private citizens simply do not, under U.S., law have the right to use deadly force to stop a fleeing criminal. Fleeing, by definition, means they have broken off the attack and are attempting to escape. If they have broken off the attack, exactly what are you defending against? Since you have only the right to use force in self-defense, shooting a fleeing person would not be considered lawful.

When then, are we justified in using deadly force in self-defense? Traditionally, there are four elements that must be satisfied before you can use deadly force against another human being. These are not complicated, and they are not hard to judge in the real world. There is nothing subtle about someone trying to kill you. If it is a legitimate self-defense action it will be obvious to you and everyone else.

The first of the four elements is **ability.** Your attacker must have the physical capability, or the means, or be able to cause your death, or serious bodily injury. Ordinarily, he must have a weapon capable of causing such damage, and you must be within the useful range of that weapon. A man waving a tire iron at you from 50 feet away, shouting obscenities, has no real ability at this point to cause you harm. A man with a tire iron at 10 feet is a different story. If your assailant has a weapon, and you are within the useful range of that weapon, he is said to have **ability.**

Weapons can generally be divided into two main categories: guns and everything else. The entire purpose of the gun is to project violence across a distance. Before guns became common, violence was typically hand-delivered. With the gun, violence can be sent by airmail. So, if your assailant has a firearm and a clear line of sight to you, you are in danger whether he is 5 feet away, 15 feet away, 50 feet away or farther because he has the **ability** to harm you from where he stands.

Most other weapons fall into the category of contact weapons. This would include knives, razors, swords, tire irons, fireplace pokers, baseball bats, sections of

Deadly force can consist of many acts other than firing a gun at a person. Stabbing or cutting a person with a knife or other edged weapon, striking a person in the head with a club, whether a nightstick or a fireplace poker or tire iron, could all be examples of the use of deadly force.

2x4 lumber, machetes, axes and hatchets and claw hammers. It might surprise you to find out that more people are murdered in the U.S. each year with hammers than with assault rifles. In fact, the third most commonly used weapon in U.S. homicides is the screwdriver. Some thugs carry one in a back pocket. It's what he breaks into your house with, what he breaks into your car with, what he starts your car with, and if you interrupt him in the course of one of these crimes he might stick it between your ribs and wiggle it around and you'll be dead. An implement does not have to be designed or intended as a deadly weapon if that is what the user is attempting. All of the weapons listed here would have to touch you to cause harm. Does that mean your assailant must be within arm's reach before an impact tool or contact weapon could be considered a legitimate threat? No!

"... you might, in fact, have to use a deadly weapon in self-defense against another person who is not armed."

The problem is people can and do move very quickly. Many years ago, my friend Dennis Tueller conducted a series of tests in which randomly selected grown men were asked to stand 21 feet from him on an open parking lot. On Dennis' signal the man would run forward and touch Dennis. Dennis would start a stopwatch when the man would start moving and stop the watch when the subject touched him. Over the course of many iterations of this experiment, Dennis found that the average grown man starting from a standing position could cover that 21-foot distance and touch him in a second and half. Thus, if you're standing on an open parking lot, someone brandishing a knife or tire iron from as much as 20 feet away could still be considered to be an immediate deadly threat because he could close that gap and cut or strike you in as little as a second and a half. Over the years, many people have

completely misconstrued Dennis' findings. This does not mean you can automatically shoot someone holding a contact weapon 20 feet away. Factors you have to consider include your assailant's apparent age and physical ability and what intervening obstacles you could place between yourself and him, which might buy you time. There is no hard and fast line at 21 feet or anywhere else. Let's say there is an adult male holding a knife, 8 feet away from you, and threatening to cut you. However, he is 85 years old and in a wheelchair. That changes the equation. Or, you have an athletic-looking, 6-foot-5-inch, 25-year-old male holding a big knife 30 feet from you on an open parking lot with no obstacles between you and him. How long would it take him to get to you? Again, the equation

A man waving a tire iron at you from 50 feet away, shouting obscenities, has no real ability at this point to cause you harm. A man with a tire iron at 10 feet is a different story. If your assailant has a weapon, and you are within the useful range of that weapon, he is said to have ability.

is changed by the exact circumstances involved.

There is another aspect of **ability** we should mention, a concept known as "disparity of force." Despite uninformed opinions you might have heard, you might, in fact, have to use a deadly weapon in self-defense against another person who is not armed. This circumstance arises when your attacker has an overwhelming advantage that forces you to move to a higher level of force in order to defend yourself. This rule will require two things on your part: unusual circumstances, and your ability to articulate your decision-making process. To keep this from being mysterious, I will give you two examples.

First, let's say a 105-pound woman has been backed into a corner by a 275-pound thug who looks like he just got out of prison, where he pumped iron four hours a day. He has made it clear, through his words, actions or combination of those that he intends to rob, rape and murder her. He does not have an artificial weapon (by the way, artificial does not mean fake, it means made by man). He does not have a gun, knife or club, but does he have the ability to kill her or cripple her with his bare hands? Of course he does. When she articulates her decision-making process, these are some of the key points she will need to point out to justify her decision to use her pistol against this "unarmed man."

First, he is male, and she is female. Males have a significant upper body strength advantage,

If someone deliberately points a gun at you, that strongly implies intent to do you harm. If someone is holding a weapon and says, "I'm going to kill you!" that establishes intent. A reasonable person would have to believe what this person is about to do is to attempt to kill or cripple you. Be prepared. (Photo courtesy Galco)

and a huge reach advantage over females. Second, he had her backed into a corner. She cannot escape to her rear and she would not be able to get past him. She is trapped. Third, he is almost three times her size, and has an enormous strength advantage. If he got his hands on her he would be able to strangle or beat her to death easily, and the only way she could be reasonably expected to stop that would be to employ her firearm. A reasonable person would conclude that she had no other choice.

Another example: An elderly gentleman is walking down the sidewalk when three 19-year-old thugs knock him down and begin kicking and stomping on him. Would he be justified in using his pistol to make them stop, although they are not armed with guns or knives? Of course he would.

Here are the reasons. There are three of them and only one of him. They are younger, tougher, stronger and meaner. They have him down on the ground in a position of extreme disadvantage - he cannot get out from under them and he cannot strike back effectively from there. If they continue kicking and stomping on him, he will almost certainly be killed or severely injured. His only reasonable alternative is to produce a pistol and shoot them in self-defense.

As you can see, it is not difficult to envision circumstances in which you would have to use deadly force against an "unarmed attacker." You have to be able to articulate why the attacker had the ability to cause your death or serious bodily harm and why your action was the only reasonable alternative.

The next element is **intent**. Your assailant must, through his words, actions, or combination of those, show what he intends to do is cause your death or serious bodily injury. I actually had a student once in a permit type class say to me, "I'm not a mind reader, so how am I sup posed to know what someone else's **intent** is?" Please! It is not hard to deduce someone's intent in this context.

Let's say a man is walking down the sidewalk outside the athletic field, toward you, with a baseball bat on his shoulder, whistling "Take Me Out to the Ball Game." What do you suppose his **intent** is? On the other hand, if an angry, screaming, cursing man draws a bat back behind his head in both hands a few feet away from you and says, "Kiss your ass goodbye!" what do you suppose is his intent? If someone deliberately points a gun at you, that strongly implies **intent** to do you harm. If someone is holding a weapon and says, "I'm going to kill you!" that establishes **intent.** A reasonable person would have to believe what this person is about to do is to attempt to kill or cripple you.

The third element is **imminent jeopardy.** You must reasonably believe that your life is in grave, immediate danger. This must be a reasonable belief, based on the facts and circumstances as you know them at that time. Please note that what you know or perceive at that moment is all that counts. If, after the incident, investigation shows that your assailant had prior convictions for manslaughter or murder, that information is not part of your justification process unless it was known to you before you fired.

Again, your conclusion that you are in **imminent jeopardy** must be reasonable, that is, it would be shared by any other normal, sane, decent person given the same facts and circumstances. For instance, if someone points a banana at you and says, "This is a Martian ray gun, I am going to disintegrate you," that would not be a credible threat, so you would not be justified in using deadly force. On the other hand, let's say an armed robber points a gun at you, puts you in fear for your life, and you shoot him. Later, it turns out that his pistol had a broken firing pin, or an empty chamber, or was completely unloaded. That does not change the fact that when you shot, your reasonable perception was that your life was in immediate danger. Again, a reasonable person would conclude that when an armed robber points a gun at you, your life is in immediate danger. The law does not require you to know things you cannot know. There was no way for you to know if the firing pin was broken, the chamber was empty, or the gun was unloaded, therefore, when you acted, your actions were reasonable.

So, if your attacker has the **ability** to cause your death or serious bodily injury, his words or actions manifest that is his **intent**, and you reasonably believe that your life is in **imminent jeopardy** then you may be justified in using deadly force in self-defense. I used the words "may be" because of the last element, **preclusion,** which simply means you had no other option. In some states, there is a statutory "duty to retreat." This is often, however, misunderstood. It does not mean you have to back away or run away from an assailant who is capable of killing or crippling you. It means you must not have some other viable alternative that would protect you. Also, you must be able to retreat in safety. Here is an example. You are sitting in your car, which is stopped. It is running and in gear. A man on foot is waving a tire iron and threatening to beat your head in. What would be your reasonable action at this point? Do you draw your gun and defend yourself or do you simply drive away? Drive away. Driving away removes you from the danger zone without risk of death or injury, so this would be required under this set of circumstances. No rocket science involved here.

"The question should never be, 'Can I shoot him?' The question should always be, 'Do I have to shoot him?'"

A lot of people try to make this far more complicated than it actually is. If someone is attempting to kill, rape or cripple you it is usually pretty obvious. "Is he capable of causing such damage to me?" "Is this what he is trying to do?" "Do I have any other option?"

Many people make the mistake of asking, "If he does (fill in the blank) can I shoot him?" The question should never be, "Can I shoot him?" The question should always be, "Do I have to shoot him?" Here are some suggestions that will go a very long way toward keeping you out of legal trouble anywhere in the United States:

• I will not seek a fight, and if at all possible, I will avoid one, but if one is forced upon me, I will do what it takes to win.

• My sidearm is neither a status symbol nor an emotional crutch. I will not reach for it unless out of dire necessity, but if I must use deadly force to preserve my life or that of an innocent person, I will use it skillfully and without hesitation.

• I will forget I have a pistol, unless I need it to stop an immediate and otherwise unavoidable deadly threat to me or to someone for whom I am responsible.

Self-Defense and Religion

If you have done any study of Western religions, you quickly learn the King James Version of the Bible is not a particularly accurate translation of the original texts. There are a lot of reasons for this, some cultural and some political, but suffice to say translating from Hebrew to Greek to Latin to old English to modern English created many opportunities for error. The Sixth Commandment is a classic example.

The word "kill" in Exodus 20:13 and Deuteronomy 5:17 should properly be written as "murder." The proper translation is THOU SHALT NOT MURDER. It is interesting that in Matthew 19:18 the King James Version correctly translates the Sixth Commandment: "Thou shalt do no murder."

The Hebrew word (ratsach) and the Greek word (phoneno) which are used in the Sixth Commandment in earlier texts both clearly mean "murder." The Hebrew language has a general word for killing (the verb muwth, meaning "to cause to die") and the Greek language has a general word for killing (the verb apokteino), but these general terms for killing are not used in the Sixth Commandment. Instead, very specific words are used which forbid MURDER. Judaism uses the same Commandments as found in the Christian Old Testament, so the same comments apply.

Thus, there is no Biblical injunction against using deadly force in self-defense or in defending the life of another. MURDER is killing unjustly, or without justification, and unlawfully. None of those adjectives describe legitimate self-defense.

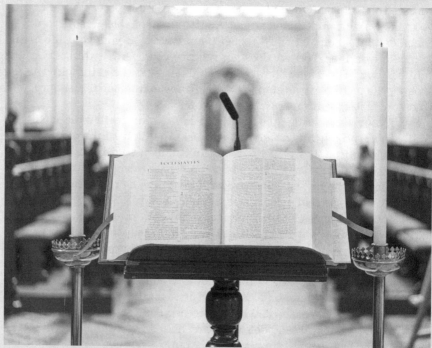

Translating from Hebrew to Greek to Latin to old English to modern English created many opportunities for error in the King James Version of the Bible. (File photos)

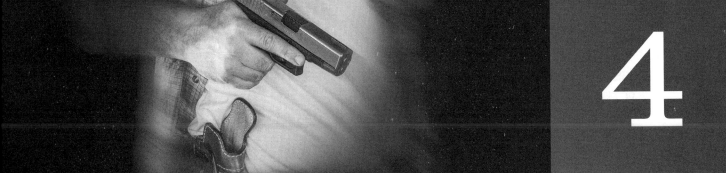

4

PRINCIPLES OF PERSONAL DEFENSE

Some years ago, Jeff Cooper wrote an excellent booklet entitled *Principles of Personal Defense*. This brief work outlined seven principles that, according to Jeff, lay the groundwork for all successful self-defense efforts. This little book is available from several online sources and should be required reading for anyone interested in personal security.

I have taken the liberty of listing the seven key words Jeff used in enumerating these principles and adding my own perspective to them. I truly believe mastery of these principles, as your standard operating procedure, is the key to personal safety. Many of us concentrate too much on hardware (specific gun model, caliber or type of ammunition, etc.) when it is this type of software issue that really decides who wins. The seven keywords used by Jeff Cooper to enumerate his Principles of Personal Defense are used here by permission of Jeff and the publisher, Paladin Press.

ALERTNESS

This one trait is the cornerstone of all physical security. You cannot defend yourself against something you don't know is there. You must learn habits of alertness and awareness, so you are always in tune with your environment.

Elsewhere in this text we cover some of the important facets of observation skills, but you must grasp the importance of this principle. If you know who is around you and what they are up to, you are in control. Always be on the lookout for people, behavior, or activity that is out of place or out of context. When you see something like that, question it. Ask yourself, "why…?" If you don't get a satisfactory answer, treat this as a danger signal.

DECISIVENESS

You are going to have to select a course of action and implement it, right now! No one is going to be there to tell you what to do. You're on your own. This is especially difficult for us these days because all decisions are made by committee, and no one likes to sign off on anything anymore. See the chapter on mental imaging to learn how to prepare to make crucial tactical decisions quickly. Always, do something, immediately.

AGGRESSIVENESS

This is another principle that is difficult for the average person, as aggressiveness is systematically being bred out of us. You have been taught all of your life that fighting is bad, human life is sacred and you should play nice. The trouble is you might be up against someone who shares none of these sentiments.

To a degree, we do a disservice to our students when we harp continually on the defensive nature of the pistol. The pistol is defensive in concept, but not in

Running a timed drill during a competition helps you develop quickness in the presentation of your pistol from the holster and your firing stroke.

Jeff Cooper wrote an excellent booklet entitled Principles of Personal Defense. This brief work outlined seven principles that, according to Jeff, lay the groundwork for all successful self-defense efforts. The author teaches these principles in his classes and adds his own perspective to them in this chapter. (File photo)

"Speed is the defining element of any form of fighting."

use. Gun fighting is just a form of fighting, and any type of fighting is, by definition, an aggressive activity. You cannot win any type of fight by being passive. Imagine yourself in a fistfight where all you do is block punches, but never throw any of your own. Going to win? The same goes for armed conflict. If I have to defend my life with a firearm, I will use it vigorously, with all of the violence, aggressiveness and commitment I can muster, because my life is at stake!

When a fight starts, failing to respond aggressively is the same as surrender. If you let evil people do evil things to you, guess what will happen? You have a duty to resist evil. You owe this duty to your family, to society and to yourself. If attacked, attack right back!

SPEED

Speed is the defining element of any form of fighting. Whoever moves faster wins. You must develop quickness in your presentation of your pistol from the holster and your firing stroke. This comes only through structured, careful, frequent practice. You also must develop quickness in your ability to assess developing situations and make sound decisions. Again, this comes from prior preparation. Play the "what if..." game to develop responses in advance of need. The time to debate strategy is not while someone is trying to kill you.

COOLNESS

If attacked, you must keep your wits about you and do what you have to do to win. You must concentrate on the task at hand, and in our context, the task at hand is to focus on the front sight and press the trigger. Invariably, when I discuss this with a group of new students, some of them look incredulous and say something like, "how am I supposed to keep cool when someone a few steps away is trying to kill me?" The answer to that is simple – every day a large number of people have to do this. I personally know a very large group of people who have done this successfully. The key is in prior mental preparation. You must consider the possibility of an armed conflict and be prepared mentally to deal with it.

Part of the answer is practice. Practice builds skill. Skill builds confidence. Confidence prevents panic. If your mind knows that you have a fair degree of skill, your confidence in that skill will help you remain calm. Police officers in this country have an average hit ratio of around 20 percent. That means in the field they hit with 20 out of every 100 shots they fire. This is due to several factors. First is startle response – from not being mentally prepared for an attack and being caught completely off guard, which, as always, is a training issue. The second is infrequent and poor practice. One major East Coast agency, for instance, fired 1,293 shots on the street in 1996, and hit only 64 bad guys! They also hit 11 bystanders. This agency gets one day of live-fire training per year, and you can bet some of the officers never touch their weapons and practice on their own time, and never do any homework. As a result, when suddenly confronted with a shooting situation they panic, stick the gun out in front of them and empty it as fast as they can. This is called the "spray and pray" method, and it almost always results in two things: an empty gun and a pissed-off bad guy.

Over a period of 18 years, the school I ran in Memphis trained some 45,000 students, and a fair number of them have been involved in shootings. As far as I can tell, they have about a 95-percent hit ratio. The very few misses that have occurred have been under very unusual circumstances. This extremely high hit rate occurs because they came here on their own time, and spent their own money, and then spent the time and effort it takes to achieve and retain basic proficiency with their weapons.

Do your homework. Repetition is the mother of all physical skill. Make time to get to the range. By constantly repeating the motions involved in your presentation and your firing stroke, you burn a neural pathway from your brain to your fingertips, eventually ingraining the proper response into your muscle memory. Sports physiologists will tell you it takes between 2,500 and 5,000 correct repetitions of any complex motor skill to automate it. To automate the skill means to be able to do it reflexively, without conscious thought or effort and this is the goal. You must concentrate your mental effort on the evolving tactical situation, not on marksmanship, and this is how you remain in control and hit under stress. Your mind must be free to work on the tactical situation, not on marksmanship.

Get some practice shooting under stress. Engage in competition shooting, like IDPA matches. Having to shoot an unfamiliar drill or scenario, under time and scoring pressure and with the peer pressure of having other shooters watching you is an excellent way to get some stress inoculation as well as some experience running your equipment under pressure. Hunt deer, wild hogs or similar game with your pistol and learn to control "buck fever." In training and practice, push yourself always to be better.

All shooters experience a degradation of skill under the extreme stress involved in a real life-and-death shooting confrontation. The more skill you have, however, the less you will lose when placed under sudden stress. The reason for this is simple. To get a higher degree of skill you had to do the work. You put in the repetitions both on the range and in dry work and have automated your physical skills. On the other hand, someone with a low skill level will drop even more skill under duress, simply because they have not driven those skills into the unconscious or automated level.

RUTHLESSNESS

To many, this seems an odd word in the context of self-defense, but in reality, ruthlessness is a vital element of fighting to stay alive. In our context, ruthlessness means absolute single-mindedness of purpose. Once the fight starts, there are absolutely no considerations other than winning. It doesn't matter why he chose you. It doesn't matter why he's a criminal. All that matters is winning. Bear in mind, in our context losing can mean dying. Hit him fast, hit him hard, hit him with everything you have, then assess and if needed, hit him some more.

SURPRISE

Surprise is put last in this list deliberately, because surprise is the first element of offensive combat.

Surprise comes in two forms: strategic surprise and tactical surprise. Strategic surprise is what the bad guy plans on. I recently got my hands on a captured copy of a bad guy's training manual, and when I opened it, I found only this: sneak up on them and jump on them. That is his entire strategy. Surprise is the only true advantage he has over you. He is typically not as smart, as well armed, or as well-trained, but if he surprises you the advantage is entirely his. How, then do we neutralize this advantage? Simple. Be alert. If he cannot surprise you, he probably cannot harm you. This is a loop that goes right back to the beginning of this chapter. Be alert and aware so you cannot be surprised.

The other form of surprise is tactical surprise, and that is your advantage. If attacked, do something he does not expect. Action is faster than reaction. Make him react to you, not you to him. You

"Surprise comes in two forms: strategic surprise and tactical surprise."

Frequent and deliberate practice at the shooting range helps build and maintain the muscle-memory skills needed to draw and fire a handgun safely. Sports physiologists will tell you it takes between 2,500 and 5,000 correct repetitions of any complex motor skill to automate it.

accomplish this by doing what he least expects, which is a violent, explosive counterattack.

He is just as culturally indoctrinated as anyone else. When he attacks what he believed to be a helpless victim, what does he expect that person to do? Whimper, whine, belly up and do whatever he is told. Think about it. If he points a gun at you and tells you to do something, what does he expect you to do? Comply, of course. The reason he didn't shoot you was because he believes you will comply. If you do something else, he has to process that information, decide what to do and only then can he act. It's over by then.

This would be a good time to mention the OODA Cycle. This was a development by Col. John Boyd (USAF, Ret.) who was a fighter pilot, a fighter-pilot instructor, a researcher and inventor and a true genius. OODA is the acronym for Observe, Orient, Decide, Act. That is the cycle the human mind goes through in order to react to something in our environment. This applies to us as well as to the other side. Whether someone's IQ is 40 or 140 his mind has to work through this sequence before any deliberate action can take place. Let's look at it in detail.

OBSERVE

For the 10th time now, you cannot do anything about a problem until you detect it. Get your head up, open your eyes and look around. Bad guys do not beam down out of the mother ship and materialize next to you, despite what violent crime victims would have you believe. Remember, you're looking for anything in your immediate environment that looks suspicious because it is out of place, out of character or out of context.

ORIENT

This means to turn your attention to the person or circumstance

that caught your eye. Assess the person as a potential threat. Evaluate your tactical position. Consider your options for dealing with the threat. Start playing the "what-if" game to determine your options.

DECIDE

Action is needed. Select a course of action to fix the problem.

ACT

Physical action in self-defense is needed. This can only occur after you have gone through the first three stages. You cannot act until you detect the threat, evaluate it and select an option for dealing with it. The time it takes to process this information and act is reduced greatly by being alert and having practiced emergency responses before the crisis.

This same OODA Cycle applies to the opposition.

When he tells you to do something, do something else. He will have to observe that action, realize it is not what he told you to do (orient to it), decide what to do about it (run, shoot, etc.) and only then can he act. By being alert and having preplanned tactical responses, you can short-circuit his reaction process.

If he is in the act stage while you are entering the observe stage, you probably have lost. Be alert. The same works in reverse. If you are acting while he is looking, you should be finished before he can move through the orientation, decision and action phases.

Practicing your shooting skills with the added pressure of shooting in a competitive match is an excellent way to get some stress inoculation as well as some experience running your equipment under pressure. Pictured here, Lynn Givens, the author's wife, (foreground) competes one-on-one against another shooter. (Photo by Tamara Keel)

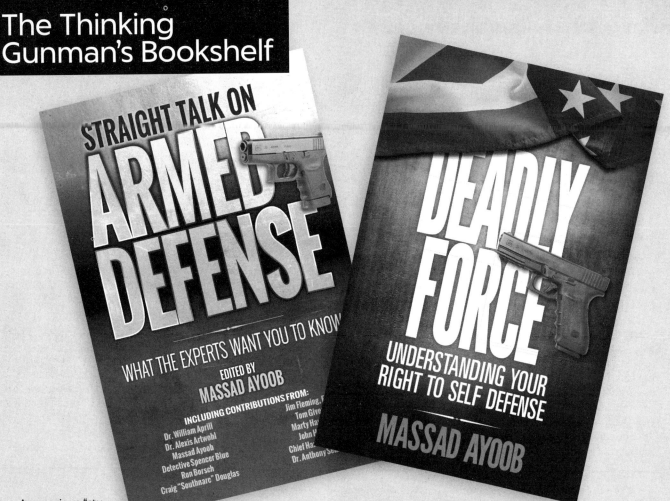

As a serious "student of the gun" for more than 40 years, I have always sought out information on every aspect of armed self-defense. Sadly, I frequently encounter people who own guns, ostensibly for self-defense, but they have no knowledge of defensive-shooting techniques or equipment. Others know something about their handguns and might even be good shots, but have never actually considered the moral, ethical and legal ramifications of using a firearm in self-defense. Still others have some understanding of these issues, but have no idea of the rich history of armed self-defense in this country, or the evolution of the techniques we take for granted today.

If self-defense against dangerous criminals is your goal, some understanding of the criminal's mentality could be very useful. Finally, some understanding of the wounding mechanisms of handgun ammunition and of human anatomy are important pieces of the puzzle. In my view, a well-rounded handgunner should have some basic knowledge and understanding in each of these areas of study.

Looking over my personal reference library, I found more than 300 books dealing with the topics listed above. Generally, they can be divided into two categories, "software and hardware." The software volumes deal with issues such as developing a proper defensive mindset, understanding the criminal mind, and basic understanding of the legal issues involved in using force. The hardware books deal with handguns, holsters, and other equipment and with the specific techniques involved in using these tools efficiently. I'll break these further into subsets based on content and make some recommendations for your reading list. Space constraints keep me from being able to give you a real book report on each, but I'll highlight why I think some of these books are important to you.

SOFTWARE

The first book on my list should be required reading for every person who even thinks about carrying a handgun for self-defense. *Principles of Personal Defense* was written by Jeff Cooper in 1972 and is a very brief work outlining the seven guiding principles of personal combat. It is available in booklet form from several online vendors. Jeff authored a number of books in his long career and many of them contain great insight into both shooting technique and mindset development. One of my favorites is Fireworks, a Gunsite Anthology.

Born Fighting, How the Scots-Irish Shaped America, by James Webb has been described as "popular history at its finest" by the American Library Association. Webb traces the influx of Scots-Irish immigrants into the U.S., and how their input shaped the American working class' sense of fierce individualism, persistent egalitarianism and strong sense of personal honor.

A wealth of great information has been written and published about handguns, concealed carry and self-defense. A depth of knowledge about all aspects of concealed carry can be as important as becoming proficient with your pistol at the range.

Deep Survival, Who Lives, Who Dies, and Why, by Laurence Gonzales is a vital description of the mental, emotional and character issues involved in surviving catastrophe, whether natural or man-made. Many years ago, Jeff Cooper wrote "the world is divided into two groups, 'copers' and 'non-copers.'" The purpose of training and personal development was to become a "coper." According to Gonzales, it appears Jeff was correct.

The Deadliest Men, by Paul Kirchner is a fascinating look at some of the most skilled and successful warriors in history. Paul spent five years researching this material and has offered some real insights into the character and actions of some of the best known as well as some relatively unknown fighters. From well-known folk heroes like Sgt. Alvin York and James Bowie to some less well-known gunmen like Delf "Jelly" Bryce and Lance Thomas, Kirchner gives us a look at what makes real warriors.

Straight Talk on Armed Defense, What the Experts Want You to Know, edited by Massad Ayoob. This is a collection of chapters written by 14 different experts in the self-defense field, each with his own area of expertise. Contributors include Mas Ayoob, Craig "Southnarc" Douglas, William Aprill, Dr. Alexis Artwohl, John Hearne, myself and others. The information covers all aspects of armed self-defense.

To this list I would add two more works dealing with the emotional and mental aspects of law-enforcement involved deadly force incidents. Both offer a great deal of information on what you can expect during and, as importantly, after a defensive shooting. They are *Deadly Force Encounters*, by Dr. Alexis Artwohl and Loren Christensen, and *Into the Kill Zone,* by David Klinger.

HISTORICAL BACKGROUND

Without comment, here is a good starting list for learning about the history and development of gun fighting in the U.S. Many are available as low-cost reprints, or you can scour gun shows and estate sales for original copies.

Fast & Fancy Revolver Shooting, by Ed McGivern

Sixguns, by Elmer Keith

Gunfighters, by Col. Charles Askins

Shooting, by J. Henry Fitzgerald

Legendary Lawman, The Story of Quick Draw Jelly Bryce, Ron Owens

HARDWARE

These are current works dealing with modern, effective shooting and gun-handling techniques. Each represents current state-of-the-art technique, but because of the different backgrounds of the authors (law enforcement, special operations military) those techniques might vary slightly.

Stay in the Fight!!, Warriors Guide to the Combat Pistol, by Kyle Lamb, recently retired from U.S. Army Special Operations.

Handgun Combatives, by Dave Spaulding, recently retired from a long and storied law enforcement career.

The Art of Modern Gunfighting, by Scott Reitz, recently retired member of LAPD SWAT, winner of several line-of-duty gunfights and experienced trainer.

Building a Better Gunfighter, by Richard Fairburn, a police firearms instructor, researcher and writer.

Training at the Speed of Life, by Kenneth Murray. Murray is one of the pioneers in simulation-based training and this book is the bible for force-on-force training.

WOMEN'S ISSUES IN FIREARMS TRAINING

More and more women are entering the field of personal self-defense training, and they bring a unique set of challenges and needs to the modern firearms trainer. Here are some excellent works to help guide women and their trainers.

Concealed Carry for Women, by Gila Hayes

Teaching Women to Shoot, by Vicki Farnam and Diane Nichol

GUNSHOT WOUNDING

Gunshot Wounds, by Dr. Vincent DiMaio, one of the most experienced and respected forensic medical examiners in the U.S.

Forensic Analysis of the April 11, 1986, FBI Firefight, by Dr. French Anderson. A detailed look at a historical shooting incident, including extensive information on the many wounds suffered by participants in this gun battle, and how those wounds affected the action.

LEGAL ISSUES

In the Gravest Extreme, by Massad Ayoob is several decades old now, but still has a solid foundation of information on the legal aspects of self-defense.

Deadly Force, Understanding Your Right to Self Defense, by Massad Ayoob. This 2014 release covers the legal issues involved in the use of lethal force in self-defense in great detail, but in language the non-lawyer layman can easily understand. Highly recommended.

CRIMINAL PSYCHOLOGY

Inside the Criminal Mind, by Stanton E. Samenow, Ph.D. (The Revised and Updated Edition). The original version of this book was published in 1984, and became a best-seller. The work was updated in 2004, after Samenow had an additional 20 years of experience in researching criminal behavior. John Douglas was one of the original profilers in the FBI Behavioral Sciences Unit, and he had this to say about Inside the Criminal Mind, "Utterly compelling reading, full of raw insight into the dark mind of the criminal."

The Dark Side of Man, by Michael Ghiglieri is a thorough and detailed look at human aggression and violence from the unique perspective of a former combat soldier and longtime primate researcher, a protégé of Jane Goodall. The Dark Side of Man offers scientific explanation for behavior such as rape, murder and genocide. Not for the fainthearted.

So, this should keep you reading for a while. When you finish these, you'll have a good basic working knowledge of the many topics involved in self-defense and I am hoping, an appetite for more. Happy reading.

5

JEFF COOPER'S COLOR CODES

Most people stumble through life, blissfully unaware of the world around them. They remain preoccupied with thoughts of work, or personal problems, or how to get a date, or other trivialities, with no thought to their immediate environment. By not paying attention to their surroundings, they place themselves in needless jeopardy.

Go sit in the intake area in your neighborhood hospital emergency room one evening, as an educational exercise. Observe the unfortunates who come in for treatment, and you will get an excellent illustration of this point. About 20 percent of the customers are actually sick, discount them. The remaining 80 percent are there because they were inattentive to their environment. These will be people who walked off loading docks, or stepped off ladders 20 feet up, or backed into running machinery, or stepped into the path of a vehicle, OR allowed a thug to walk right up to them unnoticed and bean them with a brick.

"If you should find yourself faced with a life-threatening attack by a criminal, as a typical, rational person, you will be faced by three enormous difficulties."

You can be stupid, inattentive and oblivious in your work environment day in and day out and get away with it, until one day the odds catch up with you and you are injured. The same applies on the street. You can be stupid, inattentive and oblivious and get away with it until your path happens to cross the path of a criminal. The vast majority of criminals are opportunists, who only strike when presented with a viable opportunity. Remove the opportunity and you remove the risk to you.

By learning to observe your environment, constantly evaluate it, and react appropriately to what you see, you can achieve a large degree of control over your fate. This requires you to learn to shift up and down a scale of readiness, just like shifting gears in a car, so you can match your level of awareness/readiness with the current requirements of your situation. In a car, you shift gears based on the grade encountered or the speed desired. On the street, you must learn to "shift gears" mentally, to match the threat level encountered. There is a sliding scale of readiness, going from a state of being oblivious and unprepared to a condition of being ready instantly to do lethal violence if forced. One cannot live stuck at either end of this spectrum.

Jeff Cooper, center, first publicized and taught the system called the Color Codes at the Gunsite Academy in Arizona and later gave an excellent videotaped presentation. The system consists of four mental states, which Jeff gave color names. (File photo)

If you try to live at the bottom of the scale, you will fall victim to an accident or to a criminal, eventually. It's just a matter of "when," not "if." On the other hand, you can't go through your daily routine with your hand hovering over your holstered pistol, ready to shoot if anything moves. What you must learn to do is escalate and de-escalate up and down this scale as the circumstances around you dictate. This is an easily learned system, and one that will help you be in the right frame of mind to deal with any conflict you encounter.

If you should find yourself faced with a life-threatening attack by a criminal, as a typical, rational person, you will be faced by three enormous difficulties. They are:

• Recognizing the presence of the predator in time.

• Realizing, internalizing and accepting that THAT MAN, RIGHT THERE, is about to kill you for reasons you do not understand; if you don't stop him.

• And, overcoming your reluctance to use lethal violence against a fellow human being.

Let's look at each of these in turn. First, you have to see him and realize he is a threat. Thugs are flesh and bone and are not invisible. They typically walk right up to you unnoticed because of the mental fog most people operate in daily. Learn to lift that fog and see the warning signs earlier, so you can be prepared.

Second, it is very difficult for normal, rational, socialized, civilized people to grasp that they live cheek by jowl with people who are NOT normal, rational, socialized or civilized. There are people out there who do not care about your hopes or plans for the future, they do not care about your family, they do not care about the pain and suffering they inflict. They just don't care. They might kill you for the contents of your wallet, so they can buy one more day's supply of drugs. They might rape you because they feel powerless, degraded and abused except while they are degrading and abusing someone else. They may kill you simply to move up one rank in their street gang. Guess what? It doesn't matter "Why?" A typical victim reaction is, "But why would anyone want to hurt me?" Who cares why?

Third, it will be difficult for you to put your sights in the center of a human being's chest and press the trigger, knowing you are turning a vertical, living, breathing person into a horizontal pile of meat. Don't let anyone tell you that will be easy. As a society, we don't want it to be easy, do we? This is why legally armed citizens don't shoot people over arguments, or traffic accidents and so forth. In fact, self-defense

shootings by legally armed citizens are almost always ruled justifiable by the authorities, while almost a third of police shootings are ruled questionable or improper. Private citizens are reluctant to actually shoot, even when it is necessary. You must overcome this obstacle if your life is on the line. You will have to realize there are times when lethal violence is not just excusable, or justifiable, or acceptable, but actually required.

Fortunately, there is a system available to help you overcome all three of these problems. By learning to use this system, practicing it, and making it part of your daily routine, you can be assured of seeing an attack in its developing stages, and become both mentally and physically prepared to defend yourself. Jeff Cooper, who taught it at Gunsite and later gave an excellent videotaped presentation, first publicized this system, called the Color Code. I had the great good fortune of being taught this by Jeff early in my career, and I can say without reservation that this system saved my life on several occasions. Not what kind of gun I had, nor the brand of ammo, but this mental system. I feel so strongly that this is one of the most important weapons in your arsenal, that I feel it is my duty to share it with you.

I mentioned earlier learning to move up and down a scale of readiness, just like shifting gears. The scale consists of four mental states, which Jeff gave color names. The colors simply let us conceptualize and cover the basic mental states. You must learn to go up and down this scale as the situation and circumstances around you change, as they invariably do as you go through your daily routine.

CONDITION WHITE

White is the lowest level on the escalator. In Condition White one is unaware, not alert, oblivious. This state can be characterized as "daydreaming" or "preoccupied." People in Condition White tend to walk around with their heads down, as if watching their own feet. They do not notice the impending danger until it literally has them by the throat.

You see examples of this frequently. When was the last time you saw someone in traffic roll right up to a barricade or stalled vehicle, then expect you to stop and let them into your lane? They're operating their vehicle in Condition White. When a motorist runs over a motorcyclist and kills him, what are the first words out of their mouth? "I didn't see him." They're not lying. They were so inattentive and com-

(opposite) Jeff Cooper and author Tom Givens, together in a photograph taken in 1980 in Virginia.

placent that they did not notice a 200-pound man on a 400-pound machine right in front of them. When this same guy runs past a stop sign and broadsides your car, he will say, "I didn't see it." How often do you see someone in public talking or texting on a cellphone, absolutely unaware of the people around him?

These same guys will be the victims of violent crime, because the criminal targets the inattentive, the complacent, the lazy, the distracted, the preoccupied. Why? Because the criminal wants to get to him, get what he wants from him, and get away from him, without being hurt or caught. Who would be the easiest person to do that to? Someone in Condition White. I'm sure you've seen or read about the Miranda card police officers carry. From it they read off a suspect's rights before questioning him. Dedicated victims carry a similar card in their pockets. If they are still alive when the police arrive, they take this card out of their pockets and read from it, as follows:

"Jeez, it all happened so fast. He material-ized right next to me. I never saw him."

Walking down a city street with your face buried in your cellphone would have you in Condition White: oblivious to what is going on around you. You should be in Condition Yellow: a relaxed state of general alertness, with no specific focal point. (File photo)

So, when would it be acceptable to be in Condition White? When in your own home, with the doors locked, the alarm system on and your dog at your feet. Then, you can turn off your mind, if you wish, because you have sufficient layers of protection and warning to enable you to get up, get your gear and get your head running. If you leave your home, you leave Condition White behind. The instant you leave your home, you escalate one level, to Condition Yellow.

CONDITION YELLOW

This is a relaxed state of general alertness, with no specific focal point. You are not looking for anything or anyone in particular; you simply have your head up and your eyes open. You are alert and aware of your surroundings. You are difficult to surprise, therefore, you are difficult to harm. You do not expect to be attacked today. You simply recognize the possibility.

Here's an excellent analogy. Let's say you are on a small naval patrol vessel in the middle of the Mediterranean, and the year is 1980. You are not at war with anyone today, so you do not expect to be attacked. You do, however, recognize the possibility, so you have your radar on 24 hours a day, making a continuous 360-degree sweep of the area, looking for potential problems. Suddenly, there is a blip on your radar screen. You cannot tell by looking at the small, greenish-yellow dot on the screen whether it is a good thing or a bad thing,

When in your own home, with the doors locked, the alarm system on and your dog at your feet, then you can turn off your mind, if you wish, because you have sufficient layers of protection and warning to enable you to get up, get your gear and get your head running. You are in Condition White.

"The entire difference between Yellow and Orange is this specific target of your attention."

so you ask a fighter plane to intercept the blip and check it out. If it is an Alitalia airliner 100 miles off course, the fighter pilot will wave at it. If it's a Libyan MiG headed toward your boat, he will shoot it down. He won't know whether to wave or shoot until he first assesses the blip as a threat. This is exactly the same process you go through on the ground. When you

leave home, you turn on your radar, and it continually sweeps the area around you for potential hazards. When something catches your attention, you assess it. If it's not a threat, dismiss it. If it is a threat, start getting ready mentally to deal with it.

Anything or anyone in your immediate vicinity that is unusual, out of place, or out of context, should

"In Condition Yellow, you pay attention to what is going on around you when walking down a city street. If you notice someone acting suspiciously, like he might be a threat to you, this person becomes the specific target of your attention as you move into Condition Orange."

be viewed as potentially dangerous, until you have had a chance to assess it. Someone who looks out of place, or someone engaged in activity that has no obvious legitimate purpose, should be looked over carefully. When your mental radar picks up on a blip, you immediately escalate one level on the scale, to Condition Orange.

CONDITION ORANGE

This is a heightened state of alertness, with a specific focal point. The entire difference between Yellow and Orange is this specific target of your attention. Your focal point is the person who is doing whatever drew your attention to him. It might be the fact that he is wearing a field jacket in August. It might be that he's standing by a column in the parking garage, instead of going into the building, or getting in a car and leaving. It might be that you have been in five stores at the mall and saw this same guy in every one of them. His actions have caused you to take note of him, so you must assess him as a potential threat, just as the fighter pilot assessed the blip earlier.

How do you assess someone as a threat? You have to take into account the totality of the cues available to you. His clothing, appearance, demeanor, actions, anything he says to you, are all cues. The single most important cue is body language. About 80 percent of human communication is through body language. Predators display subtle pre-aggression indicators, which are obvious when you learn to look for them. There is a huge difference in body language between a worker sitting at a bus stop waiting for a bus, and a predatory feral human hanging out at the bus stop, watching for a victim.

When you shift upward to Orange, you begin to focus your attention on this individual who caught your eye, but do not drop your general overview. You don't want to be blind-sided by his associates. You begin to watch him and assess his intentions, again looking at all of the cues available to you. Nine times out of 10, after a few seconds of observation, you will be able to see an innocuous reason for his behavior and then dismiss him. After you figure out he's not a threat, dismiss him and de-escalate right back down to Yellow. Who is the 10th one? He is the predator, who would have got you if you had been inattentive. Now that you are aware of him, you are in far less danger.

As you assess this individual, and you see things that convince you he has evil intent, you start to play the "what-if…" game in your mind, to begin formulating a basic plan. This is how we get ahead of the power curve. If he acts suddenly, we must have at least a rudimentary plan for dealing with him

already in place, so that we can react swiftly enough. By saying to yourself, "That guy looks like he is about to stick me up, what am I going to do about it?" you begin the mental preparation vital to winning the conflict. With even a simple plan already in place, your physical reaction is both assured and immediate, if the bad guy presses his intentions. If, after assessing him, you believe he is an actual threat, you then escalate to the highest level, Condition Red.

CONDITION RED

In Condition Red, you are ready to fight! You may, or may not, actually be fighting, but you are MENTALLY PREPARED to fight. In many, or perhaps even most, circumstances where you have gone fully to Red, you will not actually physically do anything at all. The entire process of escalating from Yellow, to Orange, to Red, then de-escalating right back down the scale as the situation is resolved, often occurs without any actual physical activity on your part. The key is that you were mentally prepared for a conflict, and thus could physically act if the situation demanded.

When you believe a threat is real, and you have escalated to Red, you are waiting on the Mental Trigger, which is a specific, predetermined action on his part that will result in an immediate, positive, aggressive, defensive reaction from you. This is how you achieve the speed necessary to win. By having a "pre-made decision" already set up in your mind, you can move physically fast enough to deal with the problem. Without that pre-made decision, the precious time in which you could have acted was wasted on trying to decide what to do after he starts his attack.

The Mental Trigger will differ depending upon the circumstances. It could be, "If he swings that gun in my direction, I will shoot him," for instance. It could be, "I have told him to stop, if he takes one more step toward me with that (knife/tire iron/screwdriver) in his hand, I'll shoot him." Whatever trigger is selected, it is a button that, once pushed, results in immediate action on your part.

Your main enemy is reaction time. If you are not aware of your surroundings, and fail to see the suspicious character, he might overwhelm you before you can marshal an effective defense. On the other hand, if you are thinking to yourself, "I might have to hurt that guy if he doesn't wise up," you've probably already won that fight, because you have a better understanding of what is transpiring than he does. The best fight is over before the loser fully understands what just happened. If you're caught in Condition White, you will need five to six seconds to realize what is happening, get your wits together and

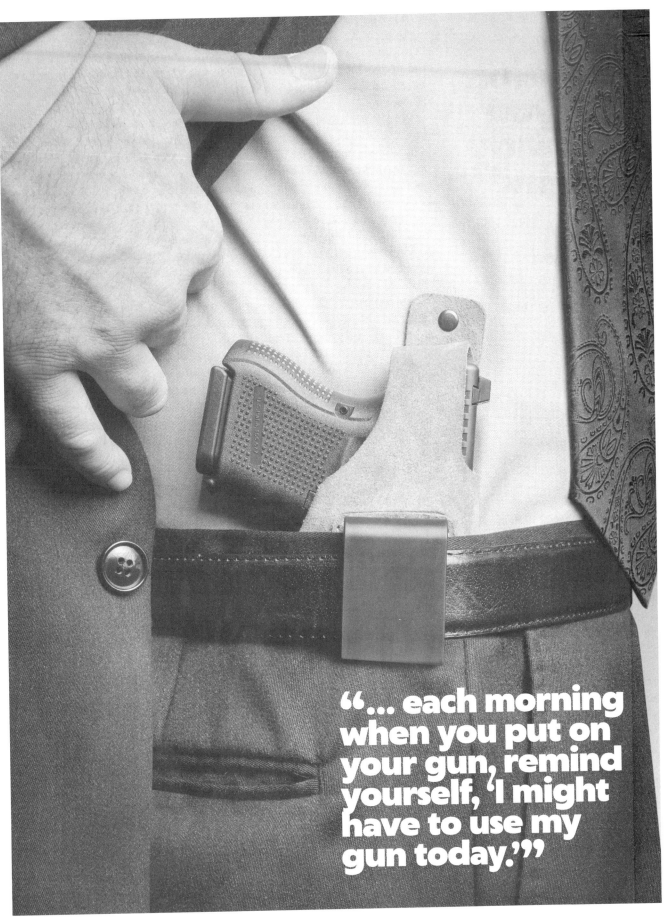

"... each morning when you put on your gun, remind yourself, 'I might have to use my gun today.'"

"In Condition Red, you are ready to fight!"

respond. You simply don't always have that much time.

There are a couple of mental tricks you can use in the early phases of your training to assist you in this. Remember one of the three problems I mentioned earlier in this chapter will be actually "doing it," actually employing lethal force when required. To help with this, each morning when you put on your gun, remind yourself, "I might have to use my gun today." This plants in your subconscious mind (which drives 90 percent of your life) that there is a reason we wear these

guns: We might actually need them to save our lives. When you pick up on that potential threat and escalate to Condition Orange, tell yourself, "I might have to shoot him today!" Believe me, if you have internalized that a specific person is an actual threat to your life, but that you have the means to stop him if need be, it gets easier to deal with the situation mentally.

Let's work through a scenario to illustrate these principles. Let's say you are working in a jewelry store today, in a small storefront shop in a strip mall in suburbia. All of the other employees went to lunch and left you here alone. There are not even any customers in the store at the moment, you're alone. What mental state are you in? (Yellow. You are not ensconced in your home; you're out in the real world.) So, you keep your head up, and occasionally you scan out through the glass storefront and check out the parking lot. Since there is no one else in the store, any problem will have to come from outside. You want to know about a problem while it's out there, not when it's standing across the counter from you.

As you glance through the glass, you see two men in their early 20s back up an old car to your store, get out in identical jogging suits, enter your door and split up. Immediately, you go to Orange. They have done nothing illegal, and nothing aggressive, but they are out of place, out of the ordinary, so you escalate your mental state and begin to think. "This looks like a holdup in the making. I might have to hurt these guys. What should I do now? If things go bad, I'll drop behind this safe and I can shoot into that wall without endangering anyone on the parking lot. I have a plan." At this point you watch them and continue to monitor their movements. If they leave, you de-escalate to Yellow when they are gone.

If they stay, they will probably get together on the far side of the store and briefly discuss what they have seen. They will then move toward your position at the counter, and after trying to distract you (Can I see that ring back there?) pull their guns and announce a stickup. If you have been using the system, you went from Yellow to Orange when they came in and went to Red as they approach your counter. You are ready. Because criminals have to be adept at reading body language (their lives depend upon this skill), they will see that you are prepared and simply leave. Most pairs will leave at this point, without a confrontation. As they drive away, de-escalate from Red, to Orange to Yellow.

What about the ones who don't leave? They might be drugged, drunk, or both, and failed to recognize your level of readiness. They might go ahead foolishly with their holdup. According to FBI studies, probably 80 percent of the ones you will actually have to fight will be under the influence of drugs and/or alcohol at the time. What's the good news? They're drunk and/or drugged, which plays hell with their reflexes, reaction time and motor coordination. They'll be relatively easy to deal with, IF you are mentally prepared (Condition Red) and have done your homework.

If they come in, and upon observing them you go to Orange, then as they approach, to Red, but then they leave, and you de-escalate, you will have gone all of the way up the scale without even reaching for your gun, which is very common. The point is, you would have been ready to reach for your gun if necessary. This is how you win fights, by being mentally prepared to win.

6

CONTROLLING FEAR AND MAKING SOUND DECISIONS UNDER STRESS

When a responsible person first begins going armed, he is usually haunted by two recurring questions, or self-doubts:

1. If I'm really attacked, and my life is at stake, will I be able to handle it?

2. What if I screw up and kill an innocent person?

This is a normal reaction, and to a degree it is healthy. We do, however, need to address these issues and resolve them, before a conflict, so they will not raise their ugly heads when we should be concentrating on winning the fight. Remember, if an unavoidable fight is thrust upon us, we MUST WIN!

The alternative can be death, or crippling injury.

The first issue to face is that of FEAR. Fear is a normal reaction to physical violence for most people. In addition, since most of us no longer have military experience and live in "civilized" surroundings, we might not have ever actually engaged in a true fight before our moment of truth in a criminal attack. This fear of the unknown is, for many, worse than the fear of being hurt or killed.

Unless you are an exceptional person, a nutcase, or a liar and you have actually been involved in armed conflict, you have tasted fear. I'm not ashamed to say I have been scared several times, and I fully expect to be scared again before my life is over. What you must learn to do is control your fear and do what you must to win.

Fear can be controlled and overcome, even in life-threatening circumstances. This is obviously true, and it is proven every day by hundreds of ordinary people all over the country. Here are some steps you can take to make this process easier:

1. Admit to yourself you are afraid, then move on. Concentrate your mental energies on the task at hand, not on your fear of death, injury, or loss of ego.

2. Avoid dwelling on the chance of failure. Concentrate on finding a way to win.

3. Take control of yourself. Autogenic breathing is the very best and most efficient way to do this.

4. Focus on getting the job done.

5. Have a Plan B. Always, always, always, expect Plan A to fail. Expect your gun to malfunction. Expect the suspect to stay up after being hit solidly. Expect to be injured. If any of these things occur, have a pre-planned option to continue (Plan B).

6. Turn anger into a motivator. Who does this clown think he is? What makes him think he has the right to (rob/rape/kill/pick on) me?

Carrying a concealed handgun requires mental preparation in addition to the physical preparation needed to draw and fire a handgun. Recognizing ahead of time that you will experience fear and stress in an armed conflict gives you the chance to address these issues so you can control and overcome these emotions when the need arises. (Photo courtesy Galco)

7. Accept an element of fate in every situation. You can get hurt by accident after doing everything right. Control everything you CAN control (selection of equipment, getting adequate training and practice, being alert, thinking tactically) so there are fewer things you CAN NOT control. Stack the odds in your favor, and fate has a lot less impact.

Courage under fire is not a matter of being without fear. It is a matter of being able to control fear and accomplish your mission, which is to stay alive. Only fools are fearless.

The other nagging self-doubt involves over-reacting and shooting someone under unjustifiable circumstances. If you are reading this, that should not happen. Citizens who are responsible enough to obtain carry permits, seek expensive training, make time for practice sessions, etc., are simply too honest, caring and self-disciplined to shoot people without just cause. Recently, in one state, there were eight fatal shootings by permit holders in three years. Every single one was judged to be justifiable and lawful by the attorney general's office. Not one of these permit holders was charged with any crime nor were they sued for anything. Why? Because every single case was clear-cut, obvious and morally, legally and ethically justified. Private citizens have a great reluctance to shoot, even when it is necessary. In fact, for many the problem they will face is the exact opposite of being "trigger happy." Believe it or not, people who are armed and know how to use their weapons, and who have a need to use their weapons to save their lives, fail to do so and die as a result. This happens to both private citizens and police officers alike.

You ask, "Why on earth would someone who is armed stand there and literally watch a thug kill him?" There are a number of reasons, and they stem from the socialization process the normal person goes through from birth (but the criminal does not). These reasons most often include:

1. Moral repugnance to taking a life: You have been taught all your life that human life is sacred, that to kill is wrong and that only bad people hurt others.

2. Failure to be mentally prepared: An astonishing number of people who go armed have never given any thought whatsoever to the fact that they might have to shoot someone. To many, the gun is a talisman, and wearing it is thought to ward off evil spirits. In fact, it is a tool, one used for regaining control of your immediate environment in an emergency.

3. Failure to understand the dynamics of armed confrontations: People armed with firearms have been killed by thugs armed with edged weapons because they failed to take the "lesser" weapon seriously; they don't understand deadly force is deadly force, whether applied by gun or knife; and they don't realize how quickly someone 10 feet away can get to them.

4. Inhibition by community pressure and fear of lawsuits: These are trivial matters compared to being killed, raped or permanently crippled. Get your priorities straight. Unless you are alive, these don't matter, anyway.

> "Courage under fire is not a matter of being without fear. It is a matter of being able to control fear and accomplish your mission, which is to stay alive."

5. Uncertainty about when deadly force is justified: This is a training issue. Be certain you understand the laws of your state as they apply to self-defense and the use of deadly force. When you have internalized this information, it is simple and easy to see when the circumstances fit the law. There is nothing subtle about someone actually trying to kill you. It will be obvious to you, to any witnesses and to the police.

The best way to be fully mentally prepared to actually press that trigger if you have to, is to develop a well-thought-out and plainly stated set of Rules of Engagement, long before you are faced with a crisis. This is referred to as a "pre-made decision," thought out, verbalized and firmly planted in your mind in advance.

I suggest the acronym IDOL, which stands for "Immediate Defense Of Life." Make a commitment that you will only fire as a desperate measure to terminate a threat to your own life, or the life of an innocent third party. If you pose an imminent and otherwise unavoidable threat to my life, or that of an associate (wife, partner, etc.) I will act swiftly and decisively to put you down and out. I will reach for my gun for no other reason, period.

Many people think about this incorrectly. They ask themselves, "If he does (insert scenario here), can I shoot him?" That is a recipe for disaster. Your question should ALWAYS be, "Do I have to shoot him?" Ask yourself, "If I don't shoot this man, right here, right now, will I be killed or crippled?" If the answer is "Yes," shoot him. If the answer is "No," try something else.

As with most things, this is a matter of training. Proper training ingrains the proper responses.

Repetition is the mother of all skill. With skill comes confidence. With confidence comes the ability to think under pressure and make sound tactical decisions.

Recent training assures retention of motor skills, which degrade quickly. The skills involved in rapidly firing a full-power weapon with precision are perishable and are lost completely without frequent practice. I suggest two or three sessions of dry practice at home each week, with at least one range session per month to maintain competency. Practice builds skill, skill builds confidence. Having a well-developed skill set, and the confidence that well-developed skill engenders, can help you keep your head and stay in control during highly stressful conflicts. "An amateur practices until he gets it right. A professional practices until he can't get it wrong."

The author recommends two or three sessions of dry-fire practice at home each week, with at least one range session per month to maintain the motor skills needed to rapidly draw and fire a full-power weapon. These skills degrade quickly and can be lost completely without frequent practice.

The Second Crime Scene

In certain types of violent crime, it is not uncommon for the bad guy to remove the victim from one place to another, usually at gunpoint. Typically, the victim is accosted in a relatively public place, like a shopping mall parking lot, and is then forced to go to a more remote and more private location. That second location is called "the

where they can be raped and/or murdered out of sight. You must not let the violent criminal remove all your options. Once you are face down on the stockroom floor, or tied hand and foot, there is little you can do. You must act before things reach that point.

Recently in Georgia, an armed citizen was able to turn the tables

in a holster," Dallas County Sheriff Harris Huffman said. "And when the customer got to the door, he turned around and shot the individual."

Of course, this was ruled a justifiable shooting. When you are being herded into a second crime scene at gunpoint, you are reasonably in fear for your life, and the time to act is NOW.

So, make up your mind now, that:

- I will NOT get on the floor.

- I will NOT get on my knees.

- I will NOT go to the stockroom.

- I will NOT be tied up.

- I will NOT get in the trunk of the car.

If you brandish a weapon and order me to do ANY of those things, you have declared total all-out war. You had better be ready for the consequences.

second crime scene" and is usually a pretty gruesome sight.

Unlike in much of the world, abductions in the U.S. are rarely ransom kidnaps, but rather are forays to obtain rape/torture/murder victims. The bad guy selected the second crime scene specifically because it is remote, or private, and will conceal his activity over a period of time. In business holdups, victims are often removed from the front of the store to a back stockroom or restroom,

on someone who was almost certainly going to kill the citizen and a store clerk. Here is part of the story from a local news source:

"Officials say the suspect walked into the store waving a gun in the air and forced a cashier and a customer (armed citizen) who was trying to leave the store toward a break room. The cashier went in first and the customer went in behind her, and the suspect had the gun on the customer and the customer had a pistol concealed

In certain types of violent crime, it is not uncommon for the bad guy to remove the victim from one place to another, usually at gunpoint. That second location is called "the second crime scene." When you are being herded into a second crime scene at gunpoint, you are reasonably in fear for your life, and the time to act is NOW.

7

VISUALIZATION AND MENTAL IMAGERY

"Only a fool learns from his own mistakes. The wise man learns from the mistakes of others."

— German statesman
Otto von Bismarck

Visualization, or imagery, is one of the most effective tools available to you for mental conditioning. This is vital to success in a fight. Under stress, your subconscious mind will immediately take over and direct your body to do whatever the subconscious has been programmed to do. If you have been programmed through training to respond correctly, you will. Panic is simply the lack of a pre-programmed response. Since your subconscious doesn't know what to do, it does nothing. (When in danger, or in doubt, run in circles, scream and shout!) Obviously, your odds of surviving improve drastically if you have pre-programmed the correct tactical responses before a crisis.

How do we program these correct responses until they become automated? There are three ways. First, you could engage in about a dozen gunfights. You would then be adept at making rapid, sound tactical decisions, if you are still alive! We don't recommend this method because the test comes first, the lesson afterward. This is a painful and expensive way to learn.

German statesman Otto von Bismarck said, "Only a fool learns from his own mistakes. The wise man learns from the mistakes of others." This is especially true in this business, where mistakes can be fatal.

The easiest way to learn from the mistakes of others is to read a big city newspaper each day as you eat your breakfast. Look in the local news and select two instances reporting the criminal victimization of some unfortunate person. Take five minutes to read these two accounts and actually analyze them. Ask yourself two questions and make yourself come up with an answer.

The first question is: "What did the victim do to put himself in this situation?" When you learn a bit about criminal behavior, you realize, above all, criminals are opportunists. They capitalize on circumstances created by inattentive, complacent, lazy, and unobservant victims. Very soon you will learn to recognize the behavior or activity on the part of the victim that facilitated or even precipitated the crime. This will hold true in probably 95 percent of the cases you study. Once you have identified the specific victim behavior that caused the attack, you are reinforcing in your subconscious that this is negative, or harmful behavior. Day after day, by doing this, you are programming your subconscious to avoid that type of behavior. If you don't present the opportunity, the criminal cannot take advantage of it.

The second question is: "All right, I was careless and got into this mess, how do I get myself out of it?" Make yourself think up a solution to the tactical situation. In this manner, you are getting practice every single day in making tactical decisions. If you make tactical decisions every day of your life, they will come easily to you if you find yourself in dangerous circumstances. If you have never practiced this decision-making process, how do you expect to do it well under extreme stress?

The last technique in imagery we will cover has to do with mentally rehearsing confrontations, to prepare beforehand for a confrontation. In your mind, as a normal, healthy person, there is a very fine line between reality and fantasy. A psychopath no longer has this distinc-tion in his mind, and his fantasies become his reality. A normal mind blurs this distinction under several circumstances. If you are an avid reader, for instance, you "see" the action of a good novel or historical account unfolding in your mind as you read. You form mental images of the characters and events, as if you had seen them yourself. How many times have you wakened from a vivid dream and took a few seconds to orient yourself? These are examples of that blurred distinction between reality and fantasy.

Be sure to spend some practice time using paper targets showing images of a realistic human form, rather than just generic round or square bull's-eye targets. Your subconscious needs to be accustomed to seeing your sights superimposed on such an image, otherwise you might lock up the first time you put your sights on a real assailant.

Airline pilots periodically receive training in a flight simulator, which is an enclosed box mounted on hydraulic jacks. Upon entering the simulator, the pilot is seated in a cockpit seat, a control panel is arrayed before him, and the "windshield" has a back-projected image on it, just like the view from a plane. As the pilot applies control movements to the stick and so forth, the "plane" responds with motion. Within a few moments, the pilot's brain is fully convinced he is flying a plane, although intellectually he knows he is bolted to the floor of the training building. At some point, the control panel will advise him of an emergency, and the "plane" will simulate the movement involved, as in a sudden dive. The pilot must immediately take corrective action to keep from "crashing." Although they are in no real danger, these guys come out of the simulator white knuckled and sweating, because the mind blurred the distinction between reality and fantasy. If, at some future date, the pilot is confronted with that actual emergency in a real aircraft, he will automatically respond, quickly and correctly, because his brain has learned that the correct action will save its life.

You can do the same thing with your mind in a self-defense context by using visualization exercises. Go to a quiet room and sit in an easy chair. Relax, and clear your mind of all thought (easy for some of us!). Now, in your mind vividly imagine a tactical scenario. Think of it as a daydream, if you like, but get into it and project yourself into the action. For every imagined action by the bad guy, direct yourself through a proper reaction. "If he does this, I'll do that." Always direct the action to a successful outcome.

Let me give you a couple examples. If you work in a retail environment, ask yourself, "What am I going to do when they stick up this place?" Visualize your workstation, and the surroundings. Where is cover? What direction could you fire in without endanger-

During training, pilots often use flight simulators to learn how to react to emergency situations. If, at some future date, a pilot is confronted with that actual emergency in a real aircraft, he will automatically respond, quickly and correctly, because his brain has learned that the correct action will save its life. You can do the same thing with your mind in a self-defense context by using visualization exercises.

ing co-workers? Is there an escape route available? Don't wait until a hold-up man is standing across the counter from you to think about this. If you are a boss, ask yourself, "What am I going to do if a disgruntled employee comes plodding down the hall with a shotgun?" Is there any other way out of your office? Is there any real cover available? Where is the secretary? You might find you want to rearrange your office. Find out now, not while under fire.

There are really only a dozen or so ways for a thug to criminally victimize you. White-collar crime has endless opportunities for innovation, but street crime is pretty straightforward. Over a period of time, you can visualize your way through just about all of the likely forms of street crime, and have pre-programmed responses filed away in the back of your mind (the subconscious) ready for deployment if faced with a similar circumstance.

One last area to address is that of paper targets used in practice. Beware of doing all your shooting practice on bull's-eye targets or only vaguely human-oid targets that look more like a milk bottle than an attacker. Do some of your work on targets printed with photographs or computer-generated images that look like a real, live, armed, threatening human being. Your subconscious needs to be accustomed to seeing your sights superimposed on such an image, otherwise you might lock up the first time you put your sights on a real assailant.

If you are faced with a life-threatening crisis in a form you have never seriously considered or given any thought to, you might hesitate just long enough to lose. If, on the other hand, you take a little time to practice these simulations, you can program ready responses and be better able to retain control of yourself and your actions. Your mind needs to know there is a way out, and that you know what it is. This avoids panic, and allows you to act decisively, which is your salvation.

8

AWARENESS GAMES, SELF-TRAINING

T he single most important element in your survival is a cultivation of your awareness skills. Many people don't realize their awareness skills are more important than their marksmanship skills. Well, you can't shoot something you don't know is there, or don't know it needs to be shot.

Awareness and alertness are not, for most people, innate behavior traits. This is a learned behavior pattern, and like most skills it is best learned through repetition. Make a conscious effort at first to be more aware and see the details around you. After a few weeks of effort, it will become second nature.

You should have been taught this as a child, but unfortunately, most children now are not taught this

Most carjackings occur at intersections, as drivers stare at the stoplight, waiting for it to change and not paying attention to what's going on around them. It's best to keep your head up, scanning your surroundings, looking for someone who might be acting suspiciously. (File photo)

or other vital social skills. One thousand years ago, all children were taught at a very early age to be aware, alert, and in tune with their surroundings. If they were inattentive, they might get eaten. One hundred years ago, children were taught to be aware and pay attention to their surroundings, or the hay bailer might tear off their arms and legs. In our time, if you fail to pay attention to your surroundings, someone might cut your throat. Each example is simply a different manifestation of the exact same problem.

On the street, you must be aware of your environment. If you know who is around you and what they are up to, you are in charge. If you do not know who is around you and what they're up to, you are meat. It's that simple.

When you walk into a room, scan around and see who is in it beside you. Don't be surprised by someone you did not see. When walking on the sidewalk, glance into storefront glass and see who is behind you. Get your head up, open your eyes and look around.

Let's look at a couple of examples. Carjacking is a very common problem right now. In fact, in my city there are about 1,000 carjackings each year, and roughly half of the victims wind up seriously hurt. This is a perfect example of how passive attempts to fight crime just make it worse, by the way. By putting steering-wheel locks, kill switches and car alarms on your car, it is now easier to drag you out of it while it is running than to steal it from your driveway as you sleep. Where do most carjackings occur? At intersections, as you wait for the light to change.

When a typical driver pulls up to a red light, he sits and stares at the light, as if it is going to sing and dance. He then hears a tap on his window and turns to look into the muzzle of a gun – too late to fix it, now. To avoid this, all he had to do was scan his surroundings instead of staring at the light. If you see a guy standing on the corner, looking at your car the way a hungry man looks at a steak, start thinking. You saw him because you are in Condition Yellow, and you go to Orange and start thinking, "What am I going to do?" "If he steps off that curb toward my car, I will accelerate around the car in front of me and be gone." Problem solved.

Another crime that really annoys me is the practice of following people to their homes in the suburbs and robbing them in their driveways as they exit their vehicles. This happens two or three times a day in my city. It cannot happen unless the victim is a willing accomplice. You have to go out of your way to have this happen to you.

I say this because not one of these victims lives on a major thoroughfare. By definition, they live in residential neighborhoods. I don't care where you have

been: bank, grocery store, ATM, theater; when you turn off the main drag into your neighborhood, look in the rearview mirror. It's not there so you can shave on the way to work, or put on makeup, it's there specifically to see what kind of car is behind you. If you make a turn into your neighborhood, again, look in the mirror. If you turn on to your street, again, look in the mirror. If you have made three turns inside your neighborhood and the same ragged old car you've never seen before is right behind you, you might have a problem. It is, however, a relatively small problem at this point. You are still mobile and in control. If, on the other hand, you are too damn lazy to look in your mirror three times,

In a retail environment, such as a fast-food restaurant, the cash register is the center of likely problems involving criminals. Be away from it, in position to see it and behind anyone who might be planning a robbery. (File photo)

pull into your driveway, open your door, and find a guy standing there with a gun in your face, you have a much bigger problem. Fix it the easy way, by being alert. Every fight you avoid, you win.

There are some exercises to help you become more aware. As a car passes you in traffic, look away and quickly describe it to yourself. What was its make, model, color, two or four door, license number? What was the gender, race, age of the driver? Of the passenger? Look back and see how much information you got right. When you walk past someone in the mall, mentally describe him to yourself. Hair color? Glasses or facial hair? Shirt, pants, shoes? Turn around and look. How much did you get right?

Right now, close your eyes. Visualize your own living room. Describe every detail to yourself as you visualize it. Describe the paintings on the wall. What is the title of the book lying on the floor by the couch? What color is the coffee cup left on the table?

What most of us refer to as vision is actually a two-part process, which involves sight and observation. Sight refers to the actual physical process of having light enter your eyes and make images on your retina, which are then transmitted to your brain. Observation refers to the process of sorting, prioritizing, and making sense of these images. This is where the typical person falls short.

Human beings are visually oriented creatures. Our eyes have been elevated off the ground with our upright posture, they have been moved to the front of our head, for stereoscopic vision, we have color vision, and our visual acuity is among the best of all living creatures. For a typical person, roughly 70 to 75 percent of all sensory input is visual. The average person, however, consciously processes only a tiny fraction of the total visual input the brain receives from the eyes. This is pathetic.

You must learn to raise this level of consciousness, through actual specific effort. You need to see the gun when it is still in his pocket, not when he pulls it out and points it at you. You need to see him standing behind that column in the parking garage, not when he is in your face. Shame on you if you get a speeding ticket. You should've seen the cop long before he could get a radar reading on you.

Let me give you a recent example of how being alert allows you to avoid problems. My wife and I stopped at a local barbecue joint for a sandwich on a recent Saturday afternoon. We were sitting in a corner booth by the entrance. Anyone who entered the store had to walk past us to approach the counter, giving us a good view and putting us behind anyone who started a problem. In a retail environment, the cash register is the center of likely events. Be away

from it, and in position to see it. Every time the door opened to admit a patron, my wife and I simply glanced up from our lunch to briefly look them over. This in no way interfered with the conversation or our lunch, but we were simply aware of our surroundings (Condition Yellow). The third man to come in was a young man of about 20. He was wearing worn denim jeans, and clearly outlined in the right rear pocket was a small semi-auto pistol. He had been sitting on it in his car and the gun's outline was clearly printing through the material of his pants. As he passed us on his way to the register, I quietly asked my wife, "Did you see the gun?" "It looks like a Lorcin .380," she replied. (She's very good at this.) Go to Condition Orange. I continue eating, but keep an eye on the young man, assessing him. As the customer in front of him paid for her order, the young man got up on his toes and checked the contents of the till over her shoulder. Condition Red!

It is obvious that he is planning a stickup. I empty my hands and mentally prepare for possible violence. Before pulling a gun and announcing a stickup, however, he decided to scan the store and take a headcount first. As he turned to me, his eyes got very wide and he ran out of the store, got in his car, and sped away, without ever doing anything remotely aggressive. What did he see that scared him so badly? I looked him right in the eye and smiled. He knew that I knew, and that I was prepared to deal with him. This is a perfect example of violence that did not happen because I was alert and aware of my surroundings. Situational awareness is often situational dominance.

The scary part was that no one else in the place, customer or staff, noticed any of this interplay. They did not see the gun, did not notice him checking the till, and did not even notice him hustling out of the place. Other than my wife and me, every single person in the store was in Condition White.

The predators are out there. They are looking for the distracted and the preoccupied. If you shuffle around, with your head down, looking at your feet, you might as well wear a sign around your neck that says, "Take me, I am a victim." Get your head up, open your eyes, and move them around. Take that damn sign off and get rid of it. It's not up to them whether you're going to be a victim, it's up to you.

9

INTELLIGENCE GATHERING FOR PERSONAL SAFETY

My dictionary defines "intelligence" as follows: "1. Capacity for understanding and for other forms of adaptive behavior; aptitude for grasping truths, facts, meanings; 2. Good mental capacity; 3. The faculty of understanding; 6. The gathering or distribution of information, especially secret information; 7. A staff of persons engaged in obtaining such information."

The selected definitions listed above accurately reflect what we mean when we refer to gathering personal intelligence. Make no mistake, the law-abiding populace of this country is at war with the criminal subculture, and the gathering of accurate intelligence on the enemy's identity, location and strength is a vital part of planning your overall defensive strategy. Unless you are aware of the threat, how can you plan to counter it?

In this chapter we will examine some of the facets of personal intelligence gathering and processing, to assist you in a realistic threat assessment of your environment, and to provide forewarning in street encounters with likely threat sources. While this will not be an exhaustive examination of every threat, it will at least expose you to the main elements of some of the more common criminal types with which you might deal.

The purpose of this endeavor is to allow you to recognize subtle danger signs that will be present prior to an assault. By recognizing these cues, you can place yourself on alert, and be thinking about a planned response. As we covered previously, being aware of a threat and having a plan in mind to deal with it greatly decreases reaction time, and helps overcome the mental inertia that slows down our response. When interacting with strangers, these subtle cues, once learned, can assist you in evaluating the proper degree of vigilance and readiness to act.

Be alert for these signs as you go through your daily routine. Forewarned is forearmed.

STREET GANGS

One of the most common threats right now is that of the violent youth street gang, whether that gang has its origins in the black, Latino, Southeast Asian or white communities. Street gangs, once confined to large metropolitan cities like New York, Chicago and Los Angeles, have now spread throughout the United States, driven largely by the lucrative market in illicit drugs, particularly heroin, cocaine and crack.

Street gangs become surrogate families of sorts for many members, providing the companionship, support, affirmation and respect missing from their home life. This mutual bond among gang members is the source of one cause of violence against non-members. "Dissing" a gang member (showing disrespect to him or his associates) causes him to lose face in the eyes of his peers, unless redeemed by violence against the person showing the real or imagined disrespect. Other attacks are motivated by desire for your money, and carjacking is a common crime

"Unless you are aware of the threat, how can you plan to counter it?"

Sometimes, graffiti is just an artful expression. Other times, it is the work of street-gang members who are marking their territory as a warning to other gangs. Knowing the difference between the two can help you be in the appropriate level of mental awareness when you see one or the other. (File photo)

among youthful offenders. In some organizations, gang members must commit a serious crime in the presence of a senior gang member to move up in the social order. Regardless of the intent, these are dangerous individuals, and they must be taken seriously as a threat.

Gang graffiti is not just vandalism; it is a form of advertising and communication. Gangsters use graffiti to mark territory and to establish dominance, just as a predator might urinate on the tree trunks around the perimeter of his home range. Gang graffiti must be taken seriously as a red flag; its appearance around your place of business means you must be on the lookout for gang members and activity.

DRUG ABUSERS

According to many authorities in law enforcement, as much as 80 percent of the crime in the United States is driven by the use of illegal drugs. From turf wars among drug dealers, to robberies for money to get money to buy dope, drug abusers are your single largest threat group. According to a recent detailed study by the FBI,

"According to many authorities in law enforcement, as much as 80 percent of the crime in the United States is driven by the use of illegal drugs."

80 percent of the offenders studied who had killed police officers were under the influence of drugs, alcohol or drugs and alcohol at the time of the fatal assault. Many types of drugs lower social inhibitions (this is why alcohol is so important to so many people at social functions). Unfortunately, these social inhibitions include the inhibition to kill a fellow human being.

The most commonly abused drugs in this country include: cocaine, crack, heroin, prescription opioids; amphetamines, methamphetamines and other nervous-system stimulants; PCP, LSD, MDMA and other hallucinogens; marijuana; and, of course, alcohol.

Different types of drugs can cause different physical symptoms, of which you need to be aware. In addition, certain drugs can cause psychological effects on the user that you must be prepared for. Remember, different people can have different reactions to drugs. A complete discussion of these drug types and their effects is outside the scope of this brief chapter, but the information is readily available.

MENTAL CASES

In any major urban area, street contacts with mentally ill or emotionally disturbed persons are practically unavoidable. According to the American Psychiatric Association, one of every three Americans will suffer some form of serious mental or emotional illness at some point in his life.

The most common group of mentally disturbed persons you will encounter is the "street person," typically a homeless drifter, usually shabbily dressed, unkempt, bearded and dirty. A lot of people will try to tell you these people are helpless, harmless victims of the failed mental-health-care system. This is not always true.

It is now extremely difficult in this country to involuntarily commit someone for a mental illness, even a serious one. Many mentally ill street people have been placed in care homes or shelters at some point, but since they could not be held there against their will, they left and went back on the street. In my experience, many of these people prefer uncertain life on the street to the structured and confining life in an institution. Of course, once on the street and broke, they have no access to medications, and no one to evaluate their progress or deterioration.

In my area, for instance, I used to patrol a residential area, which was a short distance from the main concentration of hospitals, including mental-health facilities. We would arrest these "disturbed persons" for theft, burglary or assault so many times we knew them all by name. Some were not violent, some were. In court, the judges recognized them as persistent offenders, but understood they were seriously mentally ill, so were reluctant to put them in jail. In jail, true criminals victimized these typically poorly physically conditioned people horribly. The judges were powerless to commit these individuals to mental institutions for any length of time, as the admitting psychiatrists would judge them not to be "an imminent threat to their own safety or that of others." Back on the street they went in 24 hours. One night, one of these "repeat customers" of ours, a 50-ish female of slight build, knocked a man down, sat astride his chest and cut his heart out with a steak knife. Sometimes three of four of us would have to "pile up" on one of these offenders to get him into custody without having to kill him. Harmless? Hardly. In fact, almost all of these people have an extensive criminal record, and a surprising number are registered sex offenders. They also can carry such diseases as HIV, hepatitis and tuberculosis.

A large percentage of these street people are armed, usually with crude weapons such as knives, screwdrivers, straight razors or improvised weapons. They are often very territorial about "their home," which may be a cozy spot behind your office's dumpster. They also tend to be very touchy about personal space, and inadvertently getting too close to one might be interpreted as the worst sort of aggressive attack against him, resulting in a furious assault against the "intruder."

Aside from the obvious "bum," be on the lookout for behavior such as a shuffling, uncoordinated gait; a vacant, thousand-yard stare; incoherent mumbling; talking to himself or unseen associates; and other bizarre behavior.

With anyone you suspect to be mentally disturbed, try these tips to avoid or de-escalate a contact:

1. Remember his personal space, and don't invade it.

2. Do not try to touch him, unless you are prepared to fight him.

3. Do not make sudden, rapid or startling movements.

4. Speak quietly and slowly. Do not shout.

5. Try to increase distance, and get an obstacle (parked car, fence, etc.) between you and him, as if he is armed it is probably with an edged weapon.

PLAIN-OLD CRIMINALS

Criminals must go through certain specific stages of activity before they can assault/rob/abduct/rape/etc. These stages will differ slightly in different types of crimes, but will generally fall into these categories.

1. Selection

The criminal views you as a prospective victim. He looks at your "victim potential," on two separate bases. First, do you have the type of car he wants, are you wearing expensive watches and jewelry, have you flashed a roll of cash, do you fit his rape victim profile? We think of this as, "Do you have what I want?" If the answer is, "Yes," he moves to the next question.

Then he evaluates you as a threat to him. First and foremost, are you paying attention to your surroundings? Are you aware of his presence? Do you look like you might be a physical problem? Do you look like you might be armed? I assure you he goes through these questions. We think of this as, "Can I get what I want from you, safely?"

If the answer to either question, "Do you have what I want, and can I get it from you, safely?" is "NO," then off he goes, in search of easier prey. Thugs are not looking for a fight. What they're looking for is the easy mark. Someone they can get to, get what they want from, and get away from, without being hurt and without being caught.

There were some fascinating studies done in which incarcerated career criminals were shown video of people walking down the street and asked to pick out the ones they would victimize and the ones they would pass. Although interviewed separately, the thugs almost always chose the same people to victimize. The victims walked with a less purposeful stride than the non-victims, and often had their heads down, unaware of their surroundings. People who walked with a confident stride and their heads up were deselected routinely by the criminals.

> "A large percentage of these street people are armed, usually with crude weapons such as knives, screwdrivers, straight razors or improvised weapons."

There are signs a potential attacker is evaluating you. They include:

1. Anyone who appears to be watching you should be viewed with mild alarm. If every time you look up, the same guy is looking at you, ask yourself, "Why?"

2. Anyone who is inactive until you approach, then tries to look busy.

3. Anyone whose activity is geared to yours. You speed up, he speeds up, etc.

2. Positioning

After a criminal selects a victim, he must move into a position from which an attack is possible. Always remember that to assault, rob or rape you, he must be close enough to talk to you. He will attempt to maneuver into this position by stealth (which is defeated by being alert), or by ruse. He might ask you for the time, for change, for directions, anything to distract you and preferably

"Thugs are not looking for a fight. What they're looking for is the easy mark."

Always remember that to assault you, a criminal must be close enough to talk to you. He will attempt to maneuver into this position by stealth (which is defeated by being alert), or by ruse. He might ask you for the time, for change, for directions, anything to distract you. When you look away, here comes the blow. The best course of action is to politely refuse any request, no matter what it is. (File photos)

cause you to look away from him. When you look away, here comes the blow. The best course of action is to politely refuse any request, no matter what it is. Keep your eye on him and say, "No." Anything you agree to is the springboard for the next request, which then can escalate to demands. Just say "No."

Positioning prior to the assault is vital to him, as he relies almost totally on surprise for success. If you avoid his attempts to properly position himself, you forestall the attack. Be alert and watchful for these cues:

1. Anyone who falls in behind you after you walk by;
2. Two or more people who are together, but split up as you approach;
3. Anyone staying in one place, observing, but begins to move toward you;
4. Two or more people lined up along a wall or fence; or
5. Anyone who moves to block an exit after you enter a confined space.

If you see one of these cues, cross the street, change directions, turn a corner. If he alters his course to match yours, he has tipped his hand. Get mentally prepared and start planning an escape or response.

likely candidate for physical aggression. Bear in mind, however, that 80 percent of human communication is nonverbal, and you must be aware of and watchful for these sometimes-subtle indicators.

One of the most reliable indicators of an impending assault occurs when you are in a position of authority and the offender fails to comply with or contemptuously ignores your commands. If, for instance, you encounter an intruder in your home, and he does not immediately comply with your commands, you are in for a fight.

Other definitive indicators can include these, alone or in combination:

1. Hands on hips
2. Cocked head
3. Arms folded across the chest
4. Fists clenched, or clenched and flexed alternately
5. Jaw clenched
6. Spitting
7. Deliberate avoidance of eye contact
8. Continuously looking around
9. Sustained verbal rationalizations
10. Continuous yawning and stretching
11. Target glancing

"Target glancing" refers to brief, repeated shifting of the offender's eyes to your chin, your nose, or your weapon. Repeated target glances to your chin or nose means he is gauging the distance for a punch. Target glances at your weapon indicate a gun snatch might be imminent.

Always, when the pre-attack indicators are present, shift to the highest level of mental readiness and be geared up. If at all possible, extend the distance between the two of you. Have a plan and be ready to move quickly.

3. The Attack

The attack phase can only come after the evaluation phase and the positioning phase. It is simply not possible to attack you until these first two stages have been completed. The very best defense, therefore, is to circumvent the attack by not allowing the evaluation phase and the positioning phase to be completed. Every single attack you avoid is a battle won. In every attack you fail to prevent, you are at enormous risk. A one-eyed, three-fingered jackass can miss you by 10 feet with a handgun, and ricochet a round off the pavement and into your femoral artery. Although you are "accidentally" dead, you're still dead. Be alert and use your head to stay out of dangerous situations.

BEHAVIORAL CLUES TO IMPENDING AGGRESSION

With the exception of the true sociopath, there will typically be cues, principally body language, which will assist you in forecasting aggressive activity by an individual you are observing. Being aware of these cues is vital to your accurate threat assessment.

Of course, verbalization by the offender is a critical cue. Someone cursing, shouting epithets, and generally being aggressive verbally is a

10

DEALING WITH THE AFTERMATH OF A SHOOTING

A number of people who carry a gun never give any thought to the fact that they might have to actually shoot someone in self-defense. The likelihood may be lesser or greater, depending on where you live, where you work, and what you do, but if you are involved in a shooting, you will be 100-percent involved. It is a good idea, therefore, to carefully consider the possibility and have some responses thought out in advance.

The first task you need to accomplish is getting your priorities in proper order. You should have three priorities:

1. Stay alive.
2. Stay out of jail.
3. Stay out of the poorhouse.

You can work your way out of the poorhouse. You can get bailed out of jail. You can do nothing about being dead. Stop by the cemetery tomorrow and ask them what it costs to bail someone out. They'll laugh at you. So, right now, make a commitment that you will survive, and you will do whatever that takes.

Now, let's look at a scenario. You are standing by your car on the parking lot of an apartment building. You might want to take note that 40 percent of all robberies happen at the door of a car, as the driver is getting in or out of it. A crackhead walks up, points a gun at you, and says, "Give me your wallet." As an afterthought, he then says, "To hell with it, I'll just kill you and take your wallet and your car." You consider this to be antisocial behavior, so you pull your gun and shoot him, then dive around the end of your car for cover. What now?

Remain alert. Visually check the crackhead from your position of cover behind your car. Scan the area carefully for any associates he might have. Don't forget to check behind you. Reload your pistol, so if the situation flares up again, you'll have a fully loaded gun to fight with. If you are certain it's over, at this point holster your gun and look for a safe place nearby to go.

Go? That's right. Your personal safety is of greater importance than keeping him in custody or preserving the scene. Stay where you can observe the scene, preferably with a wall to your back, but don't stand there over him. If nothing else, move to a nearby position of cover and stay behind it until help arrives. You are not fleeing; you are removing yourself from a place of great danger. As soon as you reach a safe

"Understand, once the police arrive, they own the scene and everything on it, including you."

You might want to take note that 40 percent of all robberies happen at the door of a car, as the driver is getting in or out of it.

point, stay there, call the police and await their arrival. In my experience, they are perfectly willing to meet you there. Think about it. When the police arrive, would you rather be a couple of parking spaces away from the downed suspect, gun in holster and hands visibly empty, or standing over a body with a gun in your hand?

Of course, this does not apply if you are in your own home or business when the event occurs. I am referring to street encounters, where you remain at risk as long as you remain close to the suspect(s). When you call the police, advise them someone was shot and needs and ambulance, describe yourself, and remember to tell them where you are, that you are armed and that you will wait for the police. If you cannot reposition for some reason, holster your gun as soon as you are certain the action is over, remain behind cover and be very wary and alert. OK, the police have been called, and it looks like the fight is really over. Because of your cultural background, you now think, "Oh good, the police are coming to help me." Wrong. Dismiss this thought from your mind. You are now entering the most dangerous phase of the confrontation. The crackhead was sprung, he was stupid, he had a stolen gun and didn't have a clue how to use it. The people coming now, for the most part, are straight, clean, sober and have bigger guns. You are in real danger. There are a number of dynamics arrayed against you, and you must understand that.

First, you took your phone from your pocket and called police. In most cities you spoke with the dispatcher or an operator, but not always. In my city, your call is handled by a less trained person who will relay it to a dispatcher, possibly creating confusion. Second, the call volume for any large police department is staggering. The cops in my city handle roughly 1 million service calls a year, which works out to 115 calls per hour. Yours is only one of them. Third, that information has to be relayed very briefly by radio to officers in patrol cars, blocks or even miles from your location.

The other problem involves your location, the apartment building parking lot. Several residents in the apartments might have called police, as well, perhaps reporting that a crazed individual (you) just murdered a man in the parking lot, and that you are still down there with a gun. Of course, responding police will be able to instinctively tell at a glance that you are a good guy, and not feel threatened by you, right? This is why we want to remove you from the kill zone if at all practicable.

All right, you're still there, the police arrive, what now? Understand, once the police arrive, they own

the scene and everything on it, including you. Do as you are told. If you still have your gun out and they tell you to drop it, do so. Don't try to explain, just do it. At this point they don't want to hear anything; they want to see the gun leave your hands. Next, you will be told to get on the ground. Do it. It will be a lot easier to get your Armani suit cleaned than to get all those little bullet holes fixed. Then, be prepared to be handcuffed. In my area, officers risk a suspension if they fail to handcuff everyone at the scene of a shooting until order is restored.

You will then be placed in the back of a squad car. Get in and be quiet and start to get your wits together. You will be incredibly hyper and suffering the effects of adrenaline and elevated heart rate. Take deep breaths to get your body and mind back under control. Chill out.

The next thing the officer does will endanger your life just as if he pulls his gun and puts it to your head. What will he do that is so hazardous to you? He will open the car door and say, "Now tell me what happened." Shut up! You are in no mental state to make a statement, which will be recorded and follow you from then on. Tell them politely that you will cooperate fully once your attorney arrives.

You need to identify yourself to the officer and give him the briefest possible explanation of what occurred, remembering to put the burden on the person who was shot. On every police report in the country there are two blanks at the top: 1-victim or complainant and 2-suspect. You want your name to be in the victim/complainant blank, not suspect blank. Advise the officer that you are willing to press charges against the person you shot if he survives. Point out any physical evidence, like the other guy's gun, for instance. Point out the location of any witnesses of whom you are aware. That's all.

Do not answer specific questions like how far away he was, how many shots were fired, how much time elapsed, etc. The combination of adrenaline and spiked heart rate will cause physical, mental and perceptual changes that make it impossible to accurately describe what happened for at least three to four hours after the event. In fact, in most police departments now, officers are advised to go home, get a night's sleep, and not make a statement until 24 hours later if they are involved in a shooting. The same advice would apply to you. As a normal human being, you will experience some of the phenomena associated with this stress. I'm going to describe some of these phenomena to you, so you will know what to expect and you can be prepared to recognize and deal with them. You will not experience all of them, but you are very unlikely to experience none of them.

You will have some combination, depending on your level of training, your personality, and your prior experiences.

AUDITORY EXCLUSION

This is a fancy term for deafness. Under the stress involved in a life-and-death encounter, your brain will often turn off things it does not consider vital. Hearing is often the first thing to go. You might not hear your own shots, or they might sound distant or diminished or muffled. You might not hear his shots. You might not hear someone shouting at you.

TUNNEL VISION

Again, a very common occurrence. Once your heart rate passes about 145 bpm, your entire circulatory system changes. Blood flow to the eyes is altered, affecting vision. Tunnel vision has been described as looking through a hole cut in a black wall. You might be able to see your assailant, but not people 10 feet to his side.

TIME DISTORTION

Some people describe an accelerated sense of time, "Jeez, it all happened so fast." More common is the perception of time slowing down, being unable to move quickly enough, or everything moving in slow motion.

DEPTH PERCEPTION

Related to tunnel vision in many ways. The threat might appear to be right in your face, when in fact it is some distance away.

BLOCKED MEMORY

You might physically do something during the fight, and have no conscious recollection of it afterward.

DISSOCIATION

This is a feeling of having stepped out of your body and serving as a detached witness to events, rather than a participant. In some studies, as many as 50 percent of the subjects reported this perception during a fight. If this happens to you, how could you give an accurate statement?

Again, you will likely experience at least a couple of these effects, especially in your first fight. To avoid compromising yourself, simply request your attorney and be quiet until he arrives. If you make statements about time, distance, number shots, etc., and the physical evidence contradicts your statement or independent witnesses contradict your statement, it sounds like you are lying. If the police believe you're lying about one thing they will not believe anything else you say. This is why we do not get into any specifics that you may not remember accurately due to the stress.

You may need the services of a good criminal lawyer who has deadly force training and experience. This is a specialty. Attorneys involved in this type of work have to get specialized training and keep up with evolving case law. They must know the homicide investigators and the attorney general's staff people. Your family lawyer is not qualified for this. Not one attorney in 1,000 knows any more about deadly force law than you do, because they have never handled anything remotely related to a justified self-defense shooting. Most attorneys handle business law, tax law, personal injury claims, divorce/child custody cases, real estate

"If the police believe you're lying about one thing, they will not believe anything else you say."

issues, not shootings. If you had heart problems, you wouldn't go to a foot doctor, would you?

One way to find such an attorney is to check with the local police union. The lawyer who represents local officers who have been involved in shootings will have the expertise you need. The local bar association can usually give you the names of any attorneys with specialized skills. Be sure to have the attorney's name and phone numbers in your wallet at all times. Another approach, as mentioned earlier in this book, is to be a member of a service that provides for legal assistance in the aftermath of a shooting. The ACLDN (Armed Citizens Legal Defense Network) is the one I specifically recommend, as I am personally involved on the board of advisors, know all the expert witnesses personally, and know of their success rate in dealing with members issues so far.

If you live in a reasonable part of the U.S., and you limit your use of your gun to strictly self-defense, and you keep your mouth shut afterward, you will either still be at the scene or in the detective bureau office when your attorney arrives. Go over what happened with him and follow his advice. Do not make any statement outside his presence. If the police try to question you in detail prior to the arrival of your attorney, tell them you will be happy to cooperate and you intend to make

On every police report in the country there are two blanks at the top: 1-victim or complainant and 2-suspect. If you shoot someone in self-defense, you want your name to be in the victim/complainant blank, not the suspect blank. (File photo)

a full statement, but not until your attorney arrives. They can no longer question you once you ask for an attorney.

When you do make a formal statement, your attorney will probably advise you to keep it brief, stick to things you cannot be wrong about, and put the burden on the other guy. Think back to the crackhead in the parking lot that started this episode. If I shot him, here's my whole statement, "He produced a gun. He announced a robbery. He said he was going to kill me. I feared for my life and shot him." I will not guess at the number of seconds that elapsed, or the number shots that were fired, or how many feet away he was, because I could be wrong. Simple, straight forward, direct.

A lot has been written in the past few years about the psychological toll suffered by people who are forced to shoot someone in self-defense. This post-traumatic stress is real, but it does not affect everyone. I know an awful lot of people who have shot others in self-defense, and every year three or four of my students wind up having to shoot someone. The

their moral position and not made a commitment to self-preservation. These are training issues.

In advance, long before you actually carry a gun, you must work out your own personal Rules of Engagement. You must be confident in, and comfortable with, your decision not to let some scumbag take your life away from you. If you search your heart and soul and become convinced that you could never, under any circumstances, take a human life, then do not carry a gun. It will be of no value to you, and you will needlessly endanger those around you. To carry a gun responsibly, you must recognize that you might have to use it, unhesitatingly, immediately to terminate a deadly threat to your own life or that of a loved one.

"A lot has been written in the past few years about the psychological toll suffered by people who are forced to shoot someone in self-defense. This post-traumatic stress is real, but it does not affect everyone."

Post-traumatic stress as it relates to justifiable self-defense shootings appears to be a recent phenomenon. I doubt David became impotent or an alcoholic after he slew Goliath. The difference is that in past generations, fighting was an integral part of life. One had to fight to defend the clan from marauders. One had to fight Indians to protect the homestead. Typical modern middle-class and upper-class citizens, including police recruits, have never fought in their lives, and are grossly under prepared for the realities of personal combat with a vicious enemy who does not play fair and is quite willing to hurt or kill you for reasons you cannot fathom.

Make a commitment right now. I will not seek a fight. I will do everything reasonably possible to avoid, deter or de-escalate any conflict. If, however, someone puts me or a loved one in grave, imminent danger, I will do whatever is necessary to win. I will survive.

vast majority of these people suffer mild symptoms, like occasional nightmares, or vivid memories of the event for a few months, but these are pretty tame compared to the effects of being dead or crippled. The horror stories of post-traumatic stress among civilians we hear about, with sexual dysfunction, severe depression, alcoholism, etc., appear to me to happen almost exclusively to people who fail to prepare mentally before a crisis.

As I've written before, an astonishing number of people who carry a gun have never given any serious thought whatsoever to the possibility of having to use it. They engage in a constant mental diet of denial, "It won't happen to me, it won't happen in my neighborhood." They have not considered, beforehand, the ramifications of going armed, have not considered

THREAT ASSESSMENT FOR THE ARMED CITIZEN

often hear the term "threat assessment" thrown around by people in discussions about firearms or training. Unfortunately, this is often used as nothing more than an excuse not to carry adequate equipment or not to train. For many people, there are three fallacies involved in any discussion of threat assessment, so let's examine those issues.

First, you need to recognize that in the field of personal security, your perceived threat level and your actual threat level might not be the same. For instance, let's say you live in the upscale part of a suburb with a historically low crime rate. You stay home at night, you don't do drugs and you work in a nice office in a secure building. Your perceived threat level is very low. This may well lead you to conclude there is no need to actually carry a gun daily or to devote a couple weekends to defensive training.

However, on the way to work tomorrow morning, while parking your car, two career criminals decide they need your car to get out of the area, and they are willing to kill you to get it. Your actual threat level on that day is quite high, but you are working on the assumption made in your threat assessment.

Or, another scenario: You are in your secure office building when a co-worker is fired. He believes, correctly or incorrectly, that you are responsible for the loss of his job, his pension, his health care and so forth. He decides to kill you on his way out of the building.

The problem is a life-threatening event which calls for immediate gunfire to save your life or the life of a loved one might be a low-probability event, but the negative impact of losing is so high we cannot afford to be wrong. The odds needing your handgun to stay alive might be 1-in-4, or 1-in-400, or 1-in-4,000, but if you are the one who needs it today, you'll need it very badly. I have more than 60 private-citizen students who have had to use a handgun to save their own life or the life of a loved one. All of them won their fights, and only three were injured. I do, however, know of three students of mine who were killed in street robberies. All three were executed for the contents of their pockets in separate incidents. All were unarmed at the time of their death. Their threat assessments told them they had no need to be armed on those days, they were wrong, and now they are dead. Remind yourself periodically, "It's not the odds, it the stakes."

If you live in the upscale part of a suburb with a historically low crime rate and you work in a nice office in a secure building, chances are your perceived threat level is very low. This may well lead you to conclude there is no need to carry a gun on a daily basis. Remind yourself periodically, "It's not the odds, it's the stakes."

A related misconception is that "since I have a low probability of needing a gun today, I'll just carry this little gun." I have investigated or studied literally thousands of shootings over the last four decades, including more than 60 cases involving my own students. I can assure you, in a life-threatening crisis you will be zero-percent involved, or you will be 100-percent involved. You will never be 40-percent involved in a gunfight. Either your life is in grave danger or it is not. If it is, you will be very glad you bothered to wear a mid- to full-size pistol and at least one reload for it. If you carry that gear religiously, every day for 30 years and you never have to use it, that's great. If, on the other hand, you fail to carry it just one day and you or a loved one are killed or crippled as a result, that's bad.

The final misconception is that we can eliminate risk. That is simply not possible. "Life is a sexually transmitted disease that is invariably fatal." (My favorite quote from Jeff Cooper.) What we can do is manage our risks. From a personal-safety standpoint, we can do this fairly simply by following these guidelines:

1. Follow John Farnam's Dictum: Don't go to stupid places, hang out with stupid people, or do stupid things.

2. Have a security professional look over your home and make the changes he suggests involving better deadbolt locks, window locks, lighting, and alarm system.

3. Learn to pay more attention to your surroundings when in public. Look for anything that is out of place. Watch people you don't know whenever they are nearby. Ask yourself two questions, "Who is around me?" and "What are they doing?"

4. Get some reality-based, self-defense shooting training. If you want to do a "man camp" five-day rifle course, that's fine. They are great fun. Mark that on your vacation budget, though, and set aside the time for training with a daily carry sidearm.

5. Accept the fact that to have control over your life and to properly manage your risks, you need to actually carry your defensive gear, every day. The gun in the safe at home simply won't help you on the grocery store parking lot.

> "The problem is, a life-threatening event which calls for immediate gunfire to save your life or the life of a loved one might be a low-probability event, but the negative impact of losing is so high we cannot afford to be wrong."

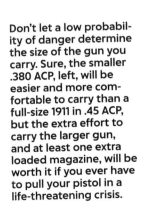

Don't let a low probability of danger determine the size of the gun you carry. Sure, the smaller .380 ACP, left, will be easier and more comfortable to carry than a full-size 1911 in .45 ACP, but the extra effort to carry the larger gun, and at least one extra loaded magazine, will be worth it if you ever have to pull your pistol in a life-threatening crisis.

The Bureau of Justice Statistics (BJS) is part of the U.S. Department of Justice. The sole function of the BJS is to gather data on crime in the U.S. and publish an annual report. The BJS considers only five crimes to make up "Violent Crime." They are murder, aggravated assault, robbery, forcible rape (as opposed to statutory rape) and assault.

According to the BJS annual report, in 2017 there were 5.6 million of those five crimes in the U.S. (That's right, 5.6 million!) To put it another way, that's one violent crime for every 30 adults. In urban areas, the rate was higher, but even in suburban areas, the rate was 1-in-50. Four out of five of these: murder, aggravated assault, robbery and forcible rape are precisely the crimes we would carry a handgun to defend ourselves against.

If you are one of the people who is victimized because you were unarmed, you run a real chance of being killed, crippled or raped. You might be left unable to work, to support your family, or you might be faced with a lifetime of regret that a family member was raped, injured or murdered because you were unarmed. Can carrying a handgun on a routine, daily basis be a pain in the butt sometimes? Yes, it certainly can. But, that is nothing compared to the aftermath of being crippled or your family having to deal with your murder. If you carry your gun religiously, day in and day out every day for the next 35 years but you never have to pull it, what harm has been done? If, on the other hand you get caught without it and you are killed or crippled or a family member is killed or crippled, what harm has been done?

Here is an exercise to help you overcome your reluctance, or hesitancy to actually go armed on a routine, daily basis. I want you to think seriously about this and list all the people who would be negatively impacted by your premature death or total disability. For most readers, that list might include a spouse, parents, your children, close friends and even co-workers. Make a list of them, and then determine just how each would be affected by your untimely death. In the case of your children, for instance, how old are they? What developmental stages in their lives would be affected by your absence? How will they turn out?

This exercise should make it plain to you that it is not just your own self-interest involved here. As a parent or spouse, for instance, you have obligations you cannot meet if you are dead or disabled. Your own safety and security are your own responsibility. Take that responsibility seriously.

> ## "If you carry your gun religiously, day in and day out every day for the next 35 years but you never have to pull it, what harm has been done?"

The Bureau of Justice Statistics, part of the U.S. Department of Justice, reports there were 5.6 million violent crimes committed in the United States in 2017. To put it another way, that's one violent crime for every 30 adults. (File photo)

12

TRAINING PRIORITIES

When setting up our own training and practice program, we are all faced with trying to determine how to prioritize the various skills we could work to improve. Which skills should have priority? Which skills are more secondary? It is my belief that when many shooters and a lot of trainers look at this issue they tend to be guided by the wrong information.

In this country, law-enforcement officers are involved in a lot of shooting incidents which are well-documented. The FBI has been gathering and collating information on these incidents since the 1930s, and each year it puts out a report referred to as LEOKA. That is the Law Enforcement Officers Killed and Assaulted Summary. Each year in the U.S., typically somewhere between 75 and 100 police officers are killed feloniously in the line of duty. The LEOKA

In this country, law-enforcement officers are involved in a lot of shooting incidents which are well-documented. The FBI has been gathering and collating information on these incidents since the 1930s. (File photo)

report has a brief, several-paragraph summary of each incident in which a police officer was killed in the previous year. For many, this serves as the basis for setting up their firearms training program.

I have a couple problems with this approach. First, we're studying the officers who, to put it bluntly, lost the fight or were ambushed. Second, the vast majority of these officers were working uniform patrol. The duties of a uniformed police patrol officer lead them to be involved in many, many dangerous incidents which, frankly, have nothing to do with the life of the typical private citizen.

The majority of shootings involving police-patrol personnel generally fall into one of three categories. The first is traffic stops. Often, an officer stops a car for a minor traffic violation without knowing the occupant is a dangerous and wanted felon. The second general area is bar enforcement. Officers go into seedy bars to enforce liquor laws, drug laws, gambling laws, prostitution laws, to break up fights and to look for parole violators. The third dangerous area consists of responding to domestic-violence calls. The cops go into the trailers, apartments and houses of people who are already drunk and fighting. As you can see, these three types of activities carry significant risk of being involved in violence. However, they have no crossover to the typical private citizen.

The problem is, the FBI report is about the only place most people know to look for information on gunfights. Although the information is not terribly relevant to the law-abiding citizen, it's all they have access to. I have done a lot of research over the past several years trying to find out exactly what is commonly involved in private-citizen, self-defense incidents and I have found a number of recurring themes. I prefer to structure my personal practice and what I teach to private citizens on these issues I see coming up over and over again in private-citizen, self-defense shootings.

Before getting into my own students' experiences, I'd like to touch on two law enforcement agencies whose experiences pretty much mirror those of the private citizen. The first is the FBI, whose special agents are required by policy to keep their weapons concealed when they're in business clothing and outside of their office. Thus, when out in public they are dressed like private citizens and carry concealed handguns. FBI agents do not make traffic stops, they don't do bar enforcement and they don't answer domestic violence calls. It surprises lots of people to find out around half of all shootings involving FBI agents occur because some thug does not realize they are law enforcement and tries to hold them up or carjack them. Therefore, their incidents closely reflect those

of the private citizen carrying a concealed handgun. Every few years the FBI does an internal audit of all of the shooting incidents involving their personnel. Their goal is to try to make certain their firearms training matches what is actually happening on the street, a laudable goal. Here are the results of a couple of their more recent internal studies:

Jan 2012 to Jan 2016

Total number of incidents: 26
Total number of rounds fired: 96
Average per incident: 3.7

Distance	Rounds Fired	Percent
0-3 yards	57	59
3-7 yards	10	11
7-15 yards	20	21
15-25 yards	9	9
+25 yards	0	0
0-7 yards		70

Drug Enforcement Administration (DEA) agents also get into a lot of plain-clothes shootings because of the nature of undercover narcotics work. In 2007, the DEA had 44 defensive shootings. The average distance involved was 14.6 feet and the average number shots fired was five.

As of May 2019, a total of 67 of my Rangemaster students reported back to me, or were reported through law-enforcement channels, after being involved in using a handgun for self-defense against armed criminals.

Of those 67 incidents, my students' record is 64 wins, zero losses and three forfeits. Of the 64 students who were armed at the time of their encounter, they all survived and only three were injured. We have, unfortunately, had three students I know of who lost their encounter and died. All three were killed in separate street robberies and all three **were unarmed** at the time of the incident, hence the term "forfeit." It's hard to win a gunfight if you did not bring your gun. Since 64 out of 64 students who were armed won their fights, we must be doing something right.

Here are some snippets of information from those 67 cases:

• Approximately 10 percent occurred in/around the home

• Approximately 90 percent occurred away from home

• In more than 90 percent, the range was 3 to 7 yards

• In two cases, there was physical contact

• Three cases involved distances at or beyond 15 yards

So, when we look at FBI agent involved shootings, DEA agent involved shootings and Rangemaster private citizen self-defense shootings, we see a lot of common factors. The vast majority of these shootings take place at 7 yards or less, although there are exceptions. Being able to get a concealed handgun out quickly and make good hits with those first few rounds seems to be the recipe for success.

So, let's look at some of the circumstances and conditions involving those fights, see how they compare to the FBI and DEA experience, and see if this information can help us structure our training programs correctly. First, the single most common type of crime resulting in defensive gun use seems to be some form of armed robbery. Whether someone is robbing your business, sticking you up on the parking lot, trying to take your car at gunpoint, or it's an armed home invasion, these are all simply variations of armed robbery.

There are a lot of common misconceptions about armed robbery. For one thing, armed robberies do not typically commence at arm's length. The whole purpose of the robber's gun or knife is to terrorize the victim into compliance from a safe distance. Once the victim is compliant, the robber moves in to take the wallet, purse, car keys, bank bag or whatever it is he's after. I often say, in our context, confrontational distances are the same as conversational distances. In our culture, we speak to people, especially strangers, from two or three steps away initially. That is also the distance from which armed robberies are often initiated.

Another common misconception is that bad guys beam down from the mother ship and suddenly appear next to you. Of course, this is nonsense. An awful lot of victims will try earnestly to convince you of this. "Jeez, it all happened so fast! He materialized right next to me! I never saw him!" I wish I had $100 for every time I've heard that exact quote from a surviving victim of violent crime. What they are admitting is that they were walking along with their head completely up their butt, totally unaware of their surroundings, and oblivious to the people and activities around them. They were walking through the parking lot texting or yakking on a cellphone

or were otherwise distracted and preoccupied and completely failed to see obvious warning signs all around them. We stress this to our students and encourage them to get their head up, open their eyes and pay attention to their environment. This is the key to dealing with the problem before it is right on top of you.

With that background information, in mind let's look at the 60-plus incidents involving our Rangemaster students. First, let's look at the distances involved. Only three incidents occurred at contact distance. In one of those cases, physical contact between the attacker and the defender was deliberate; in another, contact was purely accidental; in the third, there was no actual physical contact. This goes back to what I wrote about initiating conversations from outside contact distance, and of the advantage of being aware of your surroundings and being able to challenge someone before they are within arm's reach.

Distances beyond 7 yards were involved only in 5.2 percent of the incidents. Keep in mind, though, that that's about one incident in 20. We have had private citizen students who were forced to fire in defense of themselves or a family member at distances of 15, 17

and 22 yards. Thus, our practice regimen should include some shooting beyond 7 yards. As I was debriefing the student involved in the shooting at 22 yards, he said to me, "You know, when I had to hit that guy all the way across the street it never occurred to me that I was a statistical exception. I just had to deal with it." Truer words were never spoken. You might be the individual faced with that somewhat rare longer shot, so you should be prepared for it.

The rest of the shootings, 93.1 percent of them, occurred at between 3 yards and 7 yards with more than 80 percent occurring between 3 and 5 yards. The typical American sedan is 16 feet long, so one car length is about 5 yards. It would be safe to say then, the majority of private-citizen, self-defense shootings occur between a couple steps away and the length of a typical car. Based on that, we do the majority of our training and practice at that 3- to 5-yard distance.

Victims of armed robbery often report the criminal appeared out of nowhere. The reality, in most cases, is that they were totally unaware of their surroundings, and oblivious to the people and activities around them. They were walking through the parking lot texting or yakking on a cellphone or were otherwise distracted and preoccupied and completely failed to see obvious warning signs all around them. (File photos)

More than 90 percent of the nearly 70 shooting incidents involving the author's Rangemaster students happened at distances of 3 to 7 yards. In violent confrontations at these short distances, it's important to be able to quickly draw a handgun and get it into the proper shooting position. This takes practice.

Our shooting incidents typically involve a fairly small number of shots, say three to four rounds. We have, however, had a number of shootings that required more rounds. Right off, I can recall student shootings involving eight, 11 and 12 rounds. None of our students have had to reload during a fight, although I can think of three who went to slide lock. Fortunately, no further firing was necessary at that point. In our training, we heavily stress firing with two hands at eye level. We

only shoot with one hand if we only have one hand available. As a result, the vast majority of our students' shootings have involved two-handed, eye-level shooting and, as a result, the hit ratio is running around 95 percent.

No student has used, nor felt the need for, a flashlight in any of our shootings. This is another topic in

which there is a lot of misunderstanding among the shooting population.

There is an often-quoted statistic that claims 80 percent of pistol fights occur in the dark. This is nonsense. A more accurate statement would be that 80 percent of pistol fights occur during the *hours of darkness*. For statistical purposes the hours of darkness are from 6 p.m. until 6 a.m. Obviously, in much of the country it is not dark during that entire period. Secondly, criminal encounters do not occur in a vacuum. There is no more reason for a bad guy to be in the dark than there is for you to be in the dark. Just because it's 3 a.m. on the Stop 'n Rob parking lot does not mean it's dark. In fact, with modern commercial lighting, I have actually seen my sights more clearly late at night on one of these parking lots than in the afternoon on an overcast day. Law-enforcement officers often have to go into very dark places to search out hiding suspects. Again, it is matter of context. That is completely different than a thug approaching you on a lighted parking lot at night.

To summarize, our students' experience and those of the FBI and DEA seem to be quite similar. Shootings involve a defender in civilian clothing with a concealed handgun. The majority of the FBI's shootings occurred at 6 to 10 feet; the DEA's at an average of 14.6 feet; and the vast majority of ours at 3 to 7 yards. Typically, the number of shots fired is fairly low, but there are numerous exceptions. Shootings at 15 to 25 yards occur far less frequently, but often enough to be of concern. With this in mind I would suggest the following as the skills a private citizen should work toward competency in:

1. Fast, efficient, reliable presentation of the handgun from concealment;

2. The ability to accurately place several quick shots into an anatomically important area of the target at a distance of 3 to 7 yards;

3. The ability to place an anatomically important hit in a reasonable amount of time beyond 7 yards out to at least 25 yards;

4. The ability to reload the handgun quickly and efficiently, especially if it holds fewer than 10 rounds;

5. The ability to rapidly move off the line of force (sidestep) without hindering the presentation of the pistol from concealment.

Other skills such as malfunction remedies; alternate shooting positions, such as kneeling; the use of cover; and flashlight-assisted shooting techniques could be useful skills after mastery of the basic skills listed above has been accomplished. Early in your training, I would prefer to see all effort directed toward competency in the core skills I listed. I think the best approach is to model our training to match what we see occurring over and over again in the field, rather than hope what happens in the real world mirrors what we like to do on the range.

SHOOTING INCIDENTS: COMMON FACTORS AMONG PERSONS ARMED, BUT IN PLAIN CIVILIAN CLOTHING

1. FBI-Agent-Involved Shootings, 1989-1994

Average 20 to 30 shootings per year, typically in plain civilian clothing.

FBI agents don't do patrol work, don't police bars, don't answer domestic disturbance calls, their shootings closely parallel those of private citizens.

Roughly half of shootings involving FBI special agents occur because a criminal attempting to rob or assault someone they think is a private citizen turns out to be an FBI agent.

Ninety-two percent occurred at 6 to 10 feet.

Average rounds fired: 3.2.

At 21 to 50 feet, the average number of rounds fired jumped to 6.36.

2. Drug Enforcement Administration (DEA) Discharge Report, 2007
Shots fired in 56 incidents.

Of these, 12 were accidental discharges, usually during cleaning (clear your gun!).

Of the 44 defensive shootings:

• Average distance was 14.6 feet (about the length of a car).

• Average rounds fired: 5.

3. Rangemaster-Student-Involved Shootings

As of May 2019, 67 incidents. Of these, 10 were selected for a presentation at the 2008 Tactical Conference and the NTI. Of those 10 representative shootings:

• Five of 10 involved an armed robbery by one or two suspects;

• Three occurred on mall parking lots, only one occurred in home;

• In all but one, the range was inside the length of a large car/SUV;

• Four out of 10 incidents involved two or more suspects;

• Average number of shots fired was 3.8 (low, one; high, 11).

Common Threads:
• FBI: 6-10 feet; DEA: 14.6 feet; Rangemaster: 6-15 feet/one car length (average sedan is 16 feet long)

• FBI agents, DEA agents and civilians with carry permits wear their guns in plain civilian clothing, concealed. Plain clothing, gun concealed, but need fast access.

• High probability of more than one assailant.

• Most occur in public areas, parking lots, malls, NOT at home. WEAR YOUR GUN!

INCIDENT TRENDS AND HOW THAT AFFECTS TRAINING

At present, we are at 67 student-involved incidents with good debriefs. The current tally is 64 wins, zero losses, three forfeits. Henceforth, I will simply refer to these as incidents.

I am fully aware 67 incidents represent a statistically insignificant number. However, when we see the same things occurring over and over again, I consider that a clue.

Of our 67 so far:

• Three occurred at contact distance;

• Three occurred at 5-7 yards;

• Three occurred between 15 and 25 yards;

• And 58 occurred at between 3 and 5 yards. (86 percent).

For purposes of discussion, I suggest the following definitions pertaining to distance:

Two yards is the outer limit for confrontations happening in what the author defines as Extreme Close Quarters. Only three of the author's Rangemaster students were involved in incidents at contact distance.

Extreme Close Quarters: 0 to 2 yards. If two people are standing, facing each other, and both outstretch their arms forward, they would touch or almost touch. You have not been paying attention to your environment if the first time you are aware of the bad guy is when he is within arm's reach.

Close Quarters: 3 to 5 yards. This is essentially from just beyond two arms' reach to the length of a car. This is where 86 percent of our incidents occurred, and I believe that holds for legitimate civilian self-defense shootings in general. This is where the bulk of civilian training/practice should occur.

Five yards is the outer limit for Close-Quarter situations and is about the length of an average sedan. Eighty-six percent of the author's 67 Rangemaster students were involved in incidents at distances of 3 to 5 yards.

Open Quarters: 5 to 7 yards.
Less common, because you are leaving conversational distance. To speak to someone, as in making a robbery demand, one will usually be within one car length of the person spoken to. Conversational distances equal confrontational distances.

Mid-Range: 7 to 25 yards.
More common than Extreme Close Quarters, but still not typical. We should put some effort into training at this distance.

Seven yards is the outer limit for what the author defines at Open Quarters. Incidents at these distances are not as frequent because the people involved are beyond conversational distance.

Long Range: 25 yards and beyond. Has not come up in 67 incidents. Longest range in one of our incidents so far was 22 yards. The only scenario I can envision here for a private citizen would be an active shooter across the food court at the mall. An accomplished shooter should practice this some, for familiarization. This is probably beyond the scope for the typical CCW person.

I have started referring to distance on the training range in "car lengths" rather than in yards or meters. I find typical modern students have no concept of distance measured in yards/meters,

but all are familiar with a car length. The typical American sedan is 16 feet long, so one car length is about 5 yards. Two car lengths are 10 yards, three car lengths are 15 yards, and so on. This seems to work well.

Given the distances broken down in our incidents, I believe the bulk of our practice should be at one car length, or 3 to 5 meters/yards. One should have some familiarity with contact-distance shooting and with mid-range engagement, but since roughly 90 percent of our incidents occurred at 3, 4 or 5 yards, that is where we spend the bulk of our training effort in Rangemaster courses.

13

SIDEARM REQUIREMENTS

The sidearm is a piece of emergency-safety equipment carried on the person in anticipation of need and intended to immediately terminate a sudden, lethal attack. For various reasons, a lot of people who wear a sidearm seem to forget completely the reason it's there and focus their attention on features such as handiness, how concealable it is, its weight or even cosmetic appearance. Given the very serious purpose of the sidearm, that is sheer folly.

If you are truly convinced you don't really need a sidearm for your personal safety, why bother to wear one at all? On the other hand, if you recognize such a need, doesn't the fact that you need a firearm for protection of your life indicate that you should have a piece well-suited to the task? You might remind yourself the only reason we would draw our pistol is because we believe our own life or that of a loved one is in grave, immediate, mortal danger.

A word we need to keep in mind in any facet of this discipline is "context." When we select any tool, the first question we have to ask is, "What are we trying to do?" If you have a screw sticking out of a threaded aperture, you need a screwdriver. If you have a piece of conduit you need to cut in half, you need a hacksaw. When you need one, the other will likely do you no good. The same is true of equipment in our context. Whether selecting a handgun, a holster or other item of equipment the first thing we must ask ourselves is, "What is it for?" In our context, we need a handgun we can discreetly con-

"One often-quoted mis- conception is 'all guns are made for killing.' This is nonsense."

ceal on our person as we go about our daily routine so we can respond to a sudden, unforeseen crisis in which our life is in immediate danger. That is a pretty specific context.

The true requirements of a personal-fighting pistol run somewhat contrary to fad, fashion and the imagination of certain gun-magazine writers. A good, solid defensive pistol is apt to be less flashy, innovative or sexy than the current fad; but that should not influence your selection. Instead, as with any type of emergency safety equipment, your selection should be based on the equipment's intended purpose and the circumstances under which you might need it.

What then are the requirements for a serious personal sidearm? A sidearm must be reliable, effective, portable and ergonomic. Everything else is gravy.

Reliability is the single most important element in the selection of a personal defense weapon. The only justification for firing a weapon at a human being is to stop that person from killing or seriously injuring you or a third party. If you need a pistol for real, you need it very badly indeed. Your pistol must work each and every time you reach for it. If it doesn't, get it fixed or replace it.

For the next requirement, the pistol has to be effective. To be of use to you in a real-life fight, the pistol must be capable of rapidly and reliably putting down a grown man with as few hits as possible in as short a time as possible. Many handgun/cartridge combinations are simply not capable of this and should be avoided. Gunfights are amazingly fast, frighteningly close in affrays and any delay in incapacitating your opponent can be your undoing. Remember, in a real gunfight, it matters not who gets off the first shot. What matters is who gets the first disabling hit, and the longer your opponent is conscious and on his feet the longer you are at risk.

One often-quoted misconception is "all guns are made for killing." This is nonsense. Many, many handguns, rifles and shotguns are made for purely sporting use, many times involving only paper targets. Even if live game is involved, it is quite often small game such as squirrels or rabbits. A handgun cartridge intended to cleanly harvest a 1-pound squirrel is probably not the cartridge you need to stop a 200-pound attacker. This ought to be obvious, but apparently it is not.

Another thing to remember is, compared to a rifle or a shotgun any handgun is woefully underpowered. Handguns are not capable of many of the things attributed to them in the movies. The impact of a pistol bullet will not propel a man over the hood of a car, off the balcony or through plate glass. Handguns are governed by the same laws of physics as everything else, and as per Newton's Third Law of Motion, if I had a handgun that would knock you down if I shot you with it, it would knock me down to shoot it. Handgun bullets essentially drill holes. Those holes have to be drilled deeply, to get to the vital organs, and do as much damage as they can. We will explore this more in a later chapter.

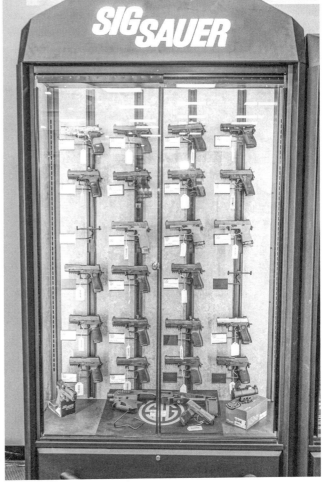

Whether selecting a handgun, a holster or other item of equipment the first thing we must ask ourselves is, "What is it for?" In our context, we need a handgun we can discreetly conceal on our person as we go about our daily routine so we can respond to a sudden, unforeseen crisis in which our life is in immediate danger. That is a pretty specific context.

The next requirement for the sidearm is it must be wearable, or portable. If you do not have it with you, it will do you no good. This will not be the same handgun for a 5-foot-tall, 105-pound female and a 6-foot-5-inch, 275-pound man. In addition to overall body size and physique, hand size has a great deal to do with handgun selection. There is no one-size-fits-all sidearm and there's nothing gender-specific about handguns. We need the most powerful and easy to shoot pistol we can adequately conceal on our person, not some tiny little gun that just makes us feel better, but will not allow us to fight effectively.

The last requirement is the handgun must be ergonomic, or user-friendly. Controls such as a manual safety, slide latch, magazine release, etc. must be located so they can be worked easily, quickly and with as little shifting of the grip as possible. Many, many handguns are very poorly designed in this regard. That is because the majority of them were not designed as defensive weapons. They were designed as hunting pistols, target pistols or plinking pistols. None of those pursuits share our extreme need to be able to get the gun into action quickly and reliably.

Accuracy can be overstated in a combat pistol. A useful level of practical accuracy is required, since you must be able to hit your assailant in the vitals in order to score regardless of the potential power of your weapon/load. In general, if the pistol can fire a group inside a 5- to 8-inch circle at 50 yards it is quite adequately accurate for defensive shooting. I am happy with a pistol for defensive use if I can shoot from a two-handed standing position and keep five shots in a 2- to 3-inch group at 25 yards. That is plenty accurate for our general use. Beware of efforts to tighten up your pistol to squeeze the last bit of accuracy out of it. This tends to reduce the pistol's reliability. Refer back to item number one, reliability is paramount.

Once again, the basic requirements for a self-defense pistol are that it has to be reliable, effective, wearable and user-friendly. Additional considerations such as finish or price are purely secondary and should be considered only after the primary requirements have been met. Remember that the choice of your sidearm is one of the few decisions you will make that could literally mean the difference between living and dying, so choose wisely.

Accuracy can be overstated in a combat pistol. The author is happy with a pistol for defensive use if he can shoot from a two-handed standing position and keep five shots in a 2- to 3-inch group at 25 yards.

Modifications and Accessories

We are fortunate in that most of the currently produced top-of-the-line, self-defense pistols come from the factory pretty much ready to use. In the past, we used to have to do all sorts of things to the stock pistol to obtain maximum performance from it. Today the things we do to those pistols are largely cosmetic or give us small personal enhancements such as sights we personally prefer.

When considering any modification on your sidearm, remember the KISS principle (Keep It Simple, Stupid). Any mechanical alteration should be considered carefully, with reliability in mind. Always remember the first requirement of the fighting pistol is reliability, and any alteration that compromises reliability must be avoided. With the exception of cosmetic touches, such as pretty finishes, all alterations should be judged on the basis of their ability to enhance the effectiveness of the piece. The tendency, for some, is to do more to the pistol than is necessary. This is sometimes encouraged by gunsmiths who make their living adding on or altering parts. If it ain't broke, don't fix it.

For a pistol that will actually be carried concealed, which means it will be riding very close to your body under your clothing, one thing that will really help is a process called "de-horning or melting." The objective is to remove all sharp corners and edges from the pistol to prevent wear and tear on the clothing, the holster and the user's hands. Newer models are pretty good in this regard, but some pistols still come with a lot of sharp edges and corners that need to be broken or beveled.

When we get into shooting technique, you will learn that high-visibility, high-contrast sights you can visually pick up quickly and easily are a great boon to high-level marksmanship. This is an area where there is a lot of personal

> **"With the exception of cosmetic touches, such as pretty finishes, all alterations should be judged on the basis of their ability to enhance the effectiveness of the piece."**

preference involved. A number of manufacturers offer aftermarket sights for semi-auto pistols. On most modern pistols both the front and rear sight sit in dovetails and can be easily replaced. If you want better or more visible sights, that is a simple and beneficial modification.

In the past, we also had to worry more about gun finishes. Many handguns were made of carbon steel with a blue finish, which is really a type of surface oxidation and provides no protection at all against rust. A handgun worn next to the body can come in contact with sweat, and a blue-steel pistol will rust very quickly. This is not so much an issue nowadays with most manufacturers. A polymer or aluminum frame will not rust, and many modern defensive pistols have either stainless steel slides, rustproof coatings or both. If

High-visibility, high-contrast sights you can visually pick up quickly and easily are a great boon to high-level marksmanship. A number of manufacturers offer aftermarket sights for semi-auto pistols. If you want better or more visible sights, that is a simple and beneficial modification.

you do decide to have your gun finished, either for corrosion protection or for aesthetic purposes, there are a few things you ought to know.

A Parkerized finish, such as many military weapons have, is a phosphating process that provides fairly good wear, is non-glare and is a little bit rust-resistant, although certainly not rustproof. Bright nickel is probably not a good choice. It is slick to the touch, reflects a lot of light, and will peel with hard use. If you want a light-colored finish either electroless nickel or hard chrome would be a better choice. Of the two, electroless nickel seems to stand up better to hard use and corrosion resistance.

There are a number of heat-cured, phenolic-resin "paint" finishes available today, including Cerakote and Duracote and others. These are relatively inexpensive, are rustproof and can be had in just about any color you desire. Where I live in the South it gets awfully hot and humid in the summer, so I use to have a pistol set up the way I wanted it, made sure that it was dehorned and zeroed, then had it hard chromed or electroless nickeled and then a black heat cured paint finish applied over the hard chrome or electroless nickel. This gave me a dark, non-glare, low-profile finish on the gun that was completely rustproof.

I would suggest you stay away from extended magazine releases and extended slide latches on a concealed-carry pistol. These extended parts are intended for competition use and, when carried close to the body, can be inadvertently activated.

Polymer-framed pistols are extremely common today. They usually have some form of texture molded into the grip frame to aid in gripping the gun consistently. I find most of these textures insufficient, especially with wet hands. A number of shops specialize in stippling, or otherwise roughening,

the texture of these polymer-grip frames to make them easier to grip in a stable manner.

Glock pistols have a somewhat rectangular grip-frame profile, and for me the bumps of the finger grooves are in exactly the wrong places. I also have fairly small hands for a man of my size. I, and many, many other Glock users send our pistols off to have what is called a "grip reduction" done on them. In my case I have the finger bumps removed, the circumference of the grip reduced somewhat and the pronounced hump at the lower rear of the Glock grip frame removed. This gives me a much more comfortable and secure grip on the pistol and when combined with a more aggressive grip texture this gives me optimal performance.

A number of shops specialize in this service, including Boresight Solutions, Bowie Custom Concepts, ROBAR and many others. My personal choice is Boresight Solutions in Davie, Florida, which does all my Glocks.

Polymer-framed pistols usually have some form of texture molded into the grip frame to aid in gripping the gun consistently. The author finds most of these textures insufficient, especially with wet hands. A number of shops specialize in stippling, or otherwise roughening, the texture of these polymer-grip frames to make them easier to grip in a stable manner.

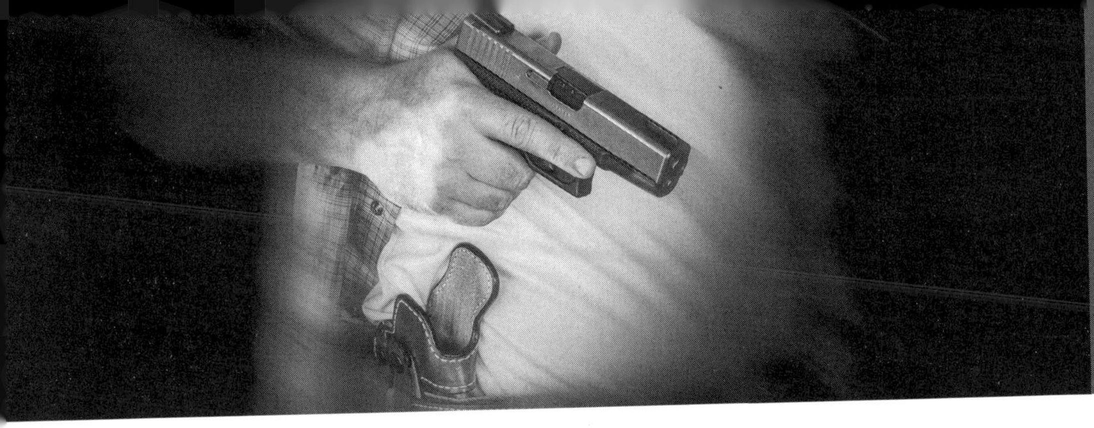

14

SELECTING A SIDEARM

Selecting an appropriate sidearm is a highly personal process, as what is right for one person might be completely wrong for another. As noted in the preceding chapter, there are a number of items we need to look at in selecting a defensive pistol. Today there is a bewildering variety of handguns manufactured, and there are quite a few that meet the criteria we listed.

Handguns are easily classifiable by action type, which would include:

- Single-shot pistols
- Single-action revolvers
- Double-action revolvers
- Single-action semi-auto pistols
- Double-action semi-auto pistols
- Double-action-only semi-auto pistols
- Striker-fired pistols

Single-shot pistols and single-action revolvers are used primarily by hunters and competition shooters. They are not suitable for our purposes. This leaves us with a double-action revolver and the various semi-auto pistol action types. Let's examine each type separately.

DOUBLE-ACTION REVOLVERS

The cylinder of the revolver rotates, or revolves, to align fresh cartridges with the barrel as the action is cycled, hence the name. Typical centerfire revolvers have five or six chambers, and the cylinder is swung out to the side of the frame to load/unload the pistol.

The term double action refers to the revolver's dual modes of operation. It can be thumb-cocked and fired by a short trigger press. Also, it can be trigger-cocked, firing the weapon by simply pulling the trigger through a longer, heavier stroke. Trigger cocking is usually, and throughout the rest of this book, referred to as double-action shooting. This is

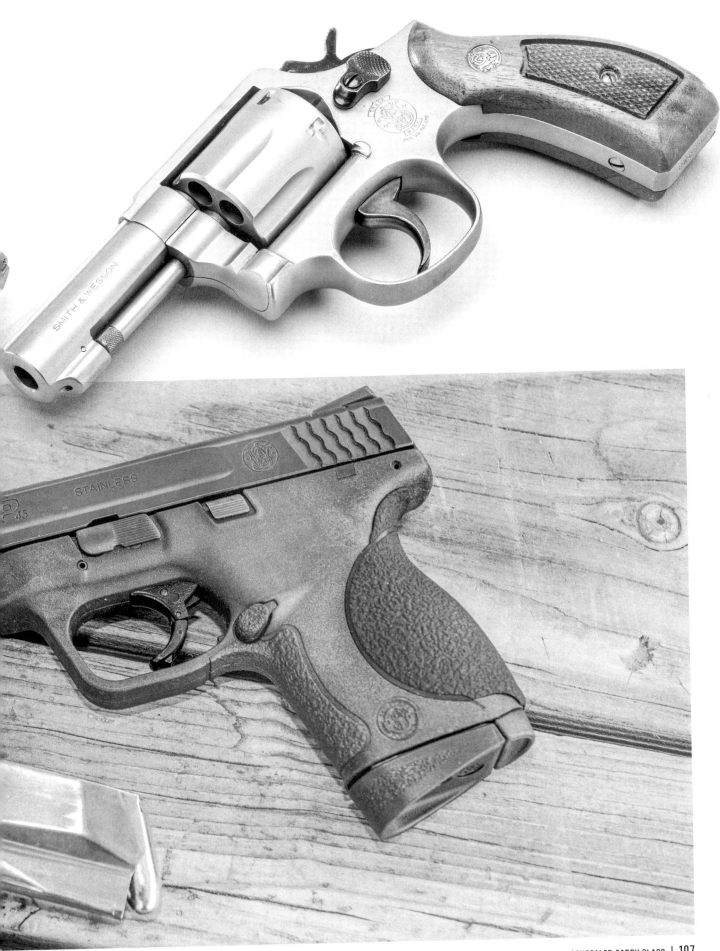

the normal mode of operation for a defensive revolver. Thumb-cocked, or single-action, shooting is reserved for rare emergencies requiring a very long shot or a deliberate shot at a small target.

Revolvers have been around a very long time, and there are hundreds of models, but many are not suited to our task. When considering revolvers as concealed-carry sidearms, we will be most interested in the small-frame to medium-frame revolvers by first-rate manufacturers, mainly in .38 Special or .357 Magnum (.38 Special ammunition can be fired in a .357 Magnum revolver, but not the reverse). We will look at the small-frame guns first. Small-frame, short-barreled .38 revolvers are often called snubbies, belly guns, pocket rockets or other cute names and are often the first type of gun the average person thinks of as a concealable sidearm. Snubnose revolvers are enormously popular, easy to conceal, and with the right ammo they can be fairly effective. The bad news is they are quite difficult shoot well under realistic conditions; they only hold five or six shots; they recoil stoutly with effective ammo; and in a typical

holster, they are really no easier to conceal or more comfortable to wear than a more effective weapon. Their true value is as a backup gun to your larger, more effective primary sidearm.

The best snubbies are made by Smith & Wesson, Colt and Ruger. Smith & Wesson's snubby line is extensive, with variations sporting concealed hammers, stainless steel construction and other desirable features. The Smith & Wesson snubbies are built on the company's J frame, and hold only five rounds, which helps keep their bulk at a minimum. The Colt Detective Special is slightly larger, but holds six rounds. Ruger's snubby is the SP-101 or the LCR. The small-frame guns weigh in the vicinity of 13 to 25 ounces depending upon construction. Some have steel frames, some have lighter-weight aluminum frames and some are even lighter with scandium or polymer frames. Of course, using the same ammunition, the lighter the gun, the heavier the recoil. Physics.

Several of these models are available with 3-inch barrels, instead of the traditional 2-inch version. The 3-inch guns are easier to shoot well and are worth considering.

A snubnose .38 Special like this one is easy to conceal and, with the right ammunition, can be fairly effective, but can be difficult to shoot accurately, especially in stressful situations. The author believes this gun's best role is as a backup gun to a larger, more effective pistol.

The medium-frame revolvers are typified by Smith & Wesson's K-frame models, which usually hold six rounds in either .38 or .357. These models can be found in 2-, 2 1/2-, 3- and 4-inch-barrel variations, with a round or square butt. Avoid the sharp-cornered square butt for concealment. I personally prefer the 3-inch barrel on K frames, as it allows a full-length ejector rod and good sight radius, while still allowing a compact package. These revolvers are available in blue, nickel or stainless steel construction, with fixed or adjustable sights.

Possibly the best model for our purposes is the S&W Model 65, with a round butt and 3-inch barrel. This stainless steel revolver weighs only 34 ounces, has good fixed sights and can use either .38 Special or .357 Magnum ammunition. In a proper holster, it can be carried all day with comfort and concealment. There are other quality revolvers including the Smith & Wesson L-frame series and the various N-frame big-bore revolvers in .41 Magnum, .44 Magnum and .45 Colt chamberings. The N-frame revolvers are too big for most people to wear actually concealed.

There are a couple of revolvers I'd like to mention that are no longer manufactured, but are nearly ideal for concealed carry. The first is the Smith & Wesson Model 12. This is the standard K-frame, medium-size, six-shot .38 Special revolver, available with a round butt and either a 2- or 4-inch barrel. It has an aluminum frame making it very lightweight for a six-shot, medium-size revolver. I have a 2-inch and a 4-inch version, and they are a delight to carry and shoot quite well. The other is the older style six-shot Colt Cobra or Agent, 2-inch-barrel snubby. These old Colt's made in the 1950s and 1960s are of very high quality and have large, easily visible front sights. They are easy to shoot well, are almost as compact as the Smith & Wesson J frame and hold six shots instead of five. Either the S&W Model 12 or the Colt Cobra can be found easily on Internet gun-auction sites or in well-stocked gun shops.

The double-action revolver does have a couple advantages. It is a very easy gun to load/unload, making the clearing process very simple and intuitive. Since it doesn't have to feed ammunition from a magazine, up a feed ramp and into the barrel it can use any bullet shape. The revolver is also more forgiving of poor maintenance practices. These are however, it's only strong points.

As a modern fighting pistol, the revolver has a number of serious drawbacks. The first is extremely limited ammunition capacity. Many small revolvers hold only five rounds and even the medium-size revolvers typically hold only six rounds. In a fight involving multiple attackers, difficult shooting conditions such as low light, or attackers hopped up on drugs, those five or six shots can be used up awfully quickly. This brings us to the next drawback. Under actual fighting conditions it is damn near impossible to get a revolver reloaded in a survivable time frame. To reload, the revolver has to be taken out of action, the cylinder opened, the empties ejected and then five or six individual chambers reloaded with fresh ammunition. Only then can the cylinder be closed, and the gun brought back into action. Speedloaders or speedstrips are faster than loading loose individual rounds, but they are still nowhere near as fast or reliable for reloading as inserting a loaded magazine into a relatively large opening in a semi-auto pistol.

Also, contrary to popular belief, revolvers are somewhat fragile and prone to failure at inopportune times. The revolver has multiple chambers that all have to line up precisely with the opening in the barrel. The timing issues involved in having the hammer fall just as these individual chambers line up precisely with the barrel require an action inside the frame of the revolver that looks a lot like an old windup watch on the inside. The ejector rod is easily bent, putting the gun out of action. A little carbon or unburned gunpowder under the extractor star will make the cylinder unable to rotate. These are just some of the common malfunctions with a revolver. Unlike the semi-auto pistol, in which malfunctions can usually be fixed quickly with a couple of hand motions, when a revolver does malfunction it typically takes time and tools to fix it.

Primarily because of the issues of very low ammunition capacity and difficulty in reloading, revolvers were completely replaced by semi-auto pistols in American law-enforcement circles in the 1980s. Revolvers are, to be frank, somewhat obsolete. In addition to the other issues, the double-action trigger pull on a quality revolver will usually run somewhere between 10 and 13 pounds. The revolver itself will weigh 1 to 2.5 pounds. This makes shooting it quickly, but accurately, more difficult than with a semi-auto pistol, which will typically have a trigger pull weighing 4 or 5 pounds on a 2.5-pound pistol. If you insist on using a revolver, plan on working harder to reach the same skill level as someone using a semi-auto pistol. Also, I would strongly suggest you consider carrying more than one revolver, since reloading one under fire is not likely to work out well.

"As a modern fighting pistol, the revolver has a number of serious drawbacks."

(above and opposite) In a semi-auto pistol, part of the energy that propels the bullet out of the gun and to the target also causes the slide to move to the rear, ejecting the spent case out of the gun (back). Then, as the slide moves forward under spring pressure, it strips a fresh round from the magazine and feeds it into the chamber ready to be fired (front).

SEMI-AUTO PISTOLS

This brings us to the semi-auto pistol. The media would have you believe semi-auto pistols are some evil, modern inventions that have only been around a few years. This is simply not true. The first workable semi-auto pistols were developed in the late 1800s. The Mauser Model of 1896, for instance, was first used in the battle of Omdurman in the Sudan by a young Winston Churchill in 1896. The Swiss Army adopted the Luger pistol in 1903 and the German Army adopted it in 1908. In 1911, the U.S. military adopted the Colt .45 semi-auto, which is often today simply referred to as a 1911.

Before we get into specific types, there are some general features all semi-auto pistols have in common. First, the revolver is a manually operated handgun. The energy that rotates the cylinder, cocks the hammer and fires the revolver all comes from the shooter's trigger finger. In a semi-auto pistol, part of the energy that propels the bullet out of the gun and to the target also causes the slide to move to the rear, ejecting the spent case out of the gun, then as the

slide moves forward under spring pressure it strips a fresh round from the magazine and feeds it into the chamber ready to be fired. The archaic term for the semi-auto pistol is the "self-loading pistol," referring to this action of loading itself by using the energy supplied by the fired cartridge.

All semi-auto weapons, whether handgun, rifle or shotgun, fire only one shot with each press of the trigger. To fire another shot, the trigger must be reset and then pressed again. In an automatic weapon, such as a submachinegun or a machine gun, the gun will continue to fire as long as the trigger is held to the rear until either the trigger is released, or the gun runs out of ammunition.

Semi-auto pistols have only one chamber, unlike the revolver. On a semi-auto pistol, the chamber is an integral part of the barrel. The semi-auto pistol uses ammunition that is housed in a detachable magazine. The magazine is not part of the pistol, it is a feeding device for the pistol. The whole purpose of the detachable magazine is to be able to carry spare magazines on your person, already loaded. This makes reloading the pistol a very simple and very quick process.

Single-action semi-autos are intended to be carried with the hammer cocked and a manual safety engaged. This type of semi-auto will not fire if the hammer is all the way down in its un-cocked position.

To reload a semi-auto pistol, one only has to push the magazine release button and let the empty magazine fall out and insert a new magazine into the magazine well. Magazines can be single column and have a single row of cartridges stacked one atop another, or they can be double column, with two rows of cartridges somewhat staggered in a fatter magazine. This allows higher magazine capacity, but tends to make the grip frame larger.

Semi-auto pistols have undergone a bit of evolution over their 130 years of existence. At present, we have essentially four mechanical families of semi-auto pistols available to us. They all operate essentially the same in that they use a magazine and a slide that reciprocates back and forth to eject the empty cartridges and load new cartridges into the chamber. The difference lies in how the trigger action of the gun operates during the firing cycle.

The oldest type of semi-auto handgun is the single-action auto. Single-action autos, as typified by the 1911 or the Browning High Power, are intended to be carried with the hammer cocked and a manual safety engaged. This type of semi-auto will not fire if the hammer is all the way down in its un-cocked position. It is fumble-prone and slower to carry this type of pistol with the hammer down and have to try to thumb-cock it as it is being presented. Rather, it is carried fully cocked with the thumb safety engaged. As the pistol is presented, the thumb safety is disengaged and the weapon is ready to fire. Each time it is fired the reciprocating slide not only ejects the spent case and loads a new cartridge into the chamber, it also cocks the hammer for the next shot. Whenever the shooter stops firing and lowers the gun to the

ready, the trigger finger immediately goes straight and the manual thumb safety is engaged. Carrying the pistol cocked with a manual safety engaged is often referred to as "cocked and locked" or Condition One carry. As previously stated, this is the mode this gun was designed to be carried in.

The Springfield Armory XD-E is designed with a double-action trigger mechanism. The trigger system works in either of two modes: double action or single action. In double-action mode, it allows the pistol to be carried with a round in the chamber and the hammer at rest, not cocked, but still be ready for action. Pulling the trigger through a longer, heavier stroke both cocks the hammer and then releases it, much like firing a double-action revolver. The first shot cycles the slide, loads a new round in the chamber and leaves the hammer cocked. Thus, all subsequent shots have a lighter, shorter, pre-cocked trigger pull, like that of the single-action auto.

In a striker-fired pistol there is no hammer. The striker is essentially a larger, more massive firing pin propelled by a strong spring. When the sear releases the striker, it moves forward to hit the primer of the cartridge in the chamber. They have a consistent trigger pull for every shot, and the trigger pull is much like that of a single-action auto, making them easy to shoot well.

The second type of semi-auto pistol evolved during the 1920s. The double-action auto was designed to allow the pistol to be carried with a round in the chamber and the hammer at rest, not cocked, but still be ready for action. Pulling the trigger through a longer, heavier stroke both cocks the hammer and then releases it, much like firing a double-action revolver. On the first shot, the cycling of the slide loads a new round in the chamber and also leaves the hammer cocked. Thus, all subsequent shots have a lighter, shorter, pre-cocked trigger pull, like that of the single-action auto. When the shooter stops firing and comes off target, he must use a de-cocker or de-cocking lever to lower the hammer back to its at-rest, carry position. In theory, this type of pistol is "safer" because it does not have to be carried cocked. Pulling the trigger through its longer, heavier trigger stroke for the first shot requires a fairly deliberate action. In actual use, however, we see an awful lot of negligent discharges with this type of pistol, largely because it is more complicated. Under stress, more complication is not desirable. The double-action auto is carried un-cocked, it requires a double-action trigger pull for the first shot, it is cocked for subsequent shots which requires a different trigger pull, and then the shooter must remember to de-cock and put the de-cocker back up before holstering the pistol. This would not be my first choice for most people.

The double-action only (DAO) semi-auto was designed in the 1930s in response to the problem noted above. In the double-action-only semi-auto the trigger is pulled through a longer, heavier stroke for every shot, first to last, just like with a double-action revolver. When the slide cycles it does not leave the pistol cocked. If there is an external hammer, it follows the slide forward and every shot is trigger-cocked. Since the pistol does not stay cocked, the DAO does not normally have a manual safety or de-cocker, as there is no need for one. The DAO auto only has one trigger action to learn and the shooter does not have to worry about engaging a safety or de-cocking the pistol before holstering. This is one of the more common pistol types in U.S. law-enforcement use.

The fourth type is generally referred to as striker-fired handguns. In a pistol that has a hammer, when the sear releases the hammer, the hammer strikes a firing pin which then strikes the primer of the cartridge, igniting it and firing the cartridge. In a striker-fired pistol there is no hammer. The striker is essentially a larger, more massive firing pin propelled by a strong spring. When the sear releases the striker it moves forward to hit the primer of the cartridge in the chamber. Striker-fired pistols, as noted, do not have a hammer. Some have a manual safety, some do not. Among the most common of the striker-fired pistols are the Glock line, the Smith & Wesson M&P line, the HK VP-9 and the SIG P320. Striker-fired pistols, in general, can be very simple and their operation is quite simple. They have a consistent trigger pull for every shot, and the trigger pull is much like that of a single-action auto, making them easy to shoot well. At present, they are the most common handguns in American law enforcement, and they are equally popular for private-citizen concealed carry.

Now that we understand the different types of semi-auto pistols, let's look at some additional considerations in selecting the one we are going to carry.

First, as mentioned in the previous chapter, your hand size will have a lot to do with fitting a pistol to you personally. You want to be able to hold the pistol in a firing grip in your dominant hand with your wrist bones and arm bones directly behind the frame of the gun, and be able to touch the center of the face of the trigger with the pad, or fingerprint, of your index finger. Ideally, you will be able to do this without rubbing the part of your finger that attaches to your palm on the frame of the gun. We want the only place your trigger finger touches the pistol to be the face of the trigger. If you cannot hold the pistol in a proper grip and place your trigger finger on the trigger properly, the grip frame of that pistol is probably too large for you. You will need a handgun with a slimmer grip frame.

In addition to making sure the handgun fits your hand, we again want to make sure it fits your overall body size. The gun needs to be of a size that you personally can carry discretely concealed.

The next issue is ammunition capacity. Personally, I don't care for a pistol for use as a primary sidearm that holds fewer than 10 rounds. Multiple-assailant engagements, and drugged up or crazy subjects make me want more rounds on board. Many people misunderstand the value of a high-capacity magazine. The purpose of a high-capacity magazine is not to allow you to shoot more. Its real purpose is to allow you to reload less often. Every time you have to reload the pistol you have to stop, take it out of action, manipulate it and get back into action. If your pistol holds more ammunition, you might not have to reload at all.

Also, you want an action type you personally are comfortable with. For instance, some people

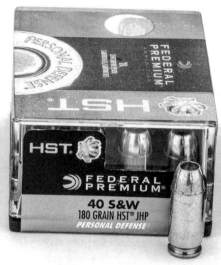
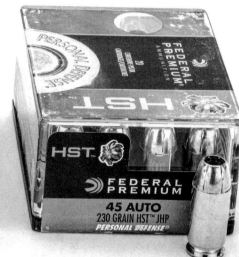

The 9mm, .40 S&W and .45 Auto calibers are readily available and there is a wide variety of good, modern, effective defensive ammunition available for them.

just simply cannot stand the sight of that cocked hammer on a single-action auto such as the 1911. The fact that the 1911 has a passive-grip safety and a manual-thumb safety doesn't mollify some people who are just terrified of that cocked hammer. If this describes you, that's probably not the right gun for you. Others are not comfortable carrying a striker-fired pistol like a Glock or M&P that has a fairly light, short trigger pull and no manual safety. This is especially true of shooters who carry their gun in the appendix position, which can point the gun at various body parts, like their own thigh, when seated. Choose an action type with which you personally are comfortable.

Of course, there's the consideration of caliber. We'll get into ammunition more deeply later on, but for now let's limit our consideration to pistols chambered for 9mm (9X19, 9mm Luger), .40 S&W and .45 Auto. These are readily available calibers and there is a wide variety of good, modern, effective defensive am-

munition available for them. The 9mm is the smallest of these cartridges, and therefore offers the highest magazine capacity. This cartridge is available in very compact pistols or in service-size pistols that hold as many as 17 or 18 rounds. The .45 Auto is an older cartridge, is quite a bit larger and therefore magazine capacity will be somewhat limited. There are .45s with double-column magazines that hold as many as 10 to 13 cartridges, however, unless you have very large hands, they will be difficult to handle well. The typical .45 Auto only holds eight to nine rounds. The .40 Smith & Wesson is a compromise cartridge that is larger than the 9mm and smaller than the .45. Typical .40 caliber handguns hold anywhere from 12 to 16 shots.

If a particular handgun is not as common others, there might be a reason. Also, the more common mainstream handguns, particularly those in widespread law-enforcement use, will have a lot more holsters and accessories readily available.

Recommended Semi-Auto Handguns

SIG Sauer P320

Glock G17

SIG SAUER
www.sigarms.com

This is a top-of-the-line company that makes a variety of top-notch defensive pistols. All SIG pistols have similar operating procedures and they are very reliable, accurate pistols.

• P229, midsize pistol in .40 S&W (13shots) TDA

• P220, full size .45 ACP pistol (9 shots) TDA

• P226, full size 9mm or .40 S&W service pistol (15-16 shots) TDA

• P320, mid or full size, hi-capacity, 9mm or .40, striker-fired

• P365, Very compact 9mm, striker-fired

SMITH & WESSON
www.smith-wesson.com

S&W makes a line of striker-fired handguns in 9mm, .40 S&W and .45 ACP calibers. Some good examples include:

• M&P, high capacity, striker-fired 9mm, .40 or .45

• M&P Compact, reduced-size version in 9mm or .40

• M&P Shield, subcompact in 9mm

GLOCK
www.glock.com

These handguns feature a polymer frame for light weight. They are simple, robust and reliable, and they come in a variety of sizes and calibers. Some of the best Glocks include:

• G43 and G48, compact, 11-shot 9mms

• G26 9mm, 13-shot subcompact pistol

• G19 Compact, 16-shot 9mm high capacity

• G17 or G22, slightly larger versions in 9mm and .40

• G30 or G36, midsize pistols in .45 caliber, 11 or 7 shots

The G19, 17 or 22 are probably the best choices among Glocks for concealed carry. They are small enough to conceal well, big enough to shoot well, and hold a lot of ammunition.

OTHER MODELS

Beretta 92/96, full size 9mm or .40 service pistols.

Kahr, extremely compact 9mm or .40 DAO handguns.

Springfield Armory single-action .45 pistols in several sizes, XD-9 and XD-40 polymer frame, inexpensive, 9mm and .40; similar to Glock.

Ruger 9mm, .40 and .45 double action or DAO; inexpensive and generally reliable, but bulky and not very ergonomic.

Walther PPS, very compact 9mm

H&K P30, service size 9mm, double action or light DAO, high capacity.

H&K VP-9, service size 9mm, striker-fired, high capacity.

Beretta M92

HOLSTER DESIGN

Proper holster design and selection is absolutely critical to effective concealed carry. A concealment holster must perform the following functions well:

It must allow you to carry the gun all day or all night in comfort.

It must conceal the pistol adequately.

It must retain the pistol securely in the event you must jump off a loading dock, struggle with an assailant or run.

And, it must instantly present the pistol on demand, to respond to a sudden, lethal threat.

Therefore, a proper concealment holster must be comfortable, concealable, secure and fast. That is a tall order. Cheap or poorly designed rigs might meet one or more of the requirements set forth here, but only a quality, professionally manufactured holster can meet all four. Quite often, I run into people who recognize they are at risk, by an expensive handgun, then insist on a $19.95, one-size-fits-none bargain holster. This is truly false economy. Since your pistol will likely be in the holster when you need it, the selection of the holster is almost as important as selection of the handgun.

To be useful, the first thing a holster must do is properly fit the weapon it will carry. No holster fits several different types or sizes of handguns; they merely accept the pistols. There is a huge difference. The holster should be carefully molded to match the contours of the pistol's exterior exactly, and this will require matching the holster to the exact make, model, barrel length and caliber of weapon you choose. This fit is necessary to prevent shifting of the pistol, which hinders the draw and causes excess finish wear. It is also necessary to retain the pistol in the holster as you engage in physical activity. Proper molding can provide adequate weapon retention to secure the pistol during normal physical exertion without the need for thumb snaps or other positive retaining devices. This is an aid to a rapid presentation. Second, the holster must fit the belt on which it is worn. The belt and holster should be precisely mated, as part of a carry-weapon system. This helps hold the gun upright on the belt, making concealment easier. It also keeps the holster from shifting back and forth on your belt as you go through your daily routine. A proper belt/holster-loop-fit locks the holstered gun in place, so you will know where to reach for it if you need it.

Third, a proper holster will allow a full firing grip by the master hand while the gun is still in the holster. This is a vital element of a proper presentation/draw stroke. All leather must be cleared away from the root of the trigger guard, and anywhere else it would interfere with a firing grip.

> **"Since your pistol will likely be in the holster when you need it, the selection of the holster is almost as important as selection of the handgun."**

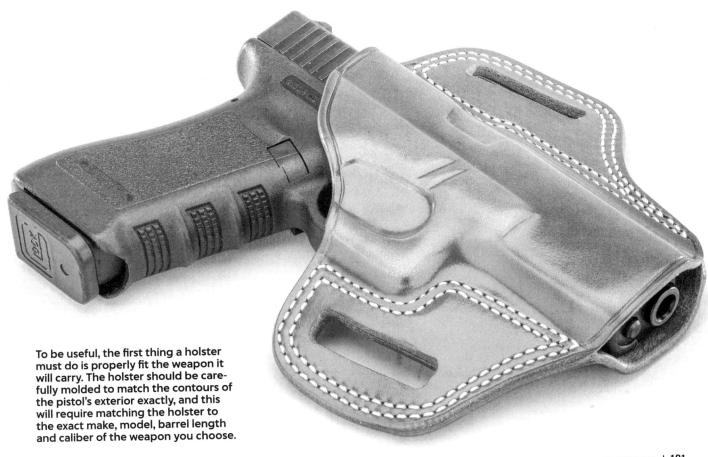

To be useful, the first thing a holster must do is properly fit the weapon it will carry. The holster should be carefully molded to match the contours of the pistol's exterior exactly, and this will require matching the holster to the exact make, model, barrel length and caliber of the weapon you choose.

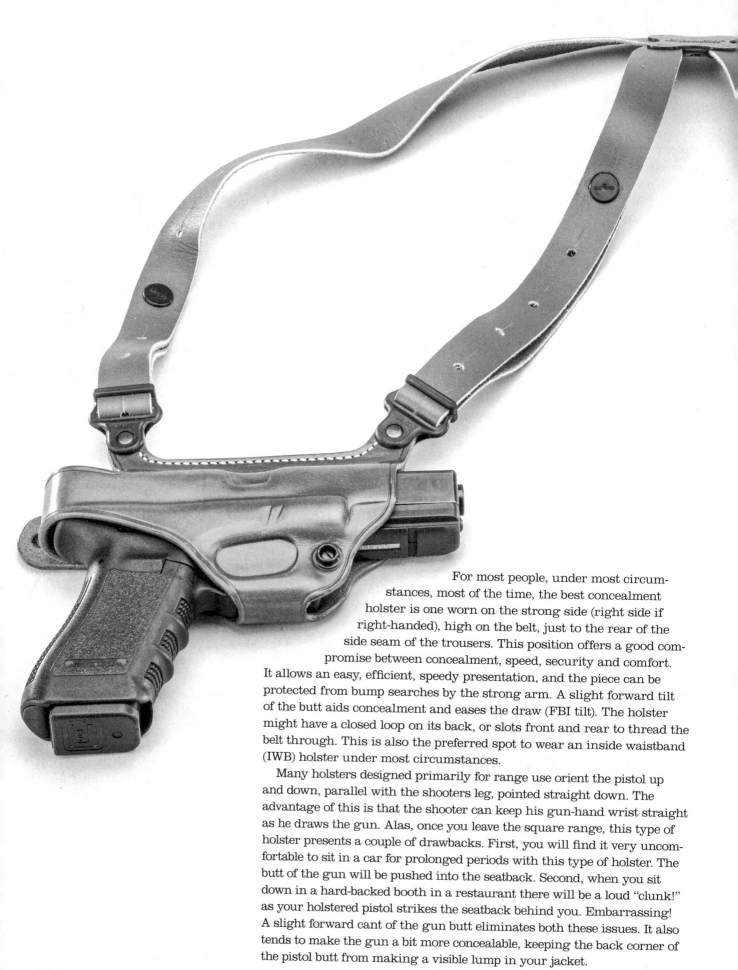

For most people, under most circumstances, most of the time, the best concealment holster is one worn on the strong side (right side if right-handed), high on the belt, just to the rear of the side seam of the trousers. This position offers a good compromise between concealment, speed, security and comfort. It allows an easy, efficient, speedy presentation, and the piece can be protected from bump searches by the strong arm. A slight forward tilt of the butt aids concealment and eases the draw (FBI tilt). The holster might have a closed loop on its back, or slots front and rear to thread the belt through. This is also the preferred spot to wear an inside waistband (IWB) holster under most circumstances.

Many holsters designed primarily for range use orient the pistol up and down, parallel with the shooters leg, pointed straight down. The advantage of this is that the shooter can keep his gun-hand wrist straight as he draws the gun. Alas, once you leave the square range, this type of holster presents a couple of drawbacks. First, you will find it very uncomfortable to sit in a car for prolonged periods with this type of holster. The butt of the gun will be pushed into the seatback. Second, when you sit down in a hard-backed booth in a restaurant there will be a loud "clunk!" as your holstered pistol strikes the seatback behind you. Embarrassing! A slight forward cant of the gun butt eliminates both these issues. It also tends to make the gun a bit more concealable, keeping the back corner of the pistol butt from making a visible lump in your jacket.

Shoulder holsters and crossdraw rigs can be considered together, as they both involve a similar draw technique. These rigs are chiefly useful if your job involves sitting at a desk or in a car the majority of the time. Good examples are easy to draw from while seated and might be more comfortable than a strong-side belt rig if you sit for hours at a time. There are several drawbacks to this type of rig, however, including:

• The presentation requires swinging the gun laterally, rather than in the target's large vertical axis. This makes rapid shooting from a fast draw more difficult.

• In an arm's-length encounter, your strong arm can be manually pinned against your chest, preventing you from drawing.

Shoulder holsters are chiefly useful if your job involves sitting at a desk or in a car the majority of the time. Good examples are easy to draw from while seated and might be more comfortable than a strong-side belt rig if you sit for hours at a time. The author reports these rigs have several drawbacks, however. (Photos courtesy Galco)

• The shoulder holster's harness cuts off air circulation under your shirt, making it uncomfortable in hot weather.

• During strenuous movement, such as running, a shoulder holster will tend to flap and move around a great deal. This is uncomfortable, but also makes it difficult to present the gun in a hurry if needed.

• To be concealable, a crossdraw rig must be worn behind the hipbone. This is a long awkward reach for most people. Competition shooters who use a crossdraw rig wear it just to the weak side of the belt buckle, which is very fast, but a gun cannot be concealed there in an open-front garment.

A carry mode gaining favor in recent years is appendix carry, especially appendix inside waistband. Worn under a loose-fitting shirt, pullover sweatshirt or sweater, this can be easily concealed and is very quick to access. The author is not a fan of this carry method because of the risk of life-threatening injury with a negligent discharge when drawing or re-holstering the pistol and because it is difficult for most people to use this method all the time. (Photo courtesy Galco)

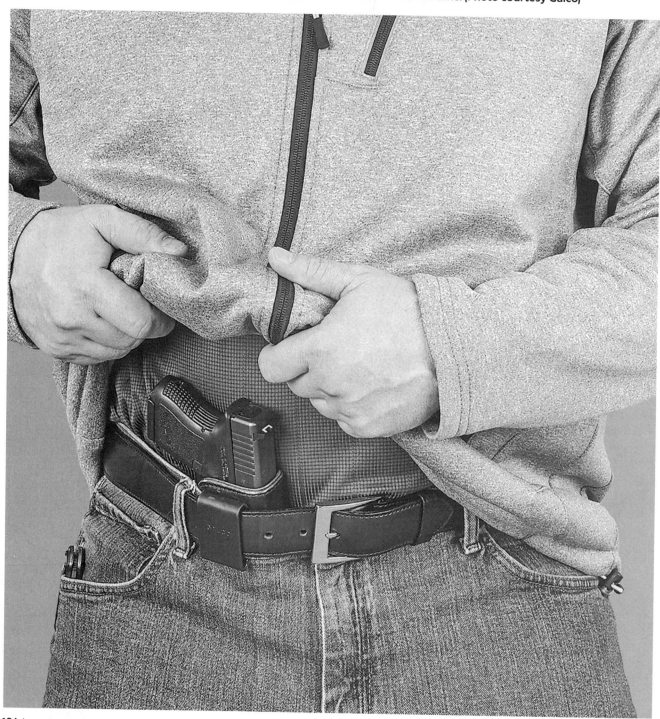

A carry mode gaining favor in recent years is appendix carry, especially appendix inside waistband (AIWB). This type of carry puts the gun just to the right of the belt buckle for a right-handed shooter. Worn under a loose-fitting shirt, pullover sweatshirt or sweater, this can be easily concealed and is very quick to access. The support hand sweeps up the garment, the gun hand obtains a firing grip on the pistol, and as soon as the pistol is lifted up both hands can get on it and drive it out. It might be easier to access the pistol carried AIWB during a physical struggle, but for many shooters the raw speed advantage is the deciding factor. I am not a fan of this carry method. The most commonly cited objection to this carry is that during drawing or re-holstering the pistol a negligent discharge would likely produce a wound to the femoral artery or other large vessel, certainly a life-threatening and often fatal injury. This risk can be reduced greatly by proper training. My objection is not the safety issue, it is that no one I know can actually carry a pistol that way all the time.

To conceal an AIWB rig requires an un-tucked shirt or other garment. There are just too many places where we have to go where we cannot dress that way. If you are wearing a sport coat, suit coat, or other open-front, dressier garment, you'll have to move the pistol behind your hip for concealment. The whole purpose of repetitive practice, such as thousands of repetitions put into your presentation stroke, is to automate that response so your hands automatically move to the right place when your brain decides it's time to draw the gun. Having your gun in more than one place from day-to-day complicates matters when you have enough to deal with already. I wear my pistol on the strong side just behind the seam of the trousers. If the belt buckle is 12 o'clock my gun is at about 4 o'clock on the belt. I can wear it there under a T-shirt with the tail out, or I can wear it that way in a suit. That way I only have one draw stroke to learn and remember.

When you have been shooting a while, you quickly learn how much more efficient a mid-size to full-size handgun is compared to a small revolver or auto. The medium- to full-size handgun will have a more ergonomic grip frame, it will have a longer sight radius, it will typically fire more effective ammunition and it will carry more ammunition than its smaller cousins. A typical medium- to full-size auto will hold 13 to 18 rounds of 9mm or .40-caliber ammo and be easy to shoot well. I have debriefed a lot of people after gunfights, and I've never had a single one say to me, "You know, when the bullets started flying I wished I had a smaller, less powerful gun, with less ammo in it." You need to remind yourself now and then that the purpose of carrying a concealed handgun is to allow you to fight for your life in a sudden, extreme emergency. If you reach for that pistol, it means your life or the life of a loved one is in grave, immediate, mortal danger.

Another thing one quickly learns is, within reason, gun size is not the determining factor in concealment. A well-designed holster will conceal a full-sized gun easier and better than a poorly designed holster will hide a small gun. As long as you stick with a reasonable-size gun, a good holster will adequately conceal it for most environments. For our purposes, when I refer to a medium-sized to full-sized gun, I mean a Glock 17/19/22/23, a Smith & Wesson M&P or M&P Compact, a Springfield XD, a Commander-size or Government Model-size 1911 or something similar. Personally, I carry a Glock 17 every day, fully concealed. That gives me 18 rounds of 9mm ammo that I can hit with well, at speed.

"A well-designed holster will conceal a full-sized gun easier and better than a poorly designed holster will hide a small gun."

The easiest way to actually conceal a pistol in this size class is the previously mentioned Inside Waistband Holster (IWB), which is available in many configurations and in many materials, including Kydex, horsehide, cowhide, nylon and plastic. In this section we will focus on IWB holsters made of cowhide, horsehide or Kydex. Leather IWB rigs might be more comfortable than some of their Kydex counterparts and are often quieter. They might also aid in retaining the gun in the holster during a struggle. Good leather IWB holsters are available from a number of sources and we will look at some of the better examples.

The Granddaddy of them all is the Summer Special as made by Milt Sparks Leather (www.miltsparks.com). The late Bruce Nelson was a career undercover narcotics agent with the California DOJ during the 1960s and 1970s as well as an early Gunsite instructor and a master-class pistol shot. On a raid one day, Nelson was suddenly confronted by a shotgun wielding dope dealer who appeared from a supposedly "secure" area after Nelson had put away his gun. Nelson was wearing a .45 Commander in one of the flimsy suede, metal-clip IWB holsters that were available then. As often happens, as Nelson drew his pistol the holster came out with the gun and Nelson had to furiously strip at the cheap holster to skin it off his pistol. The biker with the shotgun started laughing at the spectacle and surrendered having taken pity on poor Bruce. Immediately, Nelson set about designing a better holster which evolved into the Summer Special. Nelson became a leather worker

This Summer Special holster was designed by the late Bruce Nelson. They are now made by Milt Sparks Leather. Nelson, a former undercover narcotics agent, designed the Summer Special after a near-disastrous mishap with a flimsy suede holster that attached to his belt with a metal clip.

in his spare time and made this holster until his untimely death. He also granted the rights to the design to Milt Sparks and the Sparks Company still makes the holster to this day. The current updated version is dubbed the Summer Special II and is a fine choice. Dual snap loops with one-way snaps secure the rig to it cannot come out with the gun. A reinforced holster mouth makes one-handed re-holstering easy and the holster is sewn smooth-side in and rough-side out. This gives a slick, fast inner surface and the rough exterior grabs your clothing and stabilizes the holster.

Ken Null, in Georgia, is a respected leather smith who has been around for a long time (www.klnullholsters.com). One of Null's best Inside Waistband holsters is the UNS. This holster is formed by folding and stitching a large piece of leather to incorporate "wings" around the holster pouch. These leather wings mold to the wearer's body after a bit and become fitted to the individual owner. Many users claim this is the most comfortable IWB rig they have used. A belt tunnel secures the holster and the belt tugs the gun in close for maximum concealability.

This Kramer Inside the Waistband (IWB) holster is made of horsehide, which typically is thinner, yet stronger, than cowhide, and retains its shape well.

"You can get (Galco holsters) immediately to tide you over until your handmade custom rig comes in, a few months from now."

Kramer Leather makes several IWB designs in horsehide (www.kramerleather.com). Horsehide, in general, is thinner, but stronger than cowhide and is an excellent choice for an IWB rig. Horsehide retains its shape well and seems to be a bit less affected by sweat. Kramer uses Chicago screws instead of snaps. The screws allow adjustment of the loops to fit different size belts and won't come unsnapped while you're wearing the holster.

In the 1970s, Lou Alessi made a compact IWB holster for me to fit a Smith & Wesson Model 60, .38, with a 3-inch heavy barrel. This design was a great departure at the time, featuring belt loops in front of and behind the pouch of the holster. This allowed the holster to be quite thin since there was no leather added over the gun itself. I wore this gun in various undercover and investigative roles, sometimes under just a T-shirt and it concealed remarkably well. Tony Kanaley at Milt Sparks

further refined this basic concept into the Versa-Max II, which is one of the most widely emulated designs in the holster business today. By placing the belt loops fore and aft of the gun, the entire rig can be very low profile. Also, this wider "footprint" distributes the weight of the gun over a very wide section of the belt, aiding comfort. The holster conforms to the wearer's hip curvature aiding both comfort and concealment. A number of our staff, including my wife, Lynn, use a VM-II to conceal a Glock, an M&P or a 1911 quite well.

The late, great, leather master craftsman Lou Alessi, also collaborated with pistolsmith Dane Burns to design one of my all-time favorites, the GWH (www.alessigunholsters.com). For six years, I wore a full-size 1911 every day in an Alessi GWH, and my good friend Southnarc wore a full-size 1911 fully concealed in a GWH as a narcotics investigator, usually under a casual shirt. Comfortable and fast, the GWH is a subtle design. Alessi Leather is always backlogged for months as most of its production goes to government alphabet-agency customers. In looking for a substitute for the GWH, I discovered 5-Shot Leather, which offers the Inside Burton Special, a derivative of Lou's design, well-executed in quality leather. This would be an excellent choice for all-day wear with a 1911 or similar-size handgun.

Alessi also offers the Talon holster line, which combines a leather IWB with reinforced mouth with a nylon locking belt clip. The Talon clip actually secures the holster in place as the tip of the clip fits into a recess in the holster, and I've never seen a Talon holster come out of the pants with the gun. The Talon will work without a belt, although it works well with one. To be honest, I have seen the Talon clips break after extensive use. Flexing the clip while putting it on/off stresses the nylon and it will eventually break. When that happens, Alessi will cheerfully replace the clip, but that is one reason I use no equipment from any maker that clips onto the belt. My gear all slips on the belt and stays there.

Matt Del Fatti is a retired sheriff's deputy who is also a true artisan in leather. Matt's designs are thoughtful and well-executed and his attention to detail is outstanding.

Garrity's Gun Leather offers an IWB very similar to Alessi's GWH, as well as double loop IWBs similar to the Sparks VM-2. Garrity's workmanship is first rate.

Among the mass-production holster makers, Galco offers a very functional Inside Waistband holster known as the Royal Guard, which is constructed of horsehide, making it thin, but sweat resistant. In function, it is very similar to the Sparks Summer Special II. You can get these immediately to tide you over until your handmade custom rig comes in, a few months from now.

As Bruce Nelson learned many years ago, the cheap, flimsy, IWB with a cheap metal clamp should be avoided at all costs. These rigs are always poorly designed, are usually made of cheap, thin material and often come out with the gun on the presentation. Stay away from these things.

A proper IWB design is generally more concealable than any holster worn on the outside of the belt. Most of the weight of a loaded auto is in the butt and many outside the belt holsters allow the gun to tip away from the wearer's torso, making concealment difficult. In an IWB rig, the belt is on the outside, tugging the gun/holster in nice and close. Also, belt fit is crucial. Mine are 1.5-inch belt loops and a 1.5-inch belt. That locks the rig in place preventing shifting as you go through the motions involved in your daily activities. It also keeps the holster at the same angle all the time, aiding getting a firing grip on initial contact. This is, of course, a critical component of a fast, secure, concealed-carry presentation.

Be aware that the high-quality leather makers mentioned in this chapter are small shops of sometimes only four to five employees, or even true one-man shops. Their production is, therefore, severely limited. The excellent IWB holster designs recommended here, such as a Sparks VM-2, or an Alessi PCH are complex designs that cannot be built in a few minutes. The result is all of the better makers are backlogged on orders, from six months to a year or more. The end result is worth the wait.

We have taken an in depth look at leather IWB holsters for daily concealed carry. There are shooters who find the IWB design uncomfortable or who just don't like that carry mode. For them, there are a variety of OWB (Outside Waistband) holsters. Now we'll take a look at the development of this type of holster and the current options.

The concealed carry of handguns for self-defense has been going on since the development of handguns began. John Wesley Hardin designed a concealment shoulder holster in the 1880s, and pocket holsters were common at the turn of the 20th century. The first modern-looking holsters that actually concealed a handgun under typical urban men's clothing seem to have appeared in the 1920s. An awful lot of men routinely carried a handgun during this time period. There was pressure to move away from the "frontier image" of open carry, and concealed carry started becoming more and more common.

Legendary Western lawman Tom Threepersons devised a holster, originally for open carry, that was soon adapted to concealed carry by making the belt loop for a somewhat narrower pants belt instead of the 2 1/2- to 3-inch-wide gun belt normally worn for open carry. The Threepersons holster is still commonly encountered today, although there are much better designs now available. The main drawback of this design is the belt loop, which is simply part of the holster body, folded over and stitched. This allows the butt of the gun to tip away from the wearer's body, making concealment more difficult. El Paso Saddlery first made this holster to Threepersons' specifications in the 1920s and still offers it today. Various other manufacturers made very similar designs and this type was the standard up to the 1960s.

Roy Baker's original Pancake holster, although now obsolete, this design was much more concealable than the older versions, with a fold-over belt loop on the back of the holster.

In the 1960s, Roy Baker designed a radically different type of belt holster which he dubbed the "pancake." This was a very flat holster, made of two pieces of leather stitched together, with a belt slot cut in front of and behind the pistol. These dual slots allowed the gun to be pulled up much tighter and closer to the wearer's torso, aiding concealment greatly. Today, all major holster makers offer variations of this basic design. As mentioned, this design is much more concealable. It also tends to be more comfortable as the widely spaced belt slots spread the weight of the gun over a wider section of belt.

With belt slots in front of and behind the gun, this Alessi holster is more concealable than some other designs. It was constructed for the author in the 1970s.

The Galco Concealable, the Alessi Belt Slide and the Milt Sparks CC-AT are excellent examples of updated versions of the traditional pancake design. The Alessi holster pictured was made for me by Lou Alessi in the 1970s and it allowed me to carry a 4-inch-barrel, .357 revolver, fully concealed in a suit or sports coat. Note the extension that protects the clothing from the rear sight and hammer spur of the revolver, a nice touch.

Another similar design is the abbreviated belt slide, like the Galco version called the Quick Slide. This is a minimalist holster that leaves much of the gun exposed. Well-designed examples like the Galco Quick Slide still retain the gun well and allow the use of similar handguns of different barrel lengths in the same holster.

Some pancake-style holsters use slots cut to allow the belt to thread through them. Others, like an excellent holster from custom maker Matt Del Fatti, have closed loops the belt passes through. The Alessi CQC-S and its copies have snap loops fore and aft which allow easy on/off, but are still basically pancake holsters.

Modern holster pioneer Bruce Nelson not only designed the famous Summer Special IWB rig, he designed a high-riding concealment Outside Waistband holster he called the Number 1 Professional Model. This holster has a very close-fitting belt loop on the back of the holster body and a trailing belt loop or slot on an extension of leather behind the pistol. The purpose of the trailing loop is to pull the butt of the gun in closer for better concealment. The Milt Sparks #55BN (BN, for Bruce

Nelson), is a currently available rendition of Nelson's design as is the Alessi DOJ model. Don Hume makes a derivative of the Nelson design in its JIT Slide. Although it is very inexpensive and not made of the quality leather of a Sparks or Alessi rig, the JIT is a very serviceable concealment holster.

Rusty Sherrick, a custom-holster maker in Pennsylvania, makes a couple of horsehide holsters that are updated versions of the traditional Threepersons design. The Rangemaster Special was designed to carry a full-size pistol comfortably and allow a natural draw stroke without a lot of shoulder rotation. The Speed Draw was designed to give maximum draw speed from a holster that is actually concealable with a full-size gun. Both were designed by me and executed by Rusty.

Kydex is a tough, moldable form of thermo-molded plastic. Kydex holsters can be much less expensive than quality leather holsters and the wait time tends to be much shorter for Kydex, even with custom touches. Since it is a very thin material, Kydex IWB holsters can be made thinner than a comparable leather design enhancing both comfort and concealment. Where I live in the sunny South, a major advantage of Kydex is resistance to sweat. Perspiration will not soak through a Kydex holster nor will it degrade the holster over time.

> "Kydex holsters can be much less expensive than quality leather holsters and the wait time tends to be much shorter for Kydex, even with custom touches."

Kydex is a tough form of thermo-molded plastic. Since it is a very thin material, Kydex IWB holsters can be made thinner than a comparable leather design, enhancing both comfort and concealment. (Photo by Tamara Keel)

Kydex is much rougher on the finish of your pistol than leather, causing faster finish wear on the gun. Blued guns and some of the baked-on, paint-type finishes will exhibit wear very quickly when carried in Kydex, which is affected by high heat, so, never leave your rig in a parked car.

Some of the very best Kydex IWB holsters are among the very best choices for daily concealed carry wear. For the last few years I have been wearing Kydex IWB rigs daily, replacing my old leather rigs completely. Some of the very best of the current Kydex benders include:

JM Custom Kydex

www.jmcustomkydex.com
755 East Greg Street Suite 16
Sparks, NV 89431
775-686-8431

Custom Carry Concepts

www.customcarryconcepts.com
17564 Normandy Road
Lake Milton, OH. 44429
330-651-2779

Keepers Concealment

www.keepersconcealment.com

You will also need at least one magazine pouch to carry a spare magazine on your person. You should always carry at least one reload for your pistol. There are all sorts of reasons why you might need more ammo than what is in the gun. Even if you finish the fight with what's in the gun you would want to reload before holstering the pistol, just in case. Finally, there are serious malfunctions that require you to rip the magazine out of the pistol and put in a new one to get the gun back in action. For all of these reasons, you should carry at least one spare magazine. The magazine pouch is typically worn on the support side with the bullets at the bottom and bullets pointed to the front. Just remember, bullets toward the enemy, whether they are in the pouch or in the gun.

I normally carry two spare magazines, but I wear them in two single pouches, not in a double magazine pouch. A double pouch tends to be less flexible. With two single pouches, they tend to bend around the waist better and if I needed to I could put one on either side of a pants belt loop.

You will also need a proper gun belt. Many people do not realize the belt is just as important as the holster, and they both make up a carry system. The belt has to be heavy enough and stiff enough to support the weight of the pistol and keep it upright and tucked in close to your body. A cheap, flimsy belt will allow the weight of the pistol, which is mostly in the butt, to pull away from your body, making it far less concealable, allowing it to flap around as you move, and making a fast presentation more difficult.

You should always carry at least one reload for your pistol. Two reloads are better. There are all sorts of reasons why you might need more ammo than what is in the gun.

Leather belts meant for concealed carry are typically two layers of leather stitched together and might be as much as one-quarter inch in thickness. The most common width for concealed carry is a 1 1/2-inch wide belt, which will fit in the belt loops of almost all men's casual pants. There are also synthetic or nylon belts meant to wear a pistol on. These are typically reinforced with Kydex or are two layers with several rows of stitching to stiffen them.

The belt and the belt loops or slots of your holster should match perfectly, to prevent shifting and keep the gun in the same place and at the same angle all the time. A proper gun belt doesn't only lock the holster in place, it is also critical for your comfort for all-day carry. A proper, heavy gun belt distributes the weight of the equipment all around your waist and sets the weight on both hip bones. This greatly enhances comfort. You might be wearing that pistol 12 to 14 hours a day or more, so the cost of a good gun belt will be a very wise investment.

Your pistol, belt, holster and magazine pouch all form a "weapon system."

ANKLE HOLSTERS

Many of us carry a small handgun as a second, or backup gun, in addition to our larger, primary pistol. There are a number of solid reasons for this practice.

First, I teach all over the U.S., and everywhere I go I see good quality, well-maintained handguns break during classes. By "break" I do not mean malfunction. I mean a part in the gun literally fails, putting the gun out of action. If your firing pin, extractor, takedown latch, etc. breaks, the gun is a paperweight until you can procure and install a new part. If it happens in classes, it might happen in a fight. If your primary gun becomes non-functional, a second gun could be a literal lifesaver. Second, you can give the backup gun (BUG) to a trained and licensed, but unarmed, companion. Sometimes when I pick up a col-

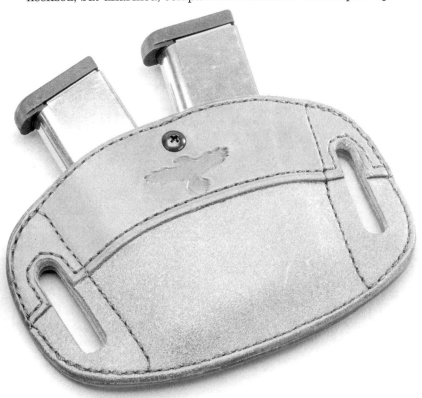

> ## "You will also need a proper gun belt. Many people do not realize the belt is just as important as the holster ..."

league at the airport, I loan them my BUG until we get to the hotel and he can unpack and put on his own sidearm. Third, in a struggle a BUG might be more accessible than your primary gun.

There are a number of ways to carry this secondary handgun, and over the years I have settled on ankle carry for mine. Here are my reasons for this decision.

Pants-pocket carry just has too many limitations. It is damn near impossible to draw a gun from a pocket holster while seated, whether in a car or at a desk or table. We spend way too much time seated, especially in the car, for this carry mode. In a tangled, hand-to-hand fight, pocket carry would be difficult to draw from, especially if you are on the ground on your back. It is also very difficult to get a gun out of a right front pants pocket with the left hand, and vice versa.

Some people simply wear the backup gun on the belt, on the support side, with the primary gun on the dominant hand side. My belt already has enough stuff on it, so I don't care much for this mode, either.

Carrying a handgun in a well-designed ankle holster solves many of these issues. The ankle gun is actually quite easy to access while seated. While driving, a gun on the inside of the left ankle

"Ankle carry works best with handguns that weigh around one pound, or very little more."

(right-handed person) is quite easily accessed by the right hand. Even on my back on the ground, I can get to my ankle gun with either hand if necessary. A well-made ankle rig is comfortable and discrete.

There are several very well-designed and well-made choices among ankle holsters. Over the years I have tried several, and have settled on some that are very comfortable, adequately secure, protect the pistol from the elements, and allow rapid acquisition. My favorites include the ankle holsters from Alessi, Ken Null, DeSantis and Galco.

If I had to rank them in order of preference, the Alessi and Null rigs would be tied for first place. Both use Velcro fasteners to secure the holster to your lower calf. Both use precise molding to secure the handgun quite well, while allowing a very quick presentation. Both have a compressed felt backer on the holster, to protect your leg. In classes, I routinely set up a double feed in my primary handgun and demonstrate dropping my primary handgun and drawing my BUG from one of these ankle rigs in less than two seconds, from "Go" signal to first shot.

The author prefers to carry his secondary gun in an ankle holster, which offers quick and easy access when standing, sitting down or even when he is on his back on the ground. If you choose to wear an ankle holster, you should practice all three scenarios during dry-fire drills.

My next choice is the DeSantis rig. This is an elastic rig that closes with Velcro. In the revolver version, an ingenious bit of leather sits behind the trigger guard to keep the gun in place until you grasp it and pull firmly. This is a very comfortable and fast ankle setup. The Galco version has a thumb-break security snap and very lightweight construction. Both the DeSantis and Galco holsters have a sheepskin pad behind the holster to cushion your leg.

Ankle carry works best with handguns that weigh around 1 pound, or very little more. An Airweight Smith & Wesson and the Colt Cobra or Agent are perfect for this role. In semi-auto pistols, the Kahr PM9 works well in an ankle rig. Wear the thing for three or four weeks and you'll hardly notice it is there from that point on. You might never need that backup gun, but if you do, you'll need it very badly.

BELLY BANDS

The belly band is a wide elastic band that closes with Velcro and has a holster built into it. It is a good way to carry a gun very-deeply concealed and will work with even minimal clothing, like running shorts and a T-shirt. The belly band is normally worn at waist level under your pants, although there are variations meant to be worn around your chest putting the gun under your arm, much like shoulder holster. I much prefer the waist-mounted version.

For really deep concealment, you can put the belly band on under your pants and tuck your shirt in over it. For this

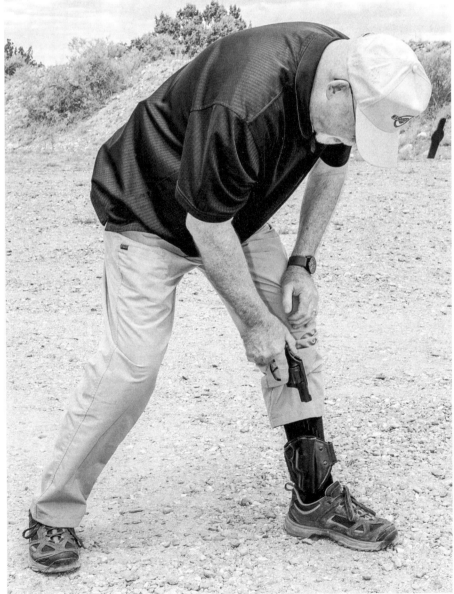

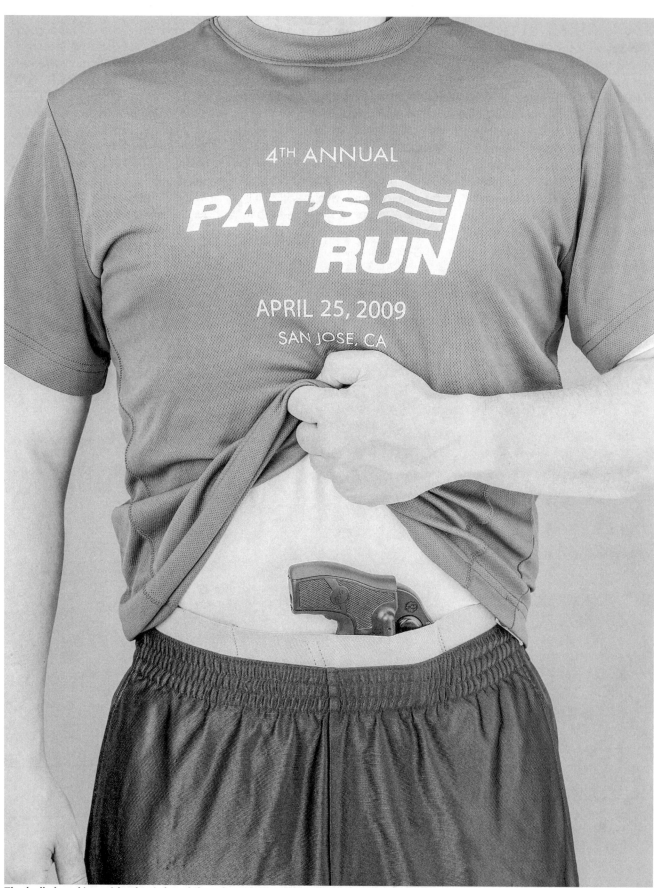

The belly band is a wide elastic band that closes with Velcro and has a holster built into it. It is a good way to carry a gun very-deeply concealed and will work with even minimal clothing, like running shorts and a T-shirt. (Photo courtesy Galco)

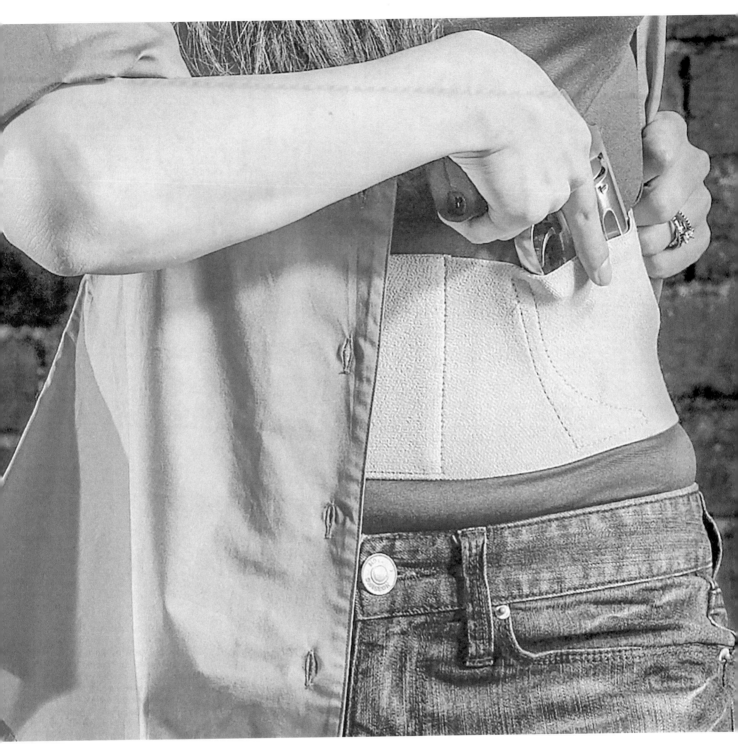

application the pistol is worn just to the left of the belt buckle (for right-handed shooters). To access the pistol, grab the shirt front and pull hard to pop the buttons and reach inside and grasp the pistol.

Belly bands seem to work particularly well for women. Many women's skirts or pants do not accommodate a belt. The belly band under a blouse or sweater covering it fixes this issue.

Some belly-band models even have other pouches sewn into them in which you can carry pepper spray, a flashlight or a spare magazine. Belly bands come in different colors. For maximum concealment use a light-colored belly band when wearing light clothing and a darker-colored belly band with darker clothing. By the way, the belly band works fine with a tuxedo, which will not accommodate a normal belt holster.

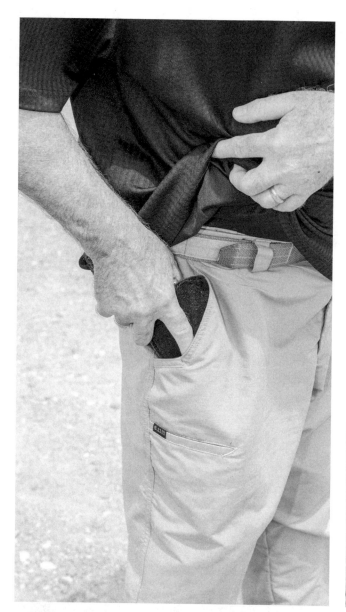

A good pocket holster will conceal the pistol adequately, will not "print" or show the pistol's outline through the pants pocket, and will provide quick and easy access to the pistol. As a general carry mode, the pocket holster has a couple major drawbacks.

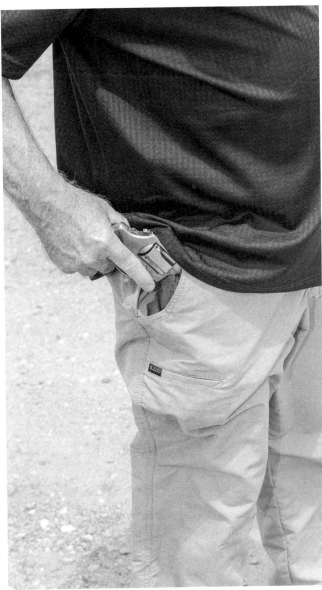

POCKET HOLSTERS

A fair number of people carry a small handgun in a pants pocket. There are actually a couple of valid reasons for this, as long as we recognize the limitations. First, this is a common carry method for a backup gun. If you wear a full-size pistol on the strong side belt, a backup gun in your support side front pocket makes a lot of sense. It would be accessible to your non-dominant hand in case your dominant hand was disabled by injury.

Another reason for pocket carry is for a lot of people who work in an office environment in casual clothing where an outer jacket would look out of place and invite scrutiny. With a tucked in shirt and no jacket the pocket holster might be a viable option.

These are specialized uses, however. As a general carry mode, the pocket holster has a couple major drawbacks. The first is you are completely unable to access your pistol while seated. Most of us spend the majority of our time seated at a desk, at a table or in a car. In fact, for many people that covers about 85 percent of your waking hours. Another drawback to pocket carry is one cannot access a pocket pistol while running, or even while vigorously sidestepping to get off the line of force. Finally, pocket carry really limits our options to a really small handgun like a Kahr PM9 or a J-frame snubby.

If you are going to carry a handgun in a pocket, however, a proper pocket holster is essential. One should never just drop a pistol in your pocket. The pistol will tend to rotate around as you move. This means the butt of the pistol will never be where it should be when you reach in the pocket for the gun. A pocket holster stabilizes the pistol, holds it upright

Never put a handgun in an everyday purse. A good purse made specifically for carrying a concealed handgun will have a separate compartment dedicated to the pistol and nothing else. A really good one will have a holster built into this compartment to stabilize the handgun and completely cover the trigger guard.

and presents the butt at a consistent location and angle for a better presentation. Also, the pocket holster breaks up the outline of the pistol so when you sit down you do not have the clearly visible outline of a handgun in your pocket. Good pocket holster designs have a hook or a sticky material on the outside so that the pocket holster stays in the pocket when you draw the gun. Good examples are available from Safariland, Uncle Mike's, Mika's Holsters and FIST Holsters, among others.

OFF-BODY CARRY

Off-body carry refers to carrying a handgun that is not attached to your person via a holster. Examples would be carrying in a purse, backpack or day planner. Off-body carry is strongly discouraged unless it is the only way you can carry a gun.

If you're going to carry a gun in a purse, it must be a purse made to carry a gun, not just your standard handbag. A dedicated gun purse will have a separate compartment to contain the pistol and nothing else. The better models actually have a holster built into this compartment, so the pistol is stabilized, and the trigger guard completely covered, for safety. The pistol compartment should be accessible completely separately from the main compartment of the purse. Never just put a handgun inside a typical purse with all the other mysterious debris women carry. The pistol will tend to rotate around, meaning you have no idea where it's pointed. Lipsticks, pencils, pens and God knows what else can find their way into the trigger guard and cause a negligent discharge.

I have personally investigated three shootings in which a handgun loose in a purse discharged and killed a bystander. In Idaho, in late 2014, a woman had a pistol in a gun purse in the shopping cart with her 2-year-old child in a Walmart. The toddler was able to unzip the gun compartment and cause the Smith & Wesson Shield in it to discharge, striking the child's mother in the head and killing her. Not only is she dead, that child will have to deal with this for its entire life. This is a perfect example of why you must maintain physical control of a purse containing a gun at all times. If there is a gun in your purse, you must have the purse in your physical control and custody at all times. This is going to require some real attention at first, until it becomes a habit. If you get up from the restaurant table to go to the salad bar, the purse has to go with you, because you and you alone are responsible for the pistol in that purse.

Another reason I discourage purse carry, is what is the first thing a bad guy goes for? If he snatches your purse from you, now he has your gun, you don't. It is just too easy to become separated from your pistol.

Another practice I would like to see abandoned is that of keeping a gun in the glove box or console of a car, rather than wearing it. There is not a single conceivable circumstance under which you could go to your car, unlock the door, open the glove box, get a gun and come back and shoot somebody in legitimate self-defense. There is, however, a legal term for going to your car, unlocking the door, opening the glove box, getting a gun and coming back and shooting somebody. It is referred to as premeditated murder. Also, this is where many of the criminal handguns on the street come from. Breaking into parked cars is an incredibly common crime and it is usually one of the gateway crimes that teenage offenders start out with. Leaving a handgun unattended in the car can wind up with it being stolen and then later used in crimes. Remember that you are responsible for that firearm. If you need it for personal protection, wear it. If you don't need it for personal protection, lock it up in the gun safe.

16

CALIBERS AND AMMUNITION

aliber is an expression of the diameter of a bullet and is used to refer to the size and type of ammunition for specific firearms. Firearms are designed for use with one specific caliber of ammunition, and only the ammunition type marked on the barrel of the firearm should be used in that weapon.

Cartridges designed in the United States are usually designated by caliber in hundredths or thousandths of an inch. The .45 ACP cartridge, for instance, uses a bullet that is 45 100ths of an inch in diameter (actually .451 inches). The caliber of European cartridges is normally expressed in millimeters, such as the 9mm Parabellum. The 9mm is actually a .36 caliber, the 10mm is .40 caliber.

Oddly, many American cartridge designs bear inaccurate caliber designations. The .38 Special, for instance, has an actual diameter of .357 inch, and .38 Special ammunition can be fired in a .357 Magnum revolver. The .380 ACP has an actual diameter of .355 inch, the same as a 9mm Luger.

To further add to this confusion, different manufacturers often refer to the exact same cartridge by different names. The standard 9mm round in American police and military use, for instance, is variously designated as the 9X19 mm, the 9mm Parabellum, 9mm Luger and 9mm NATO. All are interchangeable. A weapon chambered for the 9mm Luger cartridge should not, however, be used with 9X18, 9X21 mm or 9mm Kurtz ammunition, which all use cartridge cases different in length from that of a 9mm Luger. The .45 ACP (Automatic Colt Pistol) cartridge is also known as the .45 Auto. Ammunition marked .38 Smith & Wesson, or .38 Colt cannot be used in a revolver marked .38 Special.

As the engine is the heart of an automobile, ammunition is the heart of a firearm. The weapon can function and perform no better than its ammunition, and proper ammunition is vital to combat effectiveness. Only first-quality, commercial ammunition should ever be considered for defensive use.

The modern cartridge consists of several component parts. The cartridge case, usually of brass or aluminum, is the chassis, which holds the other components together. The case has a mouth, where the bullet is inserted, a hollow interior with a charge of gunpowder, and the head, the solid portion that holds the primer. Revolver cartridges have a protruding rim around the case, to give the extractor something to pull against to eject cases from the cylinder. One complete cartridge, ready to fire, is referred to as a round.

Pistol cartridges are either rimfire or centerfire, depending upon their ignition system. Rimfires are pretty much restricted to .22-caliber weapons used for target shooting and small-game hunting. In the rimfire cartridge, the priming compound is found inside the hollow rim of the cartridge and is ignited by a blow from the firing pin on the outer rim. All suitable defensive ammunition is centerfire, which means it has a separate primer located in the center of the head of the cartridge. When the firing pin or striker impacts the primer, the primer explodes, igniting the powder charge. The resultant gas expands violently, expelling the bullet down the barrel and out of the gun, toward the target. As these hot gases exit the gun behind the bullet, they form the flash and noise you experience upon firing the weapon.

Common concealed-carry calibers include, from left to right, the .380 ACP, which the author considers appropriate only for deeply concealed carry in a backup gun, the 9mm, the .357 Magnum revolver, the .40 Smith & Wesson and the .45 ACP.

There are several desirable characteristics in ammunition intended for use in protecting your life. First, the ammunition must be completely functionally reliable. It must go off every time, and in auto pistols, the ammunition must reliably cycle through the gun's action. This is the single most important consideration. Secondary considerations include muzzle flash (less is better), recoil, accuracy and terminal performance (the effect the bullet has on his intended target).

There has been a great deal of research and development in pistol ammunition in recent years, spurred by demands from the law-enforcement establishment for better ammo for cops. This has led to ammunition that is reliable, accurate, has less muzzle flash and better wounding effect. Stick with premium ammunition from the major manufacturers; Winchester, Federal, Speer or Remington, and you will not go wrong. For duty use, hollow point ammunition from any of these manufacturers should be used. Select one that functions reliably and shoots the best in your particular gun. Some handguns shoot different ammo types to widely different points of impact. Select a load that hits where your sights are aimed at typical combat distances of zero to 25 yards.

It is not necessary to shoot expensive carry ammunition for practice. The major factories (Winchester, Federal, Speer, Remington) all load generic ammo in defensive calibers that cost about half as much as

A .380 ACP handgun, left, can be only slightly smaller than a 9mm pistol, right, yet will offer significantly less stopping power, per round, as well as less magazine capacity.

their premium defensive ammunition. This ammo features less expensive bullets than the high-tech hollowpoint bullets used in combat ammo. These loads are fine for shooting practice targets, reserving the high dollar ammo for actual carry.

Remanufactured (commercially reloaded) ammunition is also a fine source for practice ammo. Good quality practice loads can be bought in quantity at lower bulk prices. This allows sufficient practice to obtain and maintain proficiency. To avoid damage to your guns, I would stay away from surplus foreign military ammunition. If I won't drink their water, I won't shoot their ammo.

There are handguns available chambered for a number of cartridges that are not suited for defensive use. These cartridges are of smaller caliber, or are weakly loaded, and do not have adequate power for our purposes (see chapter on stopping power). These cartridges are often used in small, cheap, poorly made handguns that are extremely poor choices as defensive weapons. Make no mistake, any of these cartridges will kill, but that is not our goal. You have accomplished nothing if your attacker dies three days later in the hospital, after having killed you or a loved one. These underpowered cartridges include the .22 rimfire, the .25 ACP and .32 ACP; and .38 Smith & Wesson, .38 Short Colt and .38 Long Colt, which are obsolete revolver cartridges.

The .380 ACP (designated the 9 mm Kurtz or 9mm Short in European arms) is a marginally powered auto-pistol cartridge, used in small handguns. In its full-metal jacket, ball loading, it is no better than the .22 Long Rifle and is not sufficient for the task. Recently, some high-

> **"Fortunately, recent developments in ammunition technology have raised the .38 Special off its knees, and the best .38 loads are fairly reliable performers."**

performance hollowpoint loads in .380 have been developed, notably the Winchester PDX-1 hollowpoint and the Federal HST hollowpoint. These better loads will not, however, transform a popgun into a hand cannon. With the best of these loads the .380 is still marginal, at best, and will rely heavily on surgical bullet placement for adequate results. In recent years, several new compact handguns in 9X19mm caliber have been designed, such as the excellent Smith & Wesson Shield, the Kahr P9 or PM9, the SIG P365 and the Walther PPS. These guns are no larger or heavier than the typical .380, but are more powerful. They are definitely a better choice than any .380. The smaller .380 pistols might have some merit as deeply concealed backup guns, to augment your primary, larger-caliber sidearm, but that is all.

This brings us to the calibers that are suitable for defensive work. These cartridges include .38 Special, .357 Magnum, and .44 Special for revolvers, and the 9X19mm, .40 Smith & Wesson, and .45 ACP in auto pistols. Let's examine each separately.

These two Smith & Wesson pistols are pretty close to the same size. The .40-caliber, right, fires a bullet that has a diameter of .40 of an inch, while the 9mm bullet has a diameter of .355 of an inch. Bigger bullet diameter equals more stopping power.

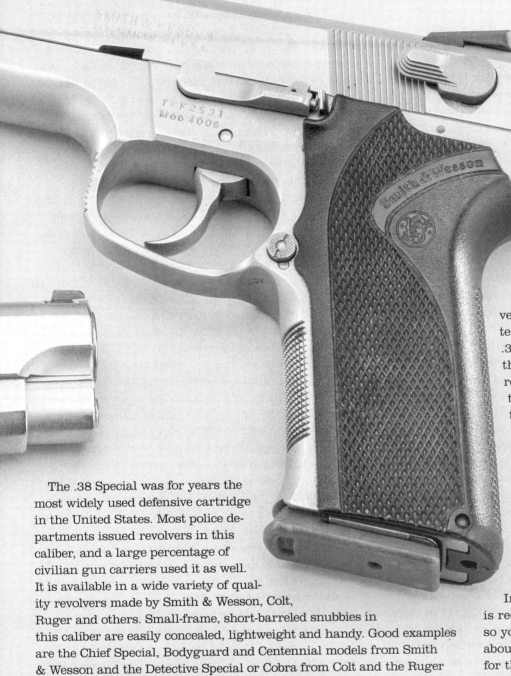

The .38 Special was for years the most widely used defensive cartridge in the United States. Most police departments issued revolvers in this caliber, and a large percentage of civilian gun carriers used it as well. It is available in a wide variety of quality revolvers made by Smith & Wesson, Colt, Ruger and others. Small-frame, short-barreled snubbies in this caliber are easily concealed, lightweight and handy. Good examples are the Chief Special, Bodyguard and Centennial models from Smith & Wesson and the Detective Special or Cobra from Colt and the Ruger SP 101. Medium-frame guns with 3- or 4-inch barrels are easily carried concealed and are very easy to shoot well. Representative models would be Smith & Wesson models 10, 64, 15 or 67, which hold six rounds and weigh around 30 to 34 ounces. These are excellent service revolvers.

In .38 Special the traditional ammunition, 158-grain, round-nose lead bullets, has a dismal reputation as a man-stopper, being called the "widow maker" in many police departments that used to issue it. Many police officers have been killed after putting five or six of these feeble loads right in the vital zone of a determined criminal. The round-nose bullets do not deform on impact and slip through tissue with little damage. One medical examiner described the wound track as a "pencil stab." Never use this type of ammunition for personal protection.

Fortunately, recent developments in ammunition technology have raised the .38 Special off its knees, and the best .38 loads are fairly reliable performers. Among the very best .38 loads are the all-lead, semi-wadcutter hollowpoint rounds offered by Winchester or Federal. In a 3-inch barrel or longer, the all-copper Barnes bullet as loaded by CorBon in its DPX line works very well. All of these loads penetrate adequately and tend to expand, or deform, creating larger wound channels. In 2-inch-barrel guns velocity is reduced by the shorter barrel so you have to be really careful about ammunition selection for these. The Speer 135-grain, short-barrel ammo was specifically crafted for these snubnosed revolvers and has a good street reputation. It does, however, have a good deal of recoil, especially in aluminum-framed revolvers. In the real lightweight snubbies, you might be just as well-off with 148-grain target wadcutters from Winchester or Federal. These are very accurate and soft shooting, and usually hit precisely on the sights. The bullets chop through flesh, making a large wound track, and they tend to penetrate plenty.

Early efforts to upgrade the poor stopping record of the .38 Special led to the development of the .357 Magnum in the 1930s. The .357 uses a basic .38 Special case, lengthened by one-tenth of an inch, and is loaded to much higher pressures. The case was made slightly longer to prevent chambering this ammunition in a .38 Special revolver. Thus, you can shoot .38 Special ammunition in a .357, but not vice versa. The best .357 loads are fairly reliable stoppers, but at a price. In a 2-, 3- or 4-inch-barrel revolver, .357 Magnum ammo has a fearsome muzzle blast and flash, and heavy recoil. Full charge .357 ammo is, therefore, quite hard to shoot well, particularly in a concealable gun. Good hits with a weapon of moderate power are far better than poor hits or misses with a weapon of greater power. This leads to the somewhat self-deluding practice of carrying a .357 Magnum revolver loaded with more comfortable .38 Special ammunition. Stamping the word Magnum on the barrel does not increase the bullet's potential for target damage.

This brings us to the cartridges for use in semi-auto pistols. At present, the most commonly encountered auto cartridge is the 9X19mm. This round is standard among the NATO military forces, including the U.S. Our military converted to the 9mm in the 1980s to have ammunition standardization with NATO. Many U.S. police departments dropped the 9mm in the 1990s or early 2000s in favor of .40- or .45-caliber pistols and have since gone full circle and are now issuing the 9mm again. Advances in ammunition performance have made the 9mm a completely different cartridge than what it was 30 to 40 years ago. The .40 Smith & Wesson is a somewhat larger cartridge that still can be used in a 9mm-sized handgun. Many federal law enforcement agencies currently issue .40-caliber pistols as do a huge number of state and metropolitan police departments. The .45 Auto is a much older cartridge, much larger than 9mm or .40 caliber cartridges. This requires a larger, heavier gun and reduces magazine capacity.

The 9mm is a compact cartridge of moderate power. It can be used in a very compact pistol, or as many as 15 to 18 rounds can be loaded into a full-size, double-column magazine pistol. The 9mm has light recoil and is quite easy to shoot in rapid fire. This makes training easy and is one of the key attractions of the 9mm for law-enforcement agencies. The best ammunition currently available for the 9mm typically is in the 124- to 147-grain

bullet weights, or the 115-grain, all-copper Barnes hollowpoint.

The .40 Smith & Wesson became commercially available in 1990. It was an overnight success because it allows a cartridge of serious power in a weapon of reasonable size and weight. In fact, many .40 Smith & Wesson pistols are no larger or heavier than similar 9mm pistols. The .40 Smith & Wesson arose from research conducted on the 10mm auto, which the .40 has pretty much made obsolete. The FBI wanted a more powerful pistol than the 9mm that could be carried concealed by special agents. The 10mm was designed to meet that need. The guns were as large and heavy as .45s, however, and therefore offered no real advantages over existing guns. The .40 Smith & Wesson, on the other hand, can use the same 10mm bullets in a shorter case and be used in a more compact gun than a .45, also holding more ammunition (typical .40s hold 11 to 16 rounds, most .45s hold eight or nine).

As mentioned above, the 10mm auto round has been made obsolete by the .40 Smith & Wesson, at least as a concealed-carry pistol round. Ammunition for the 10mm can be loaded quite hot, rivaling .41 Magnum revolver ammunition, but this ammo kicks and blasts far too much for rapid, defensive shooting. The 10mm, in its loaded-down version, referred to as 10mm FBI loads or 10mm Lite, is exactly identical in performance to standard .40 Smith & Wesson ammunition, typically launching a 180-grain jacketed hollowpoint at 950 to 1,000 fps. If you're getting identical ballistic performance, it makes sense to use it in a smaller, lighter .40 Smith & Wesson pistol.

The largest common caliber is .45, which is available from Colt, SIG, Smith & Wesson, Glock and others. Before the advent of modern, jacketed-hollowpoint ammunition, the .45 was the only auto-pistol cartridge with adequate power for defensive use. Even its full-jacketed, ball loading works pretty well, since it weighs 230 grains and makes a .45-inch hole. Modern hollowpoint rounds, like Federal HST, produce effective wounds and usually can drop an attacker with a few well-placed hits. The .45, regardless of load chosen, will not spin a man around with a hit in the little finger as in the war stories, but it will generally stop a fight with a few well-placed hits. Stay with bullets of 200 to 230 grains, as the 185-grain hollowpoints sometimes fail to penetrate deeply enough.

The last cartridge I will mention is the .357 SIG. This is a .40 Smith & Wesson cartridge necked down at the case mouth to accept a 9mm bullet. Ammunition in .357 SIG tends to have a great deal

> "American manufacturers turn out tens of millions of rounds of ammunition each day. Any product that is made by the millions per day will suffer from defective specimens."

of muzzle flash and blast, and the larger diameter cartridge case reduces magazine capacity compared to standard 9mm cartridges. Since you're shooting a bullet of the same exact diameter as a 9mm, you can't really expect more performance from it. And .357 SIG ammunition operates at high pressure and high slide velocity and is very hard on pistols, resulting in accelerated wear and parts breakage. I really don't see any need for this cartridge.

INSPECTION AND CARE OF SELF-DEFENSE AMMUNITION

Ammunition made in the U.S. is of very high quality. American manufacturers, however, turn out tens of millions of rounds of ammunition each day. Any product that is made by the millions per day will suffer from defective, out of spec, or damaged specimens and these will find their way into the boxes shipped to your local dealer. Since you literally bet your life on your self-defense ammo, it would be wise to inspect it and care for it properly.

Handguns, both revolvers and semi-auto pistols, rely completely on quality, in-spec ammunition to function. Here are just a few of the things we see go wrong frequently:

High Primer

The primer should be seated just below flush in the base of the cartridge. A "high primer" is one that protrudes above the base of the cartridge. In revolvers this can bind against the breech face, preventing rotation of the cylinder. In autos, this can keep the cartridge from sliding up under the extractor and keep the slide from going into battery.

Inverted Primer

Occasionally we find a cartridge in which the primer was inserted backward. Obviously, that cartridge won't fire.

Damaged Rim

The extractor must grab the rim of the cartridge and pull it out of the chamber so it can be ejected. The rim should be uniform, and have no bends, tears or burrs.

Damaged Case

The case might have a big dent in it, or the case mouth might have been caught by the bullet's base when the bullet was seated in the case, tearing the case mouth. These will often go into a magazine, but not feed into the pistol's chamber, causing a stoppage.

Bullets

We see bullets inserted backward in the case (they won't feed), or loose in the case, or pushed back too deeply into the case. Bad ju-ju.

We see a lot of ammo fired every year and we see these deficiencies in every brand and type of handgun ammunition. Before you trust your life to ammunition, inspect it carefully for the problems described above. I suggest doing the following for ammo you will actually be carrying:

1. Visually inspect the primers carefully. Be sure every case has a primer, that the primer is seated fully, and the primer is not dented or damaged.

2. Visually, and by feel, check the rim for damage or burrs.

3. Visually check the case, especially the case mouth.

4. Visually check the bullets, then with only finger pressure make sure they are not loose in the case. You should not be able to move the bullet at all with your fingers.

One final step many knowledgeable shooters take is to remove the barrel from the semi-auto pistol and use it as a gauge for the cartridges. Holding the barrel pointed down, drop a round into the chamber. It should go all the way in easily and stop with the base of the case even with the barrel hood. Invert the barrel over a towel. The cartridge should fall out easily. You will have confidence that cartridges that have been subjected to this test will feed smoothly in your gun.

In addition to checking your defensive ammo, you must take care of it. This branches two ways: ammo you have on hand, for instance in your home; and ammo you are actually carrying in your gun or in spare magazines. Let's look at them separately.

You should have a reserve supply of 100 to 200 rounds, at least, of your chosen defensive load at home. This should be kept in the factory boxes it comes in. The dividers or trays in those boxes help protect the individual cartridges, and identification of the ammo is easier in its original box. These should be kept inside your home, not in the garage or a detached storage shed. In those environments, the temperature and humidity vary too much. In a closet inside your home, the ammo will last indefinitely. If you want to ensure long-term viability, keep the ammo in metal GI ammo cans with a couple of packets of silica-gel desiccant inside. Ammo stored inside your home in this manner is good for 50 years or more.

Once you start carrying ammo, its service life starts counting down rather quickly. Ammo carried on your person is subjected to temperature and humidity swings, gun oils and solvents, and wear from being loaded and unloaded. Ammo that is actually carried should be shot up in practice and replaced in no more than six months. Going longer than that is just begging for trouble. Ammo routinely carried is susceptible to two major issues, which are potentially disastrous.

First, American ammo is loaded with Boxer primers. These primers consist of a metal cup, an anvil, a pellet of priming compound and a sealant.

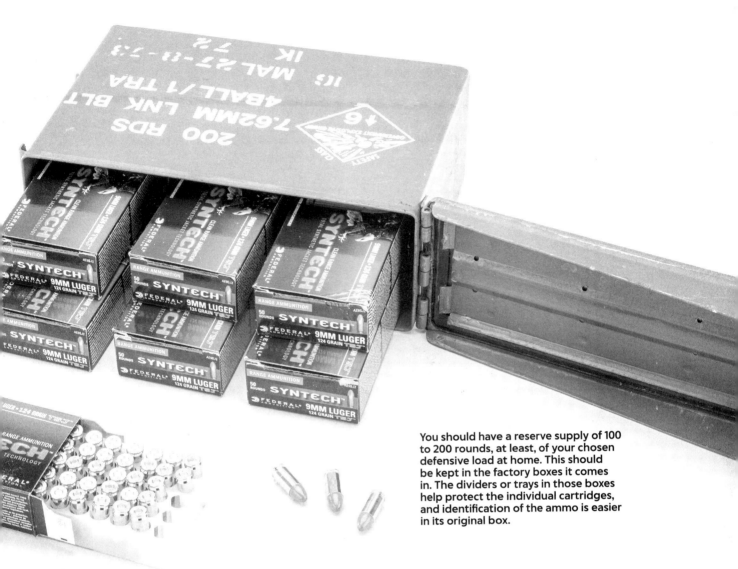

You should have a reserve supply of 100 to 200 rounds, at least, of your chosen defensive load at home. This should be kept in the factory boxes it comes in. The dividers or trays in those boxes help protect the individual cartridges, and identification of the ammo is easier in its original box.

The primer pellet is trapped between the cup and anvil, so when the firing pin or striker hits the cup, the pellet is crushed between the cup and anvil, igniting the cartridge. Every time you chamber a cartridge in a semi-auto firearm, the primer is subjected to impact by the breech face. Repeated strikes over time can cause the primer pellet to crumble. If it does, there is nothing between the cup and anvil to explode when the firing pin or striker hits, thus a misfired round. If you chamber the same round twice, I urge you to remove it from carry status and put it with your practice ammo for the next range trip.

There was a recent, well-publicized law enforcement shooting involving this very issue. An officer attempted to fire his handgun in self-defense, and the round in the chamber misfired. The officer was able to apply immediate corrective action (Tap, Rack, Bang!), and won the fight. Understandably, both he and his agency were upset that a round of premium "Law-Enforcement Only" ammo had failed to fire at a critical juncture. Examination of the misfired round showed that the primer pellet had disintegrated, as described above. Investigation revealed the officer unloaded his pistol every night and reloaded it the next day before going to work, chambering the same round over and over in the process. This caused the failure to fire. If you are worried about family members getting access to your pistol, as this officer was, lock it up, don't load/unload daily. Aside from the wear and tear on the ammo, most unintended discharges occur during loading/unloading. Load it, wear it or lock it up.

The other problem with loading/unloading is wear and tear on the bullet. When a round feeds up the ramp and into the barrel, the bullet takes a pretty solid impact. Doing this repeatedly can push the bullet back too deeply in its case. This compresses the powder charge and can result in dangerously high pressures (kaboom!).

Check your carry ammo before loading your gun or spare magazines with it, then replace the ammo every six months and you will prevent a lot of potentially serious problems down the road.

STOPPING POWER

After watching hundreds, if not thousands, of fictional shootings in violent TV shows and movies, most Americans have a grossly distorted idea of the power of handgun bullets. In the movies, people struck by pistol bullets are thrown through the air or crash through plate-glass windows. In real life, this just isn't true. In fact, in the heat of battle, a combatant might not even know he has been struck, perhaps even seriously wounded, until the action is over.

Pistol bullets are governed by the same laws of physics that control all other moving objects. Remember Newton's Third Law of Motion? For every action, there is an equal and opposite reaction. This means that if you had a pistol capable of actually knocking a man backward, it would knock you backward when you fired. In truth, the actual impact force delivered by pistol bullet is no more than the force delivered by solid punch with the fist of a man in good physical condition. How then does a pistol bullet injure or kill? The answer to that question is penetration. A pistol bullet does its work by penetrating the body, making a hole and both the amount of damage and the effect caused by the damage are controlled by three factors:

1. The size or diameter of the hole

2. The depth of the hole

3. The tissues that are destroyed or damaged by the hole made through them.

Our goal in shooting a human being is to stop his aggressive action as quickly as possible. As we learned in the chapter on use of force, we would shoot only if an assailant was undertaking aggressive, hostile action that threatens us or an innocent third party with death or serious bodily injury. This means, put simply, if we do not stop the assailant im-

mediately, we might be killed or grievously injured. We must strive, therefore, to inflict damage on the attacker that will cause him to cease his actions as quickly as possible. Ordinarily, this means damage to the central nervous system, consisting of the brain, brainstem or upper third of the spinal column (circuitry), or by letting out a lot of blood very quickly to drastically lower blood pressure and cause unconsciousness (plumbing).

Under typical gunfight conditions at close range, with rapid-dynamic movement and adrenaline-charged excitement, the brain shot is usually not a viable option. This leaves us shooting at the largest vital area of the body, the central upper torso. This area contains the heart, lungs, aorta, superior vena cava and the spine, all of which are located as viewed from the front in a somewhat circular area between the nipples, the collarbone, and the diaphragm. This area, about the size of a small dinner plate, will be your normal aiming point in a defensive shooting.

To be effective, bullets which impact in the vital zone described above must penetrate and damage life supporting organs, causing major, rapid blood loss or shock to the central nervous system by hitting

A pistol bullet does its work by penetrating the body, making a hole, and both the amount of damage and the effect caused by the damage are controlled by three factors: the size, or diameter, of the hole, the depth of the hole and the tissues that are destroyed or damaged by the hole made through them.

and damaging the spine itself. The chest cavity is protected by bone in the form of ribs and the sternum, and major organs and blood vessels lie deep within the body cavity. The spine itself may be as much is 9 inches deep from the front, and to cause damage to the spine the bullet must still have some penetrating power left when it reaches the spinal column. All of this means that to be effective, your bullets must be capable of adequate penetration to reach vital organs that lie deep within the body and then to puncture those organs and do damage to them. The first requirement, then, is to make a deep hole.

"A good hit with a marginal bullet is better than a marginal hit with a good bullet."

(opposite) Practicing with targets that show realistic human forms can help make shot placement into critical areas more likely during times of stress. Note that these Gunsite targets show vital zones in the upper chest and head with very light markings, which likely can't be seen at typical practice distances.

(below) While head shots likely won't be a viable option in a gunfight, it doesn't hurt to practice them.

Second, we want that hole through the organs to be as wide as possible, so the path of tissue destruction has the best chance of involving vital tissues. A hole an inch wide will destroy more nerve trunks, blood vessels and organ walls than a hole a half inch wide. This is self-evident, but often overlooked. The second requirement then is to make this hole as large as possible.

Making a large, deep hole does not, however, ensure success. The hole must be through vital organs. Bullet placement is the

In the 1990s, under pressure from the FBI and other large law-enforcement agencies, the ammo makers made great strides in perfecting hollow-point ammunition that both penetrates deeply and expands reliably. This raises the effectiveness of handgun ammunition greatly.

key to stopping power. You must practice until you can reliably put multiple deep, wide holes rapidly into the vital zone, to cause as much disruption of vital processes as possible in the shortest possible time. Continue to shoot as long as your assailant is on his feet or conscious, until a deadly threat is neutralized. A good hit with a marginal bullet is better than a marginal hit with a good bullet. Practice.

The essential elements of pistol-stopping power are then, in review:

1. Placement of hits in vital areas of the target's body

2. Making a bullet hole deep enough to reach underlying vital tissues

3. Making as large a hole as practicable, so as to cause maximum damage to vital organs and bring about the physical collapse of the assailant.

You must be able to rapidly and accurately fire the pistol, so you can place your shots in the vital zone quickly and reliably. If non-expanding bullets are used, such as lead semi-wadcutters in a revolver or full-jacketed, round-nosed ammunition in an auto, the larger the caliber, the more effective the hits will be. With this type of ammunition, a .40 Smith & Wesson will do more damage than the 9mm, and a .45 will outperform the .40.

Modern high-performance, hollowpoint ammunition changes this equation somewhat. In the 1990s, under pressure from the FBI and other large law-enforcement agencies, the ammo makers made great strides in perfecting hollowpoint ammunition that both penetrates deeply and expands reliably in living tissue. This raises the effectiveness of handgun ammunition greatly. When these high-performance bullets strike a living body, the bullet's nose section peels back around the body of the bullet, increasing the frontal area of the bullet. This in turn, increases the size of the bullet hole, increasing the amount of tissues damaged or destroyed in the bullet's passage through the body and allowing more rapid blood loss. In addition, the smooth, rounded original profile of the bullet now becomes irregular and jagged, increasing its tissue-damage potential. Properly designed hollowpoint ammunition increases the effectiveness of the medium caliber bullets (.38, .357, 9mm) to the level of non-expanding big-bore bullets (.41, .44, .45). Of course, one can use the same type of bullets in the big bores, increasing their performance further.

These high-performance hollowpoint bullets are available under a variety of brand names, including Winchester's PDX-1 line, Federal's HST or Tactical Bonded lines, Remington's Golden Saber, Speer's Gold Dot, and Hornady's Critical Duty (not Critical Defense). Bear in mind every ammunition manufacturer now makes hollowpoint bullets to capture a share of the burgeoning police/civilian defensive-ammo market, but not all hollowpoints perform as well as others. The specific brand names listed above all work reliably and would make good choices for defensive use.

When choosing a specific duty load for your pistol, first go to the big-name, high-performance types mentioned above. Among these ammo makers, some offer more than one bullet weight in each caliber, further complicating your choice. Generally, it is best to stick with the heavier bullet weight in any given caliber, to help assure deep penetration. Remember, adequate penetration is essential to performance. The lighter bullets, especially if they expand as intended, will tend to penetrate less than the heavier bullets in the same caliber.

18

FIREARMS SAFETY

irearms safety is the responsibility of every person who uses firearms for any purpose, whether that's sport, hunting, target shooting, plinking or self-defense. Firearms safety requires careful attention. You must constantly be aware that this is, in fact, a life-and-death issue and is a zero-tolerance activity.

Since we're writing about using firearms for self-defense, the first thing we need to do is get that into the proper context. Basically, once you are issued a permit to carry a gun or a law-enforcement commission, you have been given the power of life and death over everyone with whom you come in contact from that point on. You will be able to pick out people on the street and make them die on the

Carrying a concealed firearm comes with a lot of responsibilities; first and foremost is a complete command of the principles of firearms safety. These principles are taught thoroughly in all good concealed-carry courses, starting in the classroom. These principles are practiced and reinforced at the shooting range.

"Most negligent shootings ... are really just straightforward violations of one of the four cardinal safety rules."

spot. No appeal, no recourse, no way to fix it if you are wrong. Think about that. The president of the United States can't do that, the Queen of England can't do that, the Pope can't do that, but you will be able to. With that kind of power goes accountability and responsibility. You will be held accountable for what happens with your firearm regardless of the circumstances, regardless of your intentions and regardless of what anyone else did or didn't do.

One of these revolvers is loaded and one is unloaded, but both always should be handled and treated as if they are fully loaded. Always.

You might have to remind yourself exactly why you carry a gun in the first place. One carries a concealed firearm in case one has to shoot someone else. If you find yourself in a circumstance where your life or the life of a loved one is in grave, immediate, unavoidable mortal danger then you'd better have a gun. However, if you shoot someone, we want that to be a conscious, deliberate, willful act on your part, not a careless, stupid or inattentive act on your part. The result will be the same, the person is shot and is injured or killed as a result of your actions.

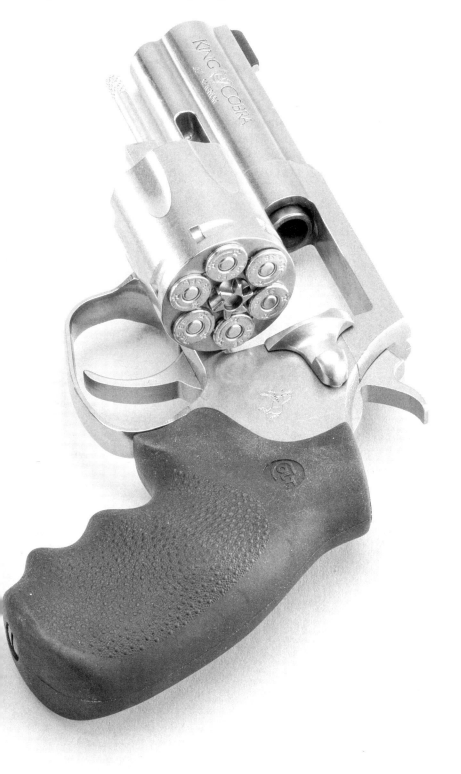

This would be a good time to cover the issue of accidental discharges and negligent discharges. In my career, I have investigated more than 200 negligent shootings, but I've looked into exactly one accident with a firearm. What's the difference? An accidental discharge involves a mechanical failure of the firearm that causes the gun to fire without input from the user, but typically without damage to anyone. An example might be a semi-auto pistol with the firing pin stuck forward protruding from the breech face due to a broken firing pin or to excessive crud in the firing-pin channel or some similar cause. When the user inserts a loaded magazine, pulls the slide all the way to the rear and releases it, the stuck firing pin protruding from the breech face can actually slam fire the primer of the cartridge being fed into the chamber resulting in an accidental discharge. The gun discharged without input from the user, such as putting pressure on the trigger, so it was an accidental discharge. However, if someone was struck by the bullet it was probably not an accidental shooting, but a negligent shooting. The gun had to be pointed toward that person when it discharged for the bullet to strike that person under typical circumstances. So, even though the discharge was accidental there was negligence involved on the part of the shooter for the projectile to strike another person, making it a negligent shooting.

Most negligent shootings, however, don't involve anything this complicated, but are really just straightforward violations of one of the four cardinal safety rules. A negligent shooting automatically involves negligence (carelessness, inattentiveness or ignorance) on the part of the shooter. As examples, holstering a handgun with a finger on the trigger can result in a bullet being fired down the shooter's leg, and is a direct violation of one of the major safety rules, i.e., having a finger on the trigger when the sights are not on the target and the shooter does not intend to fire. In the slam-fire case described in the previous paragraph, the negligence was having the gun pointed at a person when you pull the slide back and let it go. Almost all negligent shootings boil down to violating one of the four cardinal safety rules. These rules have been in use practically verbatim for about 50 years, they cover everything we can do with the gun, and strict adherence to them will prevent negligent shootings.

Before we get into the four rules, there are a few things we need to stress about them. First, we're talking about being armed on a continuous, routine basis in order to be armed when a sudden unforeseen crisis erupts. Of course, the reason we carry pistol, is in anticipation of sudden unforeseen crises in which our lives or the life of a loved one is in grave immediate danger. The key words here were sudden and unforeseen. About the only way we can be assured of having the handgun on our person when the flag flies is to make a routine habit to carry one in our daily activities. We refer to this as the armed lifestyle. This is why the four cardinal safety rules have to become literally part of our character, and they must be adhered to at all times in all places, without exception.

These four rules apply to all types of firearms, whether they are handguns, rifles, shotguns, submachine guns, flamethrowers or any other type of firearm. These rules apply all the time everywhere. They apply on the range, but they also apply in your home, in your place of business, on the street and in a gunfight. You will not be allowed to handle your weapon in a careless, sloppy manner in a fight any more than you would be on the range. Even in a fight, you will be held accountable for what happens with your weapon, so handling it properly and safely must become second nature. Now, let's look at these four rules in detail and we will see why they are so important, and how they cover just about everything we can do with a firearm.

FIREARM SAFETY RULE NUMBER ONE: ALL GUNS ARE ALWAYS LOADED.

Always treat all firearms as if they are fully loaded. This applies to every firearm you encounter. This applies to the gun you're wearing, the guns in your gun safe, your brother-in-law's gun on the shelf, the guns in the counter at the gun store and any other guns you come in contact with. If we could just get everyone to follow this one simple rule this would probably eliminate 90 percent of the problems. Don't pay lip service to this, be deadly serious about it. ALL guns, regardless of the circumstances, should be treated as loaded guns.

This leads to a simple two-way branch. If you want to shoot it, shoot it. If you wish to do anything else with it, then you must clear it first. Before you can clean it, tinker with it, paint the sights, tighten the grip screws, show it to your friend, or do anything else with it other than fire it, you must first clear it. When you clear a gun, you remove all ammunition, lock the action open, double check to make certain all ammunition is out, and leave the action open while you do any administrative handling of the firearm.

To clear a revolver, work the cylinder latch, open the cylinder, dump out all ammunition, go back and check each individual chamber to be sure all ammunition is out, and simply leave the cylinder open while you administratively handle the firearm. In this condition it cannot fire, so we can perform administrative tasks safely with it. If we clear the revolver ourselves and put it down on the table, it becomes a loaded gun again. If it has been out of our hands it has been out

of our control, therefore, we must treat it as a loaded gun. This simply means that if we pick it up again, we will clear it again. Simple! If I clear a gun right front of you and put it down, and you pick it up, then you must clear it. When you pick it up, it becomes your responsibility.

To clear a semi-auto pistol the first thing we want to do is remove the pistol's magazine. The magazine is much like the gas tank on your car, without gas your car won't go very far. Without a magazine there is nothing to feed into the chamber of the semi-auto pistol, so the first thing we will do is remove the magazine to cut off the supply of ammunition. Next, we will eject the round from the chamber, whether we think one is there or not. Next, we lock the slide to the rear and visually inspect the chamber and the magazine well to verify that all ammunition has been removed from the pistol. Once we've done that, we will simply leave the slide open while we perform whatever administrative functions with the pistol.

When you draw a handgun from a holster, you must keep your trigger finger straight and in "register" on the gun's frame. It is not enough to have the trigger finger straight and outside the trigger guard. When the trigger finger is in register, it is in a place on the pistol that is as far away from the trigger as possible, in a consistent spot, that is repeated until it becomes an automatic reflex.

> **"Unless your gun is locked up in the gun safe there are only three acceptable places for it to be: in the holster, at the ready or indexed on target."**

Do not give a handgun to someone else without first clearing it and leaving the action open. Do not accept the handgun from someone else unless they have cleared it and left the action open.

FIREARM SAFETY RULE NUMBER TWO: NEVER LET YOUR HANDGUN POINT AT ANYTHING YOU'RE NOT WILLING TO DESTROY.

The sole function of your gun is to launch bullets, the sole function of bullets is to punch holes in things. So, do not point your bullet launcher at anything you don't want to punch a hole in. This includes your body parts, persons around you and anything else of value.

With the long gun, which means typically a shotgun or rifle, this is fairly easy to keep up with since you have two different handholds on the weapon, and a much longer barrel. A handgun, however, is so short it's like an extension of your hand and it is really easy to point it at various

places without realizing it unless you pay attention. If you have your handgun out of the holster, you must constantly be aware of where it is pointed and make certain you don't point it at anything you don't want to shoot. There is a fairly simple way to keep up with this. Unless your gun is locked up in the gun safe there are only three acceptable places for it to be: in the holster, at the ready or indexed on target. Unless you need it out for a specific purpose keep the handgun in the holster. If you believe you might have to fire the gun in the next few seconds, go to the ready. At the ready position the gun is under control, you know where it is pointed and it is ready for instant use. So, if you need to shoot, get to shooting. If you believe you're about to have to shoot, go to the ready. If you don't believe you will need to shoot anytime soon, put the pistol back in the holster.

The holster is a safe, secure, readily accessible place to keep the pistol where it is under control and pointed in a safe direction, yet you can access the pistol in a heartbeat if you need it. Wandering around with the pistol in hand unnecessarily often causes problems. The longer the gun is in your hands the harder it is to keep up with where it is pointed. This is why the holster is so critically important. With the pistol safely holstered, we no longer have to worry about where it is pointed.

Muzzle awareness is a critical skill and it takes a bit of attention at first to learn it. When loading or unloading your pistol on the firing line for instance, you must keep it pointed forward, not inadvertently pointed toward people to your support side as you work the slide. If you turn to say something to an instructor, you will make certain you leave the gun pointed downrange and only turn your head to speak to that person. These are just examples of the sort of muzzle awareness you must build.

FIREARM SAFETY RULE NUMBER THREE: KEEP YOUR FINGER OFF THE TRIGGER UNTIL YOUR SIGHTS ARE ON THE TARGET AND YOU INTEND TO FIRE.

The sole function of your trigger is to release the hammer, striker, or firing pin and cause the gun to discharge. The only time we want the gun to discharge is when it's aimed at something we wish to shoot. When you draw the gun from the holster, your trigger finger must be straight. When you put the gun back in the holster, the trigger finger must be straight. When you're at the ready looking for something to shoot, the trigger finger must be straight. The only time the trigger finger enters the trigger guard is when we want the gun to fire, period.

When the gun goes on the target, the trigger finger goes on the trigger. When the gun comes off the target, the trigger finger comes off the trigger. If we draw a straight line from your eye to the center of your target that line would be called "the eye-target line". When the gun comes up to the eye-target line the trigger finger goes to the trigger and removes the slack. The instant the gun comes off the eye-target line the trigger finger must go straight and return to its register position. Gun goes on, finger goes on. Gun comes off, finger comes off.

It is not enough to have the trigger finger straight and outside the trigger guard. We must find a position on the pistol for the trigger finger that places the finger as far away from the trigger as possible and gives it a tactile indicator of where it should be located until the decision to fire has been made. This point on the pistol is referred to as the "register" for the trigger finger. When the trigger finger is in register it is in a consistent place on the pistol that is as far away from the trigger as possible, in a consistent spot, that is repeated until it becomes an automatic reflex. The register position can be the flat part of the frame above the trigger guard, it can be the flat of the slide, or it could be the edge of the ejection port. Different people have different amounts of mobility in their trigger finger due to flexibility, age, arthritis and other factors. Thus, the register position will not be the same for every shooter. The individual shooter must find a spot that gives tactile feedback for the register and is as far away from the trigger as can be comfortably maintained.

The vast majority of negligent shootings involve having the trigger finger in the trigger guard at inappropriate times. Modern handguns are equipped with various devices such as firing-pin safeties, transfer bars, hammer blocks, etc. that prevent the weapon from firing unless the trigger is pulled to the rear. If your handgun discharges, the odds are overwhelming that it did so because something put pressure on the trigger sufficient to cause the gun to fire. The object that put pressure on the trigger is almost always your trigger finger. The startle response or inter-limb reaction are well-known reasons for unintentionally pulling the trigger on a firearm. Neither will cause the gun to discharge if the trigger finger is properly in register.

The correct way to teach this is not, "don't put your finger on the trigger now, now or now." The correct way to teach it is, "only put your finger on the trigger when you have made a decision to shoot and you have your sights on your target". There is only one time when it is acceptable to have your finger on the trigger, and that is when you are aimed in and you want the gun to fire.

There is only one time when it is acceptable to have your finger on the trigger, and that is when you are aimed in and you want the gun to fire. When firing, use only the first joint of the trigger finger on the face of the trigger, and press straight backward.

FIREARM SAFETY RULE NUMBER FOUR: BE CERTAIN OF YOUR TARGET, WHAT IS AROUND IT AND WHAT IS BEYOND.

In the movies, bullets fired at someone that miss just seem to disappear. In reality, they fly until they strike something solid enough to stop them. That object might be a brick wall, a parked car, a tree trunk or a 5-year-old child. The bullet couldn't care less, it is just a chunk of metal with no soul and no will of its own. It simply goes where you send it. You will be held accountable for where it lands. Therefore, we must always be certain what we're shooting at and the background behind it so we know where our bullets will wind up. We never fire at shadows, at noises or rustles in the brush. We must know what we are shooting and why we are shooting it or we cannot fire our guns. Be aware that pistol bullets can travel as much as one mile. That creates a huge downrange danger zone. We must constantly be aware of the background behind our target.

Those four rules are basically it. They cover just about everything we can do with a firearm. If it's a gun, it's loaded unless you personally have cleared it and it is still in your control. Keep up with where the gun is pointed at all times. If you no longer need it out, put it in the holster. Keep your finger in register well away from the trigger until you bring the gun to bear on a target. Know what you're shooting at, what's around it and what's behind.

Now, can we make this even simpler? Actually, we could. There are two safety checks that all by themselves will prevent most problems. These two are:

MUZZLE DISCIPLINE AND TRIGGER-FINGER DISCIPLINE

Muzzle discipline: The firearm should always be pointed in the safest direction. That is, even if the weapon fired there would be no personal injury to anyone and only minimal property damage.

Trigger-finger discipline: The modern handgun generally will not fire unless the trigger is depressed. Keeping your finger in register at all times when you are not actually firing will prevent almost all negligent discharges. If these two safety checks are in place, no one will be inadvertently shot.

The two major causes of unintentional shootings are Ignorance and Carelessness. Ignorance is represented by that vast body of people who go out and buy a gun, obtain no training with it and, therefore, do not know how to handle it correctly. Carelessness generally refers to people who know the rules but don't follow them. The court will make no distinction between the two. The court's position is that if you have a deadly weapon it is incumbent upon you to seek proper training in its use and then to follow the rules.

Firing ranges may be run as "cold ranges" or "hot ranges." On a cold range, shooters don't wear a loaded gun unless they are actually on the firing line and are actually involved in a firing drill. The shooters only load on the command of the instructor, and at the completion of the drill, or the course of fire, all shooters will unload and holster empty guns.

(opposite) Even when running timed drills in competitions, shooters are taught to keep their trigger fingers in register on the frame of the pistol, away from the trigger guard and trigger. This is known as trigger-finger discipline.

"We never fire at shadows, at noises or rustles in the brush."

Persons on the range, but not actually on the firing line would have unloaded guns.

The cold range is typically used for the most basic types of instruction, such as a beginners' or introductory class, or a typical handgun-permit class, especially in its early stages. Since the students involved do not yet know how to handle the gun properly, they are instructed to load it and to unload it under direct supervision, and they are not allowed to possess loaded guns except while under direct supervision. Cold ranges can be very dangerous places. The problem is that once off the line everyone considers all the guns to be unloaded, which can lead to sloppy handling, and poor muzzle discipline. This leads to negligent shootings. As such, cold ranges are properly used only in those very early stages of training and they require constant supervision by an adequate number of trained instructors.

Hot ranges refer to facilities where everyone routinely wears a loaded handgun. The handguns remain holstered at all times unless actually involved in a firing drill. No guns are taken out of the holster anywhere except on the firing line. Hot ranges are probably actually much safer than cold ranges because everyone knows all the guns are in fact loaded and they treat them that way. Training beyond the introductory level should probably be conducted as a hot range.

Care, Cleaning and Maintenance

Improperly cared for equipment might fail you at a most inopportune moment. Gear that has been properly cared for and maintained, on the other hand, will last longer and work better. Maintenance of weapons, ammunition and leather gear will be covered separately.

Using the right cleaning techniques will make your firearms work better and suffer less wear from firing. Your firearms should be cleaned after each firing session, and the pistol worn on your person should be cleaned monthly whether it has been fired or not.

Using the right cleaning techniques will make your firearms work better and suffer less wear from firing. Your firearms should be cleaned after each firing session, and the pistol worn on your person should be cleaned monthly whether it has been fired or not.

The first step is to gather the appropriate cleaning materials. A cleaning rod, several lint-free rags, a supply of bore patches in the proper size, a bristle bore brush, a worn-out toothbrush, a bottle of solvent specifically intended for gun cleaning and a good lubricant are all you need. Organize these materials on your working surface, and you are ready to begin.

Obtain the weapon that is to be cleaned and unload it. Do not assume it is empty: Check it. Remove all live ammo, and place ammo as far away from the cleaning table as the size of the room will permit. This serves two purposes. First, it keeps a round from being absent-mindedly inserted into the weapon. Second, it keeps solvents and lubricants from coming in contact with the cartridges. Certain solvents and cleaning agents can penetrate the opening around the cartridge's primer, which deacti-

vates the primer for the powder charge. Be careful to keep solvents and their vapors away from all ammo to avoid dud rounds.

Once the pistol has been unloaded, disassemble it per the instructions in the factory manual. Use a patch dipped in solvent to wet the inside of the bore, chamber and each chamber of a revolver's cylinder. Use a toothbrush with solvent to clean fouling from the breech face, forcing cone of revolvers and any other surfaces that appear dirty. Use a rag to wipe off the exterior of the gun and those internal areas you can reach. If your barrel is leaded from firing plain lead bullets, use the bristle brush soaked in solvent to loosen the fouling. Run a clean patch through the bore to remove the loose fouling and repeat until the bore is clean. Lightly lubricate the pistol and reassemble. Check to be certain that the pistol's mechanism

functions properly by dry firing it and using all of the controls.

Many people tend to over-lubricate their sidearms. This is messy and will result in oil stains on your clothing when you wear the sidearm. It also leaves a lot of excess oil around in the pistol to pick up dust, lint, etc. Use oil sparingly on contact points to prevent excess friction, but do not squirt oil into every available aperture. If your pistol is made of blue steel, a very light coat of oil all over its exterior will be needed to prevent rust. A chrome, nickel or other rust resistant pistol can be left dry on the outside.

If your sidearm is a revolver, take care to clean under the extractor star because fouling here can easily result in a tied-up gun. Auto-pistol magazines should be disassembled and cleaned about once a year or if dropped in mud or sand.

Ammunition also requires care for best functioning. Each time you clean your weapon, take the ammunition aside and inspect it. Bullet noses should not be deformed, and if you use hollow-points, be sure the opening is not mashed shut or plugged with debris. Check the cases for dents and deep scratches. Observe the rims for rough dents that could cause feeding problems. Wipe off the cartridges with a clean, dry rag. Service ammunition should not be carried for more than six months. During this time, it will be subjected to the effects of weather, condensation, handling, harmful vapors, etc. Every six months shoot up your old duty ammo in a practice session and replace it with fresh cartridges.

When replacing old ammunition, inspect the new rounds carefully

"Each time you clean your weapon, take the ammunition aside and inspect it."

for defects. Modern commercial ammo is very good, but a bad round gets by the quality control people every now and then.

Leather gear also needs proper maintenance for best results. Good quality leather gear, if properly cared for, will last almost indefinitely, but neglected gear will deteriorate to the point of needing replacement in a couple of years. A damp cloth can be used to remove dirt, and a good quality paste shoe wax can be applied to outer sur-

faces to enhance appearance and help waterproof the leather. A light spray of silicone inside the holster will help keep friction down. Do not put on heavy doses of neatsfoot oil or mink oil as this will soften the leather and shorten the useful life of a good holster.

Kydex holsters can be simply wiped off with a damp cloth and require no further maintenance. Check tension screws for proper adjustment and visually inspect for cracks in the Kydex.

Closely inspect holsters, ammunition carriers and belts periodically looking for broken threads, worn rivets and other signs of wear. A shoe shop can often manage small repairs of leather goods for you.

Take good care of your equipment and it will serve you well.

Quality leather holsters, such as this sharkskin model, should be cleaned and maintained as meticulously as the pistols they house and protect. Good quality leather gear, if properly cared for, will last almost indefinitely, but neglected gear will deteriorate to the point of needing replacement in a couple years.

19

SHOOTING TECHNIQUE

Proper defensive shooting technique could be defined as "a standardized system of training and operation designed to produce rapid, accurate, decisive hits under stressful conditions."

FIRING (FIGHTING) PLATFORM

The shooter needs a balanced, poised, defensive posture, one which provides stability, flexibility and mobility. "Stability" means being able to keep steady enough to keep the sights on target as we fire, and to avoid falling down. "Flexibility" refers to being able to conform to cover, uneven ground or unusual circumstances. "Mobility" means we might need to get off this spot quickly, to avoid incoming bullets, blows or blades.

The feet should be kept shoulder-width apart, the gun-side foot back slightly, knees unlocked and upper-body weight biased slightly forward. "Keep your nose over your toes." Get your shoulders forward.

The proper firing platform delivers a balanced, poised, defensive posture that promotes stability, flexibility and mobility. The feet should be about shoulder-width apart, with the gun-side foot slightly back, knees slightly bent and upper-body weight slightly forward.

GRIP

"Grip" refers to the interface of our hands and the gun. A proper grip maximizes recoil control, minimizes muzzle rise, aids in proper trigger manipulation, builds a repeatable index and aids in retention of the pistol. The hands should be as high on the gun as possible, thumbs high and the barrel of the gun lined up with the long bones of the gun-hand forearm.

"HANDS HIGH, THUMBS HIGH."

Getting the hands as high on the handgun's stocks as possible increases recoil control and speeds shot-to-shot recovery time. Keeping the thumbs up gets them off the pistol's controls, makes it easier to move the trigger straight to the rear, and is a stronger grip in a weapon-retention struggle. The support-hand fingers should be cupped and placed on the front of the gun hand, so that all four fingers overlay the three lower fingers of the gun hand. The gun hand places front-to-rear pressure on the pistol. The support hand clamps in from the sides. This gives positive 360-degree pressure on the handgun, providing a strong, stable grip. The arms are extended until the elbows almost lock, but not quite. Slightly bent elbows allow better recoil control and stronger retention of the pistol.

The "trigger-finger biceps" must clear the frame. If the first joint of the trigger finger lies along the frame, the frame will be pushed laterally as the trigger finger arches as the trigger is pressed. This results in hits off at 9 o'clock for a right-handed shooter.

SIGHTING OR AIMING

Aiming is a two-part process consisting of sight alignment and sight picture.

Sight alignment is the optical relationship between the front sight and the rear sight. Look through the rear sight (think of it as a window) and visually place the front sight in the rear-sight notch. The front sight should be centered in the rear-sight notch (same amount of light on both sides) and the top of the front sight should be even with the tops of the rear sight.

Sight picture is the optical relationship of the sights to the target. The human eye can discern straight lines quicker and easier than any other shape. This is why traditional square-post, square-notch sights work so well.

Except in extreme close quarters, the pistol's sights are used for every shot. Consistent, conscious front-sight focus does two things:

First, it assures a well-placed hit on target, and it builds a kinesthetic "feel" for when the gun is on target.

After a bit of practice, your presentation puts the gun on target, and the sights are used to verify alignment, not to achieve it. This can be accomplished in a few hundredths of a second.

Don't let anyone tell you that at typical handgun fight distances you don't have time to aim. That is nonsense. What you don't have time to do is miss. Misses deplete your ammo, but far more importantly, they eat up your time. Time is your most precious commodity in a fight. It runs right through your fingers like water, and once it is gone you can't get it back. Anything you do that wastes time must be eliminated. The biggest waste of time is missing. Every time you miss, you waste the time it took to prep that shot, fire that shot and recover from that shot. That adds up quickly. One good hit takes less time than two misses. For precision, focus on the top edge of the front sight.

Gripping a handgun as high as possible on the stocks helps control recoil and reduces the time it takes to get the sights back on the target after each shot. Also, keeping the thumbs high in the grip keeps them off the gun's controls, and makes it easier to press the trigger straight to the rear.

Sight alignment involves visually placing the front sight in the middle of the notch in the rear sight, with the top of the front sight even with the tops of the rear sight.

TRIGGER CONTROL

Trigger control is vital. The gun must discharge while the sights are on target. Pressing the trigger must not move the sights. A typical defensive handgun weighs 2 pounds, but has a trigger-pull weight of 4 to 8 pounds. This makes trigger control harder with a handgun.

Place the fingerprint (pad) of the index finger on the center of the trigger. Press the trigger **straight to the rear.** You must remove the slack from the trigger for the first shot, then maintain contact with the trigger from shot to shot. "Trigger reset" refers to letting the trigger go forward after a shot no more than is needed to re-engage the sear and be ready to fire again. Once your finger touches the trigger, it stays on the trigger until all shots have been fired.

Your trigger finger must only contact the pistol on the face of the trigger, **not on the frame.** There must be a visible gap between the first joint of the trigger finger and the frame to avoid pushing the frame sideways as the trigger is pressed to the rear.

As an aspiring handgun shooter, you will soon learn one of the hardest things to learn for new shooters, yet one of the most important

skills, is trigger control. The shooter must learn to keep the sights on the target while smoothly moving the trigger to the rear until the gun discharges. Even in high-speed, defensive shooting, this process occurs, although the time it takes to complete the process is compressed. With a handgun, yanking and cranking on the trigger is the root cause of almost all misses, if the gun was even roughly aligned on the target when the decision to fire was made.

Larry Vickers, retired special-operations soldier, former Delta operator, and world-class firearms instructor once said, "Why is the rifle so much easier to shoot than a pistol? Easy. The rifle weighs more than its trigger pull, while the handgun weighs less than the weight of the trigger pull." That is a truly brilliant summation of the whole problem. If you have an 8-pound rifle with a 2-pound trigger, it's easy to shoot it well. Unfortunately, we often have a 2-pound pistol with an 8-pound trigger pull, hence the difficulty. Thus, proper trigger technique becomes vital.

First, let's look at the different phases of trigger operation. Manipulation of the semi-auto pistol's trigger actually consists of four separate and distinct phases, and each impacts our accuracy. These phases, in sequence, are:

"With a handgun, yanking and cranking on the trigger is the root cause of almost all misses ..."

Only the first joint of the trigger finger should come into contact with the face of the trigger when pressing it straight toward the rear of the gun to fire a round.

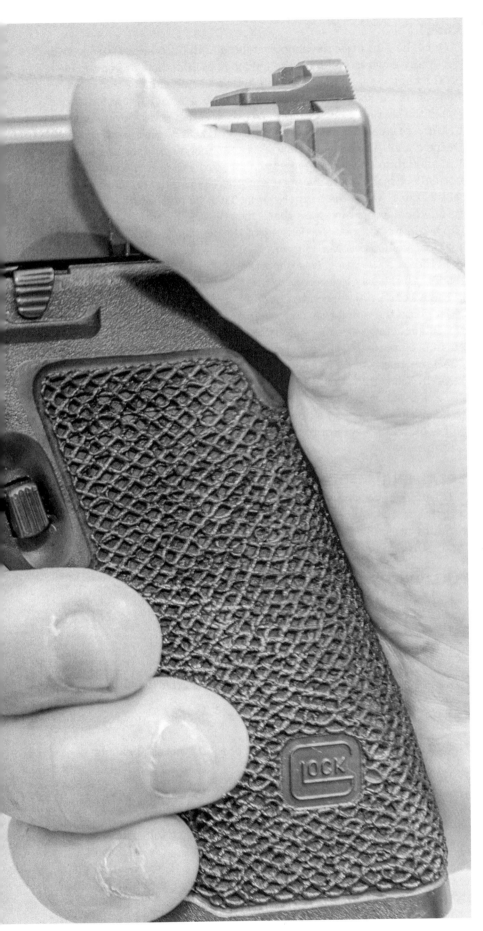

CONTACT

The "pad," or fingerprint, of the shooter's index finger should contact the center of the face of the trigger. The trigger finger should not touch the frame of the gun. Ideally, the only place the trigger finger should contact the pistol is on the face of the trigger. (That's why we call it a trigger finger.)

SLACK

Semi-auto pistols have "slack" or "pre-engagement travel" built into the action. This is a bit of rearward movement in the trigger, prior to the actual trigger pull. The shooter can feel a distinct difference in the amount of finger pressure needed to take up the slack as opposed to that pressure needed to fire the piece. Some designs have significantly more slack than others. As the gun is brought to bear on the target, the slack is taken up, so the trigger finger feels the resistance of the trigger pull. As the gun goes on target, the trigger finger contacts the trigger and removes the slack. When the gun goes on the target, the trigger finger goes on the trigger.

PRESS

Beware of semantics. The words you use form images in your subconscious, and this drives your actions. For instance, if you think "squeeze" the trigger, you will likely squeeze your entire hand while moving the trigger. We call this "milking the trigger." This results in low misses. As the lower fingers tighten their grip, the barrel is pulled downward as the gun fires. Instead, we want to "press" the trigger, with steady rearward pressure. We hold the gun with our hand; we fire the gun with our trigger finger. The student must learn to use the trigger finger independently, while maintaining a constant, consistent,

"We hold the gun with our hand; we fire the gun with our trigger finger."

unchanging grip on the pistol with the rest of the hand. When enough pressure is applied to the trigger to disengage the sear, the gun fires.

It might help to think of the trigger as the pistol's "gas pedal." Using the analogy of a car, which all shooters are familiar with, the magazine is the gas tank, the front sight is the green light and the trigger is the accelerator. When you see the green light, you apply steady, increasing pressure to the accelerator until the bullet takes off smoothly. If you stomp the gas pedal, the car takes off erratically and under less control. Same with the bullet. It won't matter if the sights are on the target if you smash the trigger and knock the sights off the target as the gun fires.

RESET

Once the gun fires, the shooter must maintain contact with the trigger. Many newbies will have the tendency to take their finger completely off the trigger the instant the gun fires, and this must be corrected. As soon as the shooter sees the front sight begin to lift, that bullet has exited the barrel and is in flight. The shooter can no longer do anything to affect that shot, so he should forget it and start concentrating on the next shot. The first step is to relax the trigger finger's pressure just enough to let the trigger return forward to its reset point. That is normally a really short distance, and there is usually an audible and tactile "click" when the trigger resets. There is no need to let the trigger go any farther forward than that. Once the trigger is reset, the shooter can begin working on the delivery of the next shot.

Double-action revolver triggers do not have slack in them, otherwise the process is the same. It is important with the revolver to move the trigger all the way to the rear to fire the gun, then let it roll back all the way out before starting on the next trigger pull. The revolver trigger must go all the way forward or you can skip a chamber or even lock up the action, a process called "short stroking." The double-action trigger should be pressed all the way through in one smooth motion.

All one needs to do to play a concerto on a piano is to hit the right keys, in the right order, at the right time. It's a simple process, but it takes practice. All one needs to do to hit anything with a pistol is to keep the sights aligned on the intended point of impact while you work the trigger smoothly to the rear. Again, a simple concept, but it takes practice.

BREATHING

Breath control is only needed for a deliberate shot at a small or distant target. For that, take a deep breath, let it out, hold the breath while you carefully press off the shot (natural respiratory pause), then breathe again. Up close and personal, don't worry about breathing, just breathe.

FOLLOW-THROUGH

Follow-through is critical, but is one of the most overlooked aspects of combat shooting. When your gun fires:

1. Keep your visual focus on the front sight;

2. As soon as you see the front sight lift, reset the trigger;

3. The front sight will rise, then fall back into the rear sight notch;

4. As the front sight descends, start pressing on the next shot.

Do not count on one shot to stop a fight, especially with a handgun. Be prepared to fire multiple accurate shots. This is why follow-through is so critical.

"Follow-through" refers to not letting anything change from the moment we press the trigger until the bullet actually leaves the barrel. The "ignition chain" is the series of events that takes place once we decide to press the trigger. This chain includes neural and muscular activity; motion of the trigger; motion of the striker or hammer; ignition of the primer; burning of the powder charge; initial movement of the bullet; and the bullet's travel down the bore to the muzzle. This takes time. We must not let our grip pressure change, move our finger on the trigger, or move anything else until the bullet has left the gun. This is follow-through.

As soon as the shooter sees the front sight rise, or lift, we know the bullet has left the barrel. As soon as the front sight lifts, reset the trigger and ride the front sight right back into the rear-sight notch. At this point we would be ready to press off the next shot. This is "recovery."

The slide of the pistol does not start to move until after the bullet has left the muzzle. As soon as you see that front sight lift, the bullet is out of the gun and on its way to the target. At that point we have to start working on the next shot.

HANDGUN MALFUNCTIONS

First, we need to define our terms. A "jam" is a serious stoppage that normally involves a broken part or something of that nature and would require tools to fix. A malfunction is some interruption in the firing cycle that can be remedied simply and quickly.

Because they operate so differently, malfunctions for revolvers and semi-auto pistols will be treated separately.

REVOLVER MALFUNCTIONS

The old beliefs about revolvers being more reliable than semi-autos arises from the ammunition that was available when autos first appeared in military and police service, circa 1900. Ammunition of that day had unstable primers that deteriorated quickly when exposed to gun oils, solvent vapors and just ordinary exposure to weather while carrying the loaded gun and ammo on the belt. The primers of that day contained mercuric salts, which gather moisture from the air and cause corrosion. These corrosive primers made cleaning the gun the same day it was fired an absolute necessity. If the gun was not cleaned immediately the mercuric salt deposits in the barrel would gather moisture and cause rust overnight. Unfortunately, these mercuric salts in the primer absorbed moisture when ammunition is worn on the belt and often failed to fire when needed.

This is no longer an issue as these mercuric primers have not been in use in the U.S. since World War II. Modern primers contain lead styphnate, not mercuric compounds. Modern primers are far less susceptible to oils, solvents and the weather. However, when auto pistols first became common, the mercuric ammunition was all that was available, and misfires were common. If a revolver misfires the user simply pulls the trigger again and a fresh round comes up for another try. If a cartridge in a semi-auto pistol misfires the user must perform an immediate action drill to get the gun back in operation. With modern ammunition, a properly maintained semi-auto pistol is about as reliable as a machine can be.

The revolver's basic design makes it far more fragile, and far more susceptible to serious malfunctions that take too long to fix in a fight. If you will think about it, a revolver has five or six individual chambers, each of which has to line up precisely with the pistol barrel upon firing. A misalignment by just a few thousandths of an inch results in part of the bullet shaving off in the forcing cone, or the primer misaligned with the firing pin causing misfires. In order to time the action so that each chamber locks in place exactly in alignment with the barrel each time, the trigger is pulled the action of the revolver has to be precisely

"Do not count on one shot to stop a fight, especially with a handgun."

timed and balanced. The inside of a double-action revolver somewhat resembles the workings of a wind-up watch. Small delicate parts, small springs and so forth require perfect fitting and no wear in order to maintain these extremely tight tolerances. Here are some of the basic malfunctions that occur with a double-action revolver and what you might be able to do to fix it in the field.

Failure to fire: You pull the trigger, nothing happens. With support hand palm, strike cylinder on left side to be sure it is fully closed. Pull trigger again. If no bang, transition to backup gun. This can be caused by a high primer jammed against the recoil shield, or a bullet lodged against the forcing cone. In either of these cases your only viable option is a backup gun.

Failure to fire: You pull the trigger, get a "click." Immediately pull the trigger again. If it clicks twice it is empty, the ammo is dead or the firing pin is broken. Speed load or transition to a backup gun. If you reload and it

goes click, the firing pin is probably broken. If you're still alive transition to your backup gun.

Cylinder won't open: The ejector rod might be backed out; high primer might be stuck; bullet might have jumped; the ejector rod might be bent. Primer metal might have flowed into the firing pin hole in the frame, locking up everything. This is most common with magnum ammunition. Transition to your backup gun.

Cylinder won't turn: You pull the trigger, but it won't move and cylinder won't turn. Debris under the extractor star has bound up the action. See first entry. Or, ejector rod is bent, or ejector rod has come unscrewed. Transition to your backup gun. Titanium guns and lead bullets don't mix; they recoil so sharply that bullets tend to jump forward under recoil and tie up the action. Transition to your backup gun.

Cylinder will not accept new ammo on a reload: You failed to eject the spent cases vigorously with the gun vertical and a spent case got under the extractor star. Transition to your backup gun. Later, if you survive, hold extractor open and pry out the case with your pocketknife.

Failure to fire: The Taurus or Smith & Wesson goofy internal lock has engaged spontaneously. Transition to your backup gun.

Failure to fire: The strain screw in the front strap of the grip has backed out due to the vibrations of recoil. If the screw backs up a couple turns, the firing pin strike will be too light to ignite the cartridges. Periodically check the screw and make sure it is tight. Also, check your firing pin frequently if you have a hammer mounted firing pin as opposed to a frame mounted firing pin. The firing pin mounted on the hammer is subject to breakage.

As you can see, there are a number of mechanical reasons why your revolver might fail, and unfortunately, most of them require time and tools to fix. In a fight you will have neither.

Firmly rapping the ejector rod with the palm of your hand while holding the revolver in a vertical position can reduce the possibility of a spent case becoming stuck under the extraction star, which could prevent the cylinder from accepting new ammo on a reload.

When a semi-auto pistol fails to fire, the most common cause is the magazine not being locked securely into place. Some occurrences are fairly obvious, and others aren't as noticeable. In either case, the solution is to firmly tap the base of the magazine with the palm of the support hand, and rack the slide vigorously to load a live round into the chamber.

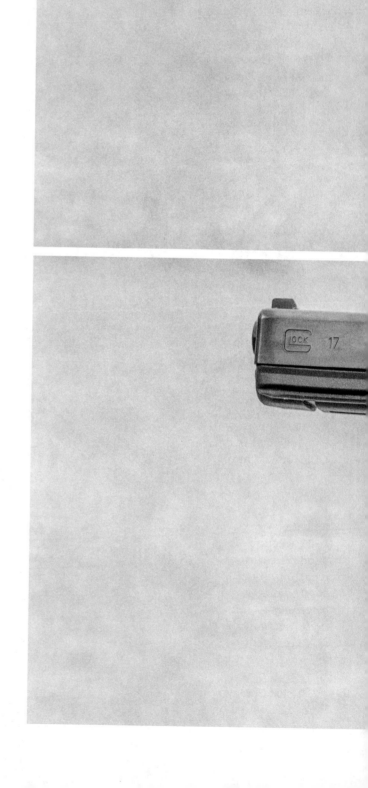

SEMI-AUTO PISTOL MALFUNCTIONS

The single most common malfunction with a semi-auto pistol is the failure to fire. Almost 99 times out of 100, this is due to the magazine not being locked in. The 100th time is due to a misfired cartridge. In either case:

1. TAP the base of the magazine with the support hand to ensure that it is locked in.

2. RACK the slide vigorously.

3. BANG fire the pistol, if the situation still calls for gunfire.

The most common reason for the gun to fail to fire is that there is simply no round in the chamber. You might have forgotten to chamber a round the last time you loaded the gun, or the magazine might have come unlocked. If the magazine came unlocked and you fired the round that was in the chamber the slide will cycle without picking up a new round from the magazine. Thus, the next time you press the trigger you will get "click" instead of "bang."

Also, American ammunition manufacturers make literally tens of millions of cartridges each day. Several of the major plants, like Remington, Winchester and Federal each turn out several million cartridges every day. No matter what you are making, when you are making millions of them you will turn out some bad ones. One major manufacturer sets a standard of four misfires per 10,000 rounds loaded. As long as ammunition meets that standard it is shipped out for sale. That means you might have a fresh, factory-loaded, premium round of ammunition in the chamber of your pistol right now and when you pull the trigger the next time it might go "click" instead of "bang."

Whether the chamber is empty because you didn't put a round there, or because the magazine came unlocked, or you have a misfired cartridge in the chamber, a simple TAP/RACK/BANG will fix it and get the gun back in action immediately.

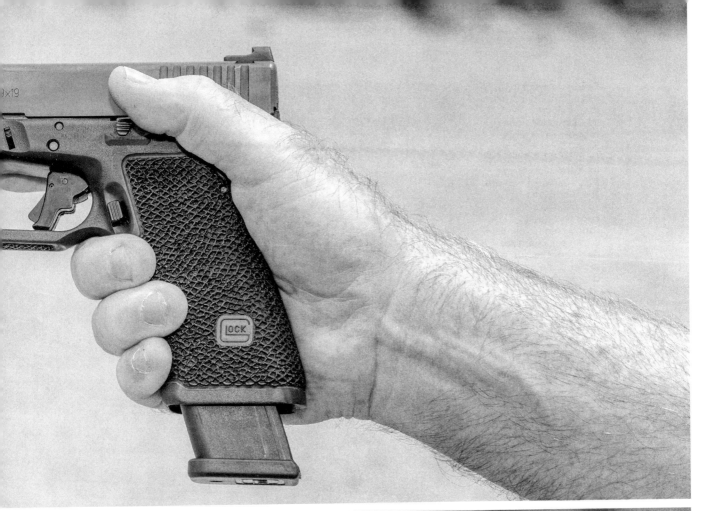

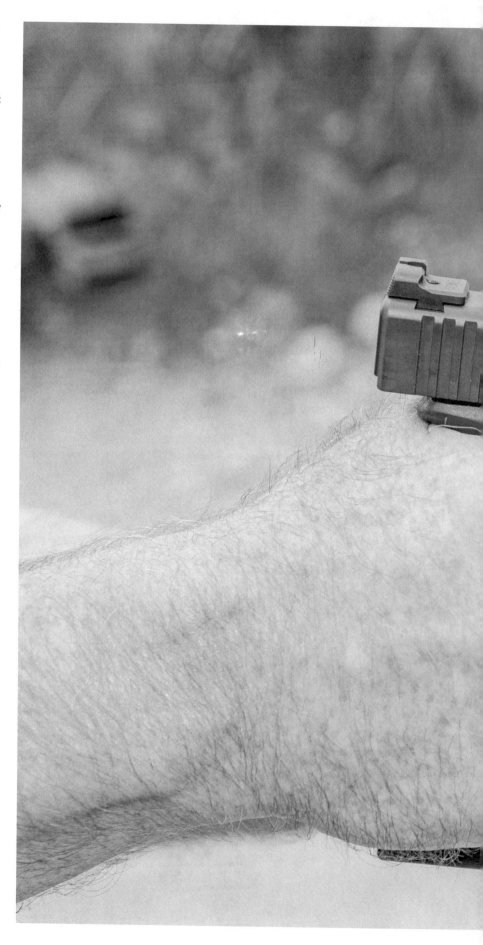

Failure to eject involving a fired case stuck in the ejection port of a semi-auto pistol is known as a "stovepipe." To fix the situation, the shooter must rack the slide forcefully rearward and tilt the gun to the right, so both the spent case and the live round that followed it into the chamber fly out of the gun to prevent the possibility of a double feed.

Failure to eject: The failure to eject, or stovepipe, malfunction consists of a fired case caught in the ejection port, preventing the slide from going into battery. TAP/RACK/BANG! The "rack" portion of the immediate-action drill must be done forcefully, pulling the slide to the rear hard while spinning the gun a bit to the right. We must eject not only the spent case but also the live round from the chamber. I have watched literally millions of rounds of ammunition fired and I've never seen a stovepipe malfunction in which there was not a live round in the chamber. So, when we remedy this malfunction we must do so forcefully, so that both the spent case and the live round in the chamber fly out of the gun or we will create a much worse malfunction, if only the fired case and not the live round in the chamber come out. As the slide goes forward it will take another round from the magazine and create a double feed. The best way to do this is to push the frame away from you with your gun hand, and pull the slide toward you with the support hand HARD, while spinning the gun to the right so that both the empty case and the live round in the chamber come out, clearing the way for the next round to go into the chamber.

Failure to extract: The failure to extract is also called a double feed. This can be caused by an underpowered round, a bad magazine, a poor firing grip on the handgun, a broken extractor and really, really bad luck. Your reflexive response should be an immediate TAP/RACK/BANG. If that fails to fix it, that is your sign that you have a double feed. If you have a backup gun transition to it immediately as this malfunction will require a bit of time to fix.

The traditional fix for this is LOCK/RIP/WORK/TAP/RACK/BANG. The first step is to manually lock the slide open to take the pressure off the system. Push in the magazine-release button and with the support hand rip out the magazine and discard it. Work the action vigorously three times, pulling the slide to the rear hard each time. Insert a new loaded magazine, rack the slide again to chamber a round, and get back into the fight. Locking the slide open first, takes the pressure off the system and allows the magazine to be pulled free. We worked the slide three times because the cartridge in the chamber was struck by the other cartridge that was trying to feed and is jammed into the chamber pretty tight. The stuck cartridge sometimes comes out on the first rack, usually on the second and almost always by the third.

Since a bad magazine can be the cause of this malfunction, as long as we have another magazine available, we want to discard the one that was in the gun and reload. If you have the hand strength, you can skip the lock step. If you depress the magazine-release button, with the support hand grasp the magazine fore and aft with index finger and thumb, and rip it out of the gun, so you can go straight to the "work" step. This is entirely

Since a bad magazine can be the cause of a malfunction, as long as we have another magazine available, we want to discard the one that was in the gun and reload.

"The best response to a double feed is simply to transition to a backup gun."

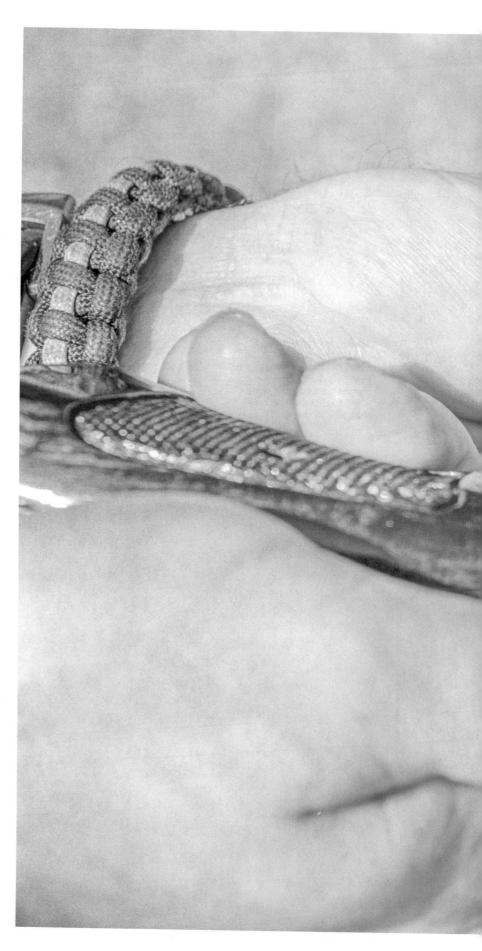

hand-strength dependent. A simpler way to describe this might be to say, unload/reload. Your first reaction would be to get the magazine and the chambered round out of the gun (unload) and to insert a new magazine and run the slide (reload).

The best response to a double feed is simply to transition to a backup gun. If you are well practiced and you know what is about to happen, a double feed requires between four and five seconds to fix. In the field, it will likely take more like to 10 seconds to fix. Either move to cover and then fix the gun, or transition to your backup gun and continue the fight.

A properly maintained auto pistol, with good magazines and good ammo will very rarely malfunction. You should set up malfunctions in your practice sessions and get used to fixing them quickly, as your gun is actually more likely to malfunction in a fight than in a calm, clean pristine training environment.

EFFECTIVE DRY PRACTICE

"Dry firing" or "dry practice" consists of practicing firearms manipulations without the presence of any live ammunition. There are a couple excellent

Safe dry-fire practice requires re-moving all live ammunition from the practice area, and then double-check-ing to make sure the practice gun is unloaded.

"In dry practice, you can more easily feel the slack take up, the trigger break and reset."

reasons for engaging in this practice. For one thing, the rising cost of ammunition and the time burden of traveling to and from a live-fire range often limits the amount of practice we can get. More practice equals more skill. Dry work can be accomplished in your own home and with no expenditure of ammunition, so there is zero cost.

Second, dry work is actually a better way to ingrain many skills. Without live fire, the shooter does not have the noise of a weapon's discharge, the noise of other shooters' guns firing, flying brass, reciprocating slides and the myriad other distractions on a typical firing range. Quiet, mentally focused dry work is an excellent way to learn the feel of your trigger, for instance, or to perfect your presentation from the holster.

During the 1970s, the old apartheid government of South Africa was under a United Nations arms embargo and could not import ammunition. The country's domestic production could not keep up with demand. As an experiment, the South African Army had one group of new recruits go through the usual handgun training program, while another group went through doing only dry practice. The "dry" group did not fire a single shot until qualification day. When the scores were tallied, the dry group slightly outperformed the group which had done all the usual live fire practice.

In my view, you go to training to learn new skills, but you perfect and ingrain those skills through thousands of correct repetitions. It is easier and quicker to amass 5,000 repetitions if you engage in dry work between range sessions.

Since you will be handling a real gun in your home there are certain precautions you will need to observe. Here is a checklist for you. Make a ritual out of going down this checklist every time, and before long these will be habits.

1. Dry practice should only be conducted in one designated, established area and nowhere else in your home. That area should have a "safe wall," that is a wall that will actually stop bullets in the event of an unintended discharge. A brick exterior wall or a stone fireplace can work, or you can use a body-armor vest as a backstop. Do not dry fire toward an interior drywall.

2. When you enter the dry-fire area, clear the gun and remove ALL live ammunition from the area. This includes loaded magazines or speedloaders, rounds in your pocket, or rounds in the desk drawer. Take all live ammunition to another room, then come back and clear your gun again.

3. You will need a target, which is simply an object to aim at while you dry fire. You can use an actual commercial target, a hand-drawn, reduced-scale target or something similar. Remember to place the target on the safe wall or body-armor backstop.

4. A session of mentally focused practice should probably not last more than 10 to 15 minutes. If you try to stretch out the session, you will tend to get bored and sloppy. Sloppy practice is worse than no practice. Remember our goal is to rack up a huge number of correct repetitions over time, to build reflexive skills. "Muscle memory," kinesthetic programming, conditioned reflexive responses and habit all actu-

ally mean the same thing. All are born of consistent repetition.

5. If you get interrupted during the session by a phone call or other distraction, start all over again, back at step 1. Failure to do this is an invitation to disaster, unintentionally using a loaded gun for dry work.

6. There are two points in this process where there is actually a danger of an unintended discharge. Those two points are the very beginning and the very end of the session. Failure to clear the gun, move all ammo out of the room, and then clear the gun again can result in an unwanted discharge. The most common error seems to be finishing the session, loading the gun, and then saying, "Just one more rep." When the session is over, say out loud to yourself, "This session is over. No more practice." Leave the dry-fire area for a while. Later, go back, load the gun and say out loud to yourself, "This gun is now loaded." At that point, it can be safely put back in the holster, or wherever you keep it.

There are certain skills that lend themselves well to dry practice. Here are some that I suggest you practice frequently. By the way, these should be practiced dressed exactly as you are when going armed, including using a cover garment for concealment.

1. Work on your presentation from the holster.

In the real world, whether you wind up drawing to ready to challenge someone, or draw to shoot, you will have to produce your pistol before you can do anything else with it. Both options should be practiced until they are second nature.

2. Work on trigger control. In dry practice you can more easily feel the slack take up, the trigger break and reset. If you press the trigger and the gun goes "click" with the sights still sitting on your point of aim, that would be a hit in live fire. If the sights move off the point of aim as the gun goes "click," that would be a miss. Keep working.

3. Empty gun reloads can be easily practiced with a couple of dummy rounds (again NO live ammo). Start with the gun in hand, slide locked open, empty magazine in the gun. Have a spare magazine with one or two dummy rounds in it. Punch out the empty magazine, insert the magazine with dummies, and close the slide. Get your hands back on the gun and get a sight picture. The dummy rounds allow the slide to go forward, simulating an actual reloading sequence.

Those are some of the obvious skills you can polish in dry work. Use your imagination as your skills progress. Recoil recovery and building a tolerance to the noise and concussion of gunfire are really about the only skills we cannot improve by dry practice, so get to work.

20

PRESENTATION FROM THE HOLSTER

New students of the handgun have to learn a number of critical skills. One of the most important of these skills is the "presentation," or drawing the handgun from the holster for use. Defensive shooters must be able to execute a swift, safe and efficient presentation. Once the need for the gun has passed, the shooter must be able to re-holster the handgun safely. This entire process of drawing and re-holstering the handgun is the most hazardous process involved in using the pistol, unless one learns to do these things properly.

I have often read on Internet discussion boards that a fast draw is seldom needed, and if trouble is brewing, one should have a gun in hand. This approach overlooks a couple of very real circumstances we face in actual defensive gun uses. First, police officers often enter potentially dangerous situations with gun in hand. They are usually, however, responding to a radio call that forewarned them of a hazardous situation. The private citizen, on the other hand, is usually reacting to an immediate-threat stimulus from an attacker, quite a different situation.

Also, if the cop turns out not to need his gun, he re-holsters it and that's the end of it. In many jurisdictions, a permit holder can be in serious trouble for drawing prematurely, or if it turns out the situation does not call for lethal force. Third, if firing is called for, the more time it takes you to get your gun out, the less time you have to make sound decisions and fire accurately. The ability to safely, quickly and efficiently produce your handgun can be a life-saving skill, and it's one that requires some effort to master.

Let's look at the requirements I mentioned. Presenting the handgun "safely" means getting the gun out without endangering the shooter, or any other innocent party in the process. Improper draw technique often muzzle-sweeps the shooter's own body or other persons in the immediate vicinity, and trigger-finger discipline has to be ingrained as part of the drawstroke. Presenting "quickly" means getting the gun on target in the least amount of time possible. An "efficient" presentation is one that gets the gun into a stable firing platform with minimal steps and motions, ready to deliver accurate fire.

A safe presentation depends on several factors. First and foremost is trigger-finger discipline. All properly designed holsters will completely cover the handgun's trigger guard, keeping a finger or other object from entering the trigger guard while the gun is holstered. Once the student starts the gun moving upward, though, the trigger will be exposed. Thus, the shooter's trigger finger must be straight, and indexed above the trigger guard, alongside the pistol's frame, where it remains until the gun is on target. Second, the motions involved in drawing the gun and moving it to the shooting position should not allow the muzzle to sweep over parts of the shooter's body, or other persons. This is a real and constant problem with shoulder holsters, for instance. Third, the support hand must be positioned so that it is not in front of the muzzle at any time during the process. I suggest placing the support hand flat on the chest, at sternum height, thumb up, fingers together. Teaching the presentation in a "one step at a time" process at first helps to ingrain these proper hand positions and prevent accidents.

An "efficient" presentation requires as little motion as possible. Speed does not come from "hustle," it comes from smoothness and economy of motion. Every unnecessary motion just adds time to the whole process. Ideally, the handgun will move through only two planes: straight up and straight out. To use a strong side belt holster as an example: The handgun is drawn straight up the shooter's side until the thumb touches the pectoral muscle, at which point the muzzle is rotated toward the target, the support hand joins the gun hand, and the gun is thrust into the eye-target line and extended toward the target. This simple set of motions gets the gun on target as quickly as possible, in the line of sight, so visually indexed fire can be delivered immediately.

Here is the typical strong-side, belt-holster presentation, broken down into four simple steps. As mentioned, learning these steps as "building blocks" helps the shooter absorb and replicate the correct motions.

"The ability to safely, quickly and efficiently produce your handgun can be a life-saving skill, and it's one that requires some effort to master."

STEP ONE

The gun hand obtains a full firing grip on the gun, in the holster. This is critical. If you miss your master grip, re-grip the gun first, then draw it. Once the gun is out of the holster, trying to shift your grip will eat up time and create the possibility of dropping the gun, so get your master grip in the holster. At the same time, the support hand moves to the sternum, thumb up, fingers flat on your chest. Both hands move simultaneously.

STEP TWO

The gun hand raises the pistol from the holster. Shooter should drag his thumb up his rib cage until it touches his pectoral muscle. This ensures that the gun is free from the holster and gets the gun closer to the eye-target line. When the shooter's thumb touches his pectoral index, the muzzle is rotated up toward the target and the gun-hand wrist is locked. (In a bad-breath-distance confrontation, the gun can be fired from here. This is often referred to as a retention position, as a result.) Once the handgun is pointed toward the target in this position, the hands are only a few inches apart.

STEP THREE

The gun hand is moved toward the shooter's centerline, at the same time the support hand slides over toward the gun hand. As the fingers of the support hand overlay the fingers of the gun hand, a two-handed firing grip is established. We want to get both hands on the gun as early in the process as possible.

Both hands are now on the gun, and the gun is just below the shooter's line of sight. A straight line from the shooter's eyes to his intended target is called the "eye-target line." In Step Four, the gun is immediately brought up to the eye-target line and thrust toward the target.

STEP FOUR

If the decision to fire has been made, as the gun moves to full extension the trigger finger contacts the trigger and the eyes visually verify that the gun is on target, by use of the sights or a rough gun silhouette on target, depending on the distance and the degree of precision called for by the circumstances. The first shot breaks just as the gun reaches full extension.

This simple four-step process gets the gun out of the holster, under control and on target as quickly and efficiently as possible. If the support hand is otherwise occupied or unavailable, the same basic movement of the gun hand would still be used. Now, this was the process for the presentation from an exposed holster. When we add a cover garment, we have to add one step to the presentation. We're not going to change the process just described, we're only going to add one thing, which is getting the garment out of the way. How this is done depends on the type of garment worn to conceal the gear.

The author in Step Three of the presentation sequence.

The author in Step Four of
the presentation sequence.

Garments that open down the front (jackets, vests, windbreakers, over-shirts) are swept out of the way with the gun hand on the way to the holstered pistol. Stab the fingers into your chest on your vertical centerline. Use these fingers, dragged across the chest, to aggressively throw the garment out of the way, to allow a full, unimpeded grasp on the handgun. Once the garment is out of the way, proceed with steps one through four.

Step One: The gun hand obtains a full firing grip on the gun, in the holster.

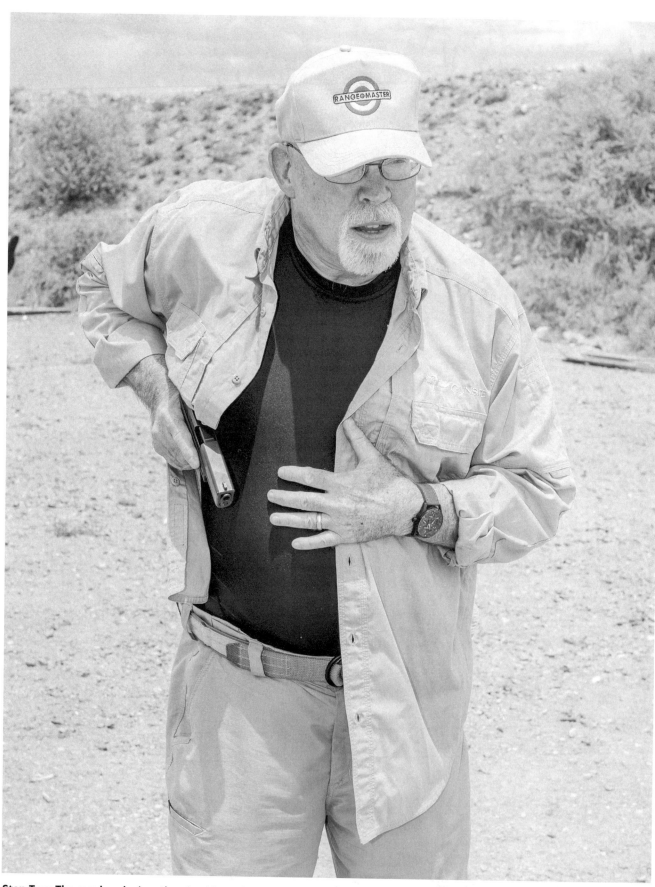

Step Two: The gun hand raises the pistol from the holster. Shooter should drag his thumb up his rib cage until it touches his pectoral muscle.

Step Three: The gun hand is moved toward the shooter's centerline, at the same time the support hand slides over toward the gun hand. As the fingers of the support hand overlay the fingers of the gun hand, a two-handed firing grip is established.

Step Four: If the decision to fire has been made, as the gun moves to full extension the trigger finger contacts the trigger and the eyes visually verify that the gun is on target, by use of the sights or a rough gun silhouette on target.

Pull-over garments require a slightly different technique. The support hand is used to pull the garment up sharply and hold it out of the way until the gun is free from the holster. You want to pull the garment upward hard, then toward your centerline, so your support hand winds up in its proper place for Step Two of the drawstroke. Again, once the garment is out of the way, proceed with steps one through four. This is Step One.

Step Two.

Step Three.

Step Four.

Garments that open down the front (jackets, vests, windbreakers, over-shirts) are swept out of the way with the gun hand on the way to the holstered pistol. The most efficient method seems to be to hold all the fingers of the gun hand as if holding a small ball in your fingertips. Stab the fingers into your chest on your vertical centerline. This ensures that we'll catch the edge of the garment on the first try. Use these fingers, dragged across the chest, to aggressively throw the garment out of the way, to allow a full, unimpeded grasp on the handgun. Once the garment is out of the way, proceed with steps one through four, as described previously.

If your cover garment has a pocket at the side, like most jackets, put a couple loose cartridges, your car keys, or a similar object in the gun-side pocket for a bit of weight. This will help throw the garment out of the way, and cause it to hesitate briefly, giving you time to draw the gun before the garment swings back into place. If there is no pocket, consider sewing a couple of stainless steel washers into the bottom hem, to serve this same purpose.

Pull-over garments require a slightly different technique. The support hand is used to pull the garment up sharply and hold it out of the way until the gun is free from the holster. You want to pull the garment upward hard, then toward your centerline, so your support hand winds up in its proper place for Step Two of the drawstroke. Again, once the garment is out of the way, proceed with steps one through four.

Holstering your handgun is the exact opposite of the presentation. First, be sure we don't need the gun out anymore. Beware the tendency to "speed holster." Come down to the ready and look, then holster deliberately. First, be sure your trigger finger is indexed properly, then retract your support hand to your chest, to the same place it goes to on Step One. Then bring the gun back to your pectoral index, turn the muzzle down, and holster. If you have an open-front cover garment, the little finger of the gun hand can be used to move the garment out of the way as you holster. If using a pull-over, leave the gun out in front as you retract the support hand and pull up the garment. The gun is not brought back to the pectoral index until the support hand is back on the chest, holding the garment out of the way. Most accidental discharges involving working from the holster occur on re-holstering, not on the drawstroke. So, take care and be conscious of trigger-finger discipline and muzzle direction while holstering.

Fortunately, the presentation is a skill that can be mastered in dry practice, at no cost. Use this as a guide for your dry work, and in short order your presentation skills should be good to go.

Clothing for Concealed Carry

Properly carrying a concealed firearm requires some thought be given to clothing selection. A pistol of appropriate size and a holster of proper design must be coordinated with intelligent apparel selection to form a truly effective system of carry.

Obviously, the clothing selection must be appropriate for your social or business environment. If you wear a suit to work, you must select suits in colors, fabric and fit that will enable you to discreetly carry a pistol. In general, darker colors, like navy blue, charcoal gray and black will make the contours of your holstered pistol less obvious to casual observers. You might wish to have the suit altered slightly, to allow a bit more room in the area where the pistol is worn. At times you might have to button your jacket, so be certain the pistol does not print, or reveal its outline, when the jacket is buttoned. Most business-suit pants have narrow belt loops that will only accommodate a belt 1 1/4 inches wide. You will either have to get these loops altered to accept a larger belt or obtain a special narrow gun belt. Galco makes a 1 1/4-inch dress belt that features two layers of leather laminated over a fiber reinforcement. This stiffens the belt to allow it to fully support a gun, spare ammunition, etc., while still being a stylish stress belt. I have used one of these extensively when wearing a suit and it works well.

In a suit or sports coat, your pistol and spare ammunition should be worn behind the side seams of the trousers. This prevents flashing the piece if your jacket falls open as you reach or if the wind catches it. If you decide on a shoulder holster, make certain the harness does not show above your jacket's collar or print through the material across your back.

Casual clothing affords much greater latitude in concealed-carry options. One casual option is the pullover shirt, the Hawaiian shirt or similar loose-fitting shirt. Paired with an IWB holster or a belly band, this can be an effectively concealed and comfortable rig for warm to hot weather. As in suits, darker colors work better, and bulkier fabrics will conceal your handgun better than light ones.

If you wear a pistol with rubber grips, like Pachmayrs, be aware that the tacky surface feel of the grips, which enhances shooting performance, might also stick to certain fabrics in shirts or jacket liners. If you reach or bend over, the material can be drawn over the gun, staying bunched up

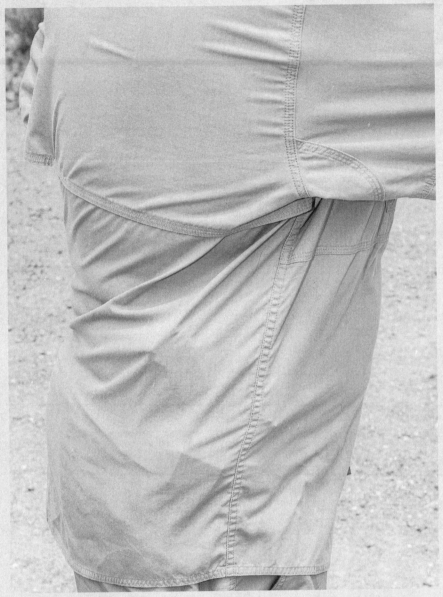

While this loose-fitting shirt appears to be a good choice for concealed carry, note that when the author extends his arm, the pistol on his right hip clearly "prints," showing through the fabric. It's a good idea to check for this in a full-length mirror before leaving the house for the first time when wearing a new concealed-carry garment. And remember: Bulkier fabrics conceal a handgun better than light-weight fabrics.

"There are also manner-isms to avoid while carrying concealed, as these actions will betray the presence of your weapon in spite of sound clothing selection."

everyone, even if it is, in fact, properly concealed. They are so convinced everyone around them knows their awful secret that they adopt a furtive, guilty look. This in turn invites scrutiny and becomes a self-fulfilling prophecy.

Bear in mind awareness of the same mannerisms in others can be subtle clues for you to use in assessing the people around you. It works both ways. Another practice to avoid is wearing items of clothing or accessories that scream to observers, "I am likely to be armed." These include ball caps emblazoned with the logo of firearm or ammunition manu-facturers, belt buckles shaped like guns, black basket weave garrison belts or T-shirts bear-ing pro-gun slogans or phrases like, "I don't dial 911, I call 357."

In a lethal confrontation, your sidearm will be most effective if it is presented in an unexpect-ed, sudden, startling reaction to being attacked. Telegraph-ing your armed status can in-vite a bullet to the back of the head without warning.

there as you straighten up. This is a dead giveaway. You might have to replace the stocks with harder, smoother ones for best concealment.

There are also mannerisms to avoid while carrying con-cealed, as these actions will betray the presence of your weapon in spite of sound clothing selection. Persons new to concealed carry often subconsciously touch the pistol through their clothing, either with the hand or the inside of the forearm. This is probably to reassure themselves it is there. Avoid hitching up your pants, a la Jimmy Cagney, or grabbing your belt on the gun side and tugging upward. Finally, until the newness wears off, most civilian gun carriers feel as if the gun is blatantly obvious to

21

RELOADING THE SEMI-AUTO PISTOL

The advantages of the semi-auto pistol over the revolver are usually described as: increased ammunition capacity; easier, faster reloads; and autos are easier to shoot well than revolvers. For the purposes of this discussion, we'll limit our focus to the first two items.

Ammunition capacity can be an important feature. Although many, if not most, civilian self-defense shootings involve a fairly small number of shots fired, they don't always. Bill Davidson of Tac Pro in Mingus, Texas, was involved in a number of handgun fights while doing executive protection and related security work in southeast Asia and Africa.

For concealed carry purposes, semi-auto handguns have several advantages over revolvers. They generally have higher ammunition capacities; they are faster and easier to reload; and they are easier to learn to shoot well than revolvers.

He is of the opinion that a self-defense handgun should hold at least 10 rounds, based on his experiences. Among our students here in the U.S., we have had shootings requiring eight, 11 and 12 rounds in the past few years. Fortunately, the students involved had guns that held enough ammo. Multiple attackers are becoming more and more common, and it often takes several shots per assailant to solve the problem. A high-capacity handgun helps avoid the dreaded disease Ammunition Deficit Disorder, which can be fatal.

As noted in the opening paragraph, one advantage of the auto is that loaded spare magazines are very easily carried on the person, and they make reloading a fast, simple procedure. In this chapter

The author demonstrates the Speed Reload in this series of images. To start, get your gun-hand thumb onto the magazine release and grab a fresh magazine with your support hand.

The goal is to get the new magazine right up by the gun and exchange it quickly, so the gun is not unloaded for any extended length of time.

Note that the author never takes his eyes off his target while reloading.

Being able to reload a semi-auto without looking at the gun or the loaded magazine takes practice.

Firmly finish inserting the loaded magazine into the magazine well.

let's examine two reloading techniques, the Speed Reload and the Emergency Reload, which serve different functions.

The Speed Reload could also be called a Proactive Reload. If you have fired your handgun in defense of your life, odds are that you will be somewhat excited and will not be able to count shots fired. After decades of investigating shootings, it appears to me most people fire more shots than they realize. This means your gun is probably closer to being empty than you realize. So, at the first lull in the action, get a spare magazine into your support hand, get it right up by the gun, then jettison the partial magazine from the handgun and insert a new, fully loaded one. Your reload is completed when both hands are back on the gun and you are ready to fire again, if needed. The goal is to get the new magazine right up by the gun and exchange it quickly, so the gun is not unloaded for any extended length of time.

Imagine a line extending forward from your nose and your chin. This space, right below the line of sight, is the best place to conduct the reload. This keeps the gun in the shooter's peripheral vision and prevents looking down at the gun, thereby losing track of the assailant(s).

If the handgun runs out of ammunition while you are still engaged in the fight, that requires an Emergency Reload, which is also called a Reactive Reload. If you look in your dictionary for the word "emergency," it reads "Your gun is out of ammo and someone needs to be shot right now!" The procedure is largely the same as for a Speed Reload. Keep the handgun in the "work space" described above. At the same time, get your gun-hand thumb onto the magazine release and grab a fresh magazine with your support

"The purpose of a high capacity magazine is NOT to let you shoot more, it is to let you reload less."

hand. Eject the spent magazine as the new one comes to the gun. Insert the full magazine, continuing upward with the support hand to grasp the slide and jerk it rearward, chambering a fresh round. Get your hands back on the gun and go back to shooting.

Claude Werner, formerly the chief instructor at the famed Rogers School, opines that the main reason people need to reload is because of missing the target. He's right. Learn to shoot well and practice frequently to maintain your skills. Throw in multiple attackers, partial targets obscured by cover, movement and the chaos and stress of real life-and-death encounters, and the need for more ammo than your gun holds might materialize at the worst moments. Knowing how to reload quickly and efficiently is the remedy.

Remember, any time you stop to reload, you are, by necessity, taking the gun out of action until the reload has been completed. This is why we prefer to do a Speed Reload at the first opportunity, rather than letting the gun run dry.

Speed Reload: Also can be called the Proactive Reload, a Partial Reload, a Voluntary Reload, an In-Battery Reload or a Slide-Forward Reload

Emergency Reload: Also can be called the Reactive Reload, an Empty-Gun Reload, an Involuntary Reload or an Out-Of-Battery Reload.

Practicing the Speed Reload during a timed drill while competing against other shooters builds the muscle-memory skills needed to complete the task during times of stress.

22

RELOADING THE DOUBLE-ACTION REVOLVER

ne of the key arguments used by proponents of the semi-auto pistol for defense over the revolver hinge on two ammunition-related topics: extremely limited capacity and extremely difficult reloading under stress. The typical revolver holds five or six shots. The shooter with even mediocre skill will fire one shot each quarter second. That means the revolver is empty within 1.25 to 1.5 seconds. Running out of ammunition so quickly leads to the next problem, getting the gun reloaded within a survivable time frame.

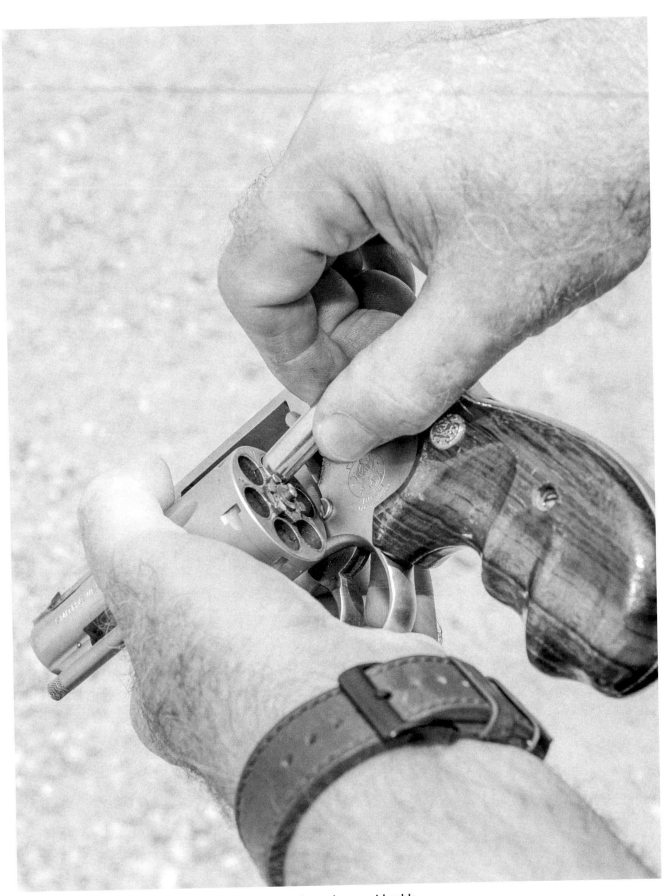

Loading individual cartridges into the cylinder of a revolver takes considerable time and can be even more difficult in times of stress.

A speedloader, which holds all five or six rounds in the proper configuration for loading into the cylinder, can greatly decrease the amount of time it takes to reload a revolver.

Speedloaders (top, middle), speedstrips (bottom, middle) and other cartridge holders (left and right) contain ammunition in an organized way that makes it easier to reload a revolver.

It is relatively easy to insert a pistol magazine into a fairly large opening in the semi-auto pistol. This greatly speeds the semi-auto reload and makes it a far more reliable process. With the revolver, one has to insert a number of small objects into a number of correspondingly small openings, which complicates matters greatly. Given the modern likelihood of multiple assailants and/or assailants who are drugged or mentally ill or both, the prospect of only having five or six shots and no ability to reload quickly is a serious issue.

If, however, you have a revolver we must teach you how to reload it efficiently. The following is a description of our preferred technique for both a right-handed operator and a left-handed operator.

METHOD 1: RIGHT-HANDED SHOOTER

Step One

Cradle the revolver in your left palm, slide your right-hand thumb around and depress or push the cylinder-release button and pop the cylinder out with the two middle fingers of the left hand. The two middle fingers of the left hand and the left thumb encircle the cylinder and hold it fully open.

Step Two

Turn the revolver until the muzzle is pointing straight up then strike the extractor rod sharply with your right hand, (preferably the heel of the hand). NOTE: Oftentimes, on a snubby the expended cases might not all fall out, if that is the case, flick them out before moving to step three.

Step Three

While still holding gun in left hand, invert 180 degrees, and while pointing the gun at the ground, (nearly at your feet, but not quite) load with speedloader or speedstrip, using your right hand. Note: This method requires the speedloader or speedstrip to be kept on the right side of your body, either in a pocket or on the belt.

The butt of the revolver should be placed against your abdomen to stabilize the gun and hold it still as you try to get small cartridges in the small chamber openings. If using a speedloader don't try to line up all six rounds at once. Pick the outside two cartridges on the speedloader, line them up with the outside two chambers. The rest will be lined up automatically. Release the cartridges into the cylinder.

Step Four

Once the rounds are seated in the cylinder, firmly close the cylinder with left hand, and obtain a firing grip on the pistol first with the right hand and then with the left. You are now back in action.

METHOD 2: LEFT-HANDED SHOOTER

Step One

Use the left index finger to operate the cylinder latch. Use the right thumb to push the cylinder out of the frame window, running the thumb right through the opening in the frame. The cylinder is held fully open by the thumb and middle finger of the right hand.

Step Two

Holding the revolver in the right hand as described

above, turn the muzzle straight up. Use the heel of the palm of the left hand to strike ejector rod sharply, ejecting the empty cases.

Step Three

Rotate the revolver in the right hand so that it is pointed straight down. Use the left hand to feed cartridges into the cylinder, whether using a speed-loader or speedstrip.

Step Four

Once all chambers are loaded obtain a firing grip on the revolver with left hand. Bring the fingers of the right hand up from beneath the trigger guard and push the cylinder into the frame fully, be certain that it locks in place. Slide right hand back on to the left hand in a two-handed firing grip. You are now back in action.

Important Notes:

When ejecting empty cases, the revolver must be pointed straight up, and the ejector rod smacked

Like a speedloader, a speedstrip reduces the amount of time it takes to reload a revolver. The author recommends loading two rounds at a time when using a speedstrip.

sharply with the other hand. There are several reasons for this procedure. First, fired cases often will not just fall out of the chamber. A sharp slap on the ejector rod will forcefully eject the empty cases and get them out of the way. Second, ejecting the empties in a less vigorous fashion often results in a case getting under the extractor star, resulting in a difficult to clear malfunction. Third, not all of the gunpowder burns when you fire a cartridge. If you do not point the revolver straight up when you remove the empties one or more cartridge case might dump burned or unburned gunpowder into the recess the extractor star seats in. This can also cause a serious malfunction.

We want to hold the revolver in the non-dominant hand while reloading it. The reason for this is the dominant hand is much more likely to be able to fit the small cartridges into the small chamber openings in the cylinder under duress. That hand will be shaky enough, the support hand even more so. This is also why we touch the butt of the revolver to the abdomen while reloading. That helps hold a revolver still while we line up the small cartridges and small chamber openings.

You are encouraged to use either a speedloader or a speedstrip to reload the revolver, rather than loose rounds in a pocket. If using a speedstrip, it seems to be best to load and peel off two rounds at a time.

> **"When ejecting empty cases, the revolver must be pointed straight up, and the ejector rod smacked sharply with the other hand."**

23

READY POSITIONS

A ready position refers to the procedure for having a pistol out of the holster, in your hands in anticipation of use in the immediate future. Note that a ready position is not a relaxed or casual position. We anticipate we might have to use the gun in the next few seconds. If you don't need the gun out anymore, put it back in the holster. In this discussion of ready positions, we are assuming we have drawn the gun with anticipation of having to shoot someone if the circumstances don't change.

There is a lot of misunderstanding about ready positions among the general shooting public. I often hear the untrained ask questions like, "Why would I ever draw my gun if I'm not going to shoot it?" Well, there are a lot of reasons. We might be responding to the proverbial bump in the night, believing we might have a problem that could require gunfire, but we have not found a target yet. It might be that we have identified a potential assailant, and although the situ-

ation is tense, we are not yet justified in firing. For instance, if someone is threatening us with a contact weapon (knife, ax, tire iron), but is on the other side of an automobile or fence, we might want to draw to a ready position and challenge him, to give him an opportunity to drop the weapon. I can tell you I have drawn my gun numerous times in a law-enforcement setting to challenge individuals and give them an opportunity to surrender before the situation escalated to gunfire. I've also had to do that three times so far in my life as a private citizen, during activities not even related to law enforcement.

There are a couple considerations at work here. First, if you look competent and confident as you draw to the ready, the odds you will have to fire the gun drop greatly. If we can successfully manage the problem without gunfire that is always going to be better. The other thing is, until we make an actual decision to fire, we have to make certain we are not pointing a gun at someone. Remember the two Cardinal Rules of gun safety: muzzle discipline and

A ready position refers to the procedure for having a pistol out of the holster, in your hands, in anticipation of use in the immediate future. The traditional ready position is low ready. In low ready, both hands are on the gun if possible, the trigger finger is straight and in register and the pistol is pointed at the ground in front of us at about a 40- to 45-degree angle.

"...if someone is threatening us with a contact weapon (knife, ax, tire iron), but is on the other side of an automobile or fence, we might want to draw to a ready position and challenge him, to give him an opportunity to drop the weapon."

trigger-finger discipline? The very best way to avoid shooting people unintentionally is not to point a gun at them when you don't want to shoot them. Thus, any ready position that is legally defensible in our U.S. civil-self-defense world will require that the muzzle not cover someone we are challenging or assessing as a threat.

The traditional ready position is the one that seems to work best for our needs, and that is low ready. In low ready, both hands are on the gun if possible, the trigger finger is straight and in register and the pistol is pointed at the ground in front of us at about a 40- to 45-degree angle. In this position we are not pointing the gun at our adversary and we have an unrestricted view of our potential assailant.

One important thing to remember is whether it is a rock or a rifle he cannot hurt you with it until he gets it in his hands. This means that anytime we are challenging or assessing people as a threat we must be able to see their hands at all times. If a weapon is not already in his hands the odds are extremely high that a weapon would come from his waistline if he were to attempt to produce one. So, we absolutely must be able to see his hands and his waistline. The problem with many currently fashionable high ready positions is that your own gun and your own hands tend to block your view of the two things that are the most critically important to us, the suspect's hands and waistline.

Another popular ready position is referred to as a high-compressed ready. Both hands are on the gun and the gun is held a few inches from your chest just below collarbone level, pointed straight forward. The theory is that it would be very quick from here to pop the gun up into the eye-target line and as the gun is thrust toward the target, get the slack out of the trigger and get the sights lined up. The problem is, you are pointing a loaded gun at everyone you look at, whether you could justify firing at them or not. This is a real problem. It is dismissed by the trainers who espouse this ready, but they almost invariably have a competitive shooting background and no field experience. On the street, you will learn fairly quickly that pointing guns at people you are not legally entitled to shoot can wind you up in a great deal of legal trouble. This trouble will be magnified greatly if you unintentionally shoot someone without justification. I strongly suggest you restrict any ready position that points the gun at your target to competitive use where all the people downrange are made of cardboard.

In the traditional low-ready position, the muzzle is pointed at the ground and the trigger finger is in register. This satisfies the requirements of the two Cardinal Safety Rules, muzzle discipline and trigger-finger discipline. All one has to do to get on target is raise their hands a few inches to bring the gun into the eye-target line. As the gun starts to intrude in your peripheral vision, the trigger finger moves from its register position to the trigger and removes the slack. At the same time, visual focus is pulled in from the target to where the front sight is going to be. Accurate fire can be delivered from this ready in a half second or less with a bit of practice. That is as fast as we need to be. We want to be careful about "outrunning our headlights" and shooting faster than we can make accurate observations and critical decisions.

One tip that will help you deliver an accurate first shot faster is really simple. No matter how many times you bring your gun up from the ready, your front sight is always going to be in the same place, right there on the end of the slide or barrel. We know where the front sight is going to be once the gun is in the eye-target line. So, as soon as a decision to fire is made and the hands start moving upward, go ahead and bring your visual focus in to where you know the front sight is going to be. In other words, bring your vision in to meet the front sight as it comes on target. With just a moderate amount of practice, your pistol does not come up and then have to be moved on to the target. After practice, the pistol comes up on the desired part of the target with the sights already pretty roughly aligned. With practice, we do not use the sights to achieve alignment of the pistol with the target. We use the sights to verify alignment with the target. This can be done in just a few hundredths of a second.

What we need to learn to do is compress the time needed to fire our first shot by learning to do things simultaneously. As the gun comes up from the ready, touch the trigger with your trigger finger and get the slack out of the mechanism. At the same time, bring your focus in to meet the front sight. By the time the gun is in the eye/target line and has stopped motion, you should have the trigger prepped and the sights aligned on the desired point of impact. All you have to do now is press the trigger.

In your early practice, periodically chant this to yourself:

1. Take up the slack

2. Focus on the front sight

3. Press the trigger

4. Follow-through

Aircraft recognition training studies during World War II found that with a bit of training and practice, aircraft spotters could catch a glimpse of the silhouette of an airplane far overhead and in just a few hundredths of a second correctly identify the type, model and country of origin of that airplane. This was a critically important skill as both sides bombed the crap out of each other. The same thing applies to using your sights. We do not use the sights in the traditional target-shooting, perfect-sight picture. At typical engagement distances all we need is a quick glimpse of the sights to verify that the gun is in fact pointed at the precise part of the target we want to hit, prior to pressing the trigger. This can be done in as little as five one-hundredths of a second with a little bit of practice. This is called the "flash sight picture" and applies whether we are presenting the gun from the holster or from the ready.

The low ready does not sacrifice any meaningful amount of time as compared to ready positions that start with the gun pointed at the target, but the low ready gives us an important safety cushion by keeping the muzzle under control and off anyone downrange until a decision to fire has been made. Remember, if we do shoot someone, we want that to be a deliberate act on our part, not a negligent one.

The author strongly suggests you restrict any ready position that points the gun at your target to training sessions or competitive use where all the people downrange are made of cardboard.

24

TRAINING DISCIPLINES

There are three different areas, or disciplines, in which the armed person must train. These are mindset, gun handling and marksmanship. Each is equally important, and you must be at least competent in all three areas.

First, let me point out that training does not necessarily consist of going to the range. Training can consist of reading a book like this one, watching a DVD, conducting dry practice at home, or a live-fire range session. Training can even include sitting in an easy chair and having an introspective conversation with yourself about some of the issues involved in self-defense. We must use all of these training tools to achieve mastery of the subject of fighting.

Mindset refers to all of the mental issues involved, including your commitment not to be a victim, and the cultivation of your awareness skills. You must develop a survivor's attitude.

Gun handling refers to the skills involved in managing your weapon and related equipment. Imagine your embarrassment if you aimed your gun at a bad guy, pressed the trigger and it went "click" because it wasn't loaded. The presentation, reloading and malfunction clearance techniques are all gun-handling skills.

Practicing your skills in a shooting competition is one way to improve your gun-handling and marksmanship skills. The third area an armed person must work on is developing the mindset needed to be fully prepared for the responsibilities of carrying a concealed weapon. (Photo by Tamara Keel)

Marksmanship refers to the simple physical, mechanical act of hitting your target. It can be referred to as directing bullets from Point A to Point B rather than just tossing them out and hoping for the best. This is the simplest of the skill areas to master, but it does require both live fire and dry practice.

Most of us make the mistake of concentrating our effort on one of the skill areas and neglecting the other two. We tend to concentrate on marksmanship. Why? Because it's the only part that is fun. We get immediate positive feedback and ego reinforcement from shooting well, and that is what humans live for.

Devote adequate time and attention to the other areas, as well. They are the legs of a three-legged stool. Unless all three are strong, you will fall on your butt.

ESSENTIAL ELEMENTS OF DEFENSIVE SHOOTING

Our shooting system is founded on the premise that there are three equal elements involved. These are speed, power and accuracy. Each is of equal importance.

Speed

One can be a wonderfully accurate shot and have a very powerful weapon, but if he cannot get a shot off quickly enough, he might die. We have to learn to move very quickly. In a fight, time is your most precious commodity. We must practice removing wasted motion and anything that needlessly eats up time. Speed does not come from hustle. Speed comes from smoothness and economy of motion.

Power

It is not enough to hit your opponent; he must be hit hard. It does you no good if your opponent collapses seconds after he killed you. This is why we want to carry the most powerful weapon we can adequately control, shoot accurately and shoot quickly.

Accuracy

A rapidly fired, powerful bullet that misses is a joke. Only hits count. You cannot miss fast enough to catch up. In addition, you are legally responsible for every round you fire, regardless of where it goes.

To be successful in an armed encounter, then, one must quickly strike a hard blow, precisely delivered. This is the essence of gun fighting.

COMPETITION AS TRAINING

Shooting in competition is not the same as being involved in a gunfight. For one thing, if you lose a pistol match you get to try again next month.

> **"One can be a wonderfully accurate shot and have a very powerful weapon, but if he cannot get a shot off quickly enough, he might die."**

Speed, power and accuracy are the three equal and essential elements required for successful defensive shooting. All three can be worked on in live-fire competitions.

Competitive shooting can, however, be an excellent form of practice, giving you a chance to practice combat marksmanship and gun-handling skills under pressure. Strangely, some people will work harder not to look bad in front of their peers than they will to stay alive. This self-induced stress, or pressure, gives the shooter a chance to practice the skills in a stressful environment, as well as a chance to try out equipment under difficult circumstances.

To achieve the maximum benefit from this exercise, you must choose the most realistically ori-ented form of shooting competition. At present, this is represented by the International Defensive Pistol Association (IDPA), which was formed in 1996 to give pistol shooters a venue in which they could compete, under simulated defensive conditions, with everyday, street-carry guns, holsters and related equipment. IDPA rules forbid compensators, optical sights and low-slung cutaway holsters that are prevalent in some other shooting sports. IDPA matches require essentially carry gear, with guns, holsters, etc., suitable for all-day, concealed carry for self-defense.

IDPA match-design guidelines call for shooting to be conducted at close range, 20 yards maximum, on a fairly realistically laid out cardboard silhouette target. Multiple targets are often involved, along with the use of cover and movement, and the presence of no-shoot targets. Major matches usually require the gun to be worn concealed, just like on the street. Athletics are held to a minimum, and strings are usually four to 12 rounds. The skills needed to win in IDPA competitions are some of the same skills you might be called upon to use in a gunfight.

I would urge you to use the actual gun you carry daily, in your everyday carry holster, and dress the way you do in your normal routine. This gives you a chance to "pressure test" your actual carry gear and find out about any deficiencies before you find yourself in a real emergency. Doing this in a match environment with other people watching will tell you a lot about your equipment and how you and it interface under pressure.

For more information or to find a club in your area, go to www.IDPA.com or contact them at (870) 545-3886. Odds are good that there is a local club in your area. There you will find like-minded individuals and, if you don't already have one, you might be able to find a training partner so you can help each other progress in your skills development.

Competitive shooting can be an excellent form of practice, giving you a chance to work on combat marksmanship and gun-handling skills under pressure. The International Defensive Pistol Association (IDPA) was formed in 1996 to give pistol shooters a venue in which they could compete, under simulated defensive conditions, with everyday, street-carry guns, holsters and related equipment.

Range Etiquette: How Not to be That Guy!

If you have had any formal firearms training, you are familiar with the Four General Firearms Safety Rules. In addition to those rules, however, there are some established and customary range practices you should be familiar with.

1. Once you're on the firing line, stay there until you are dismissed by the instructor. It is very poor form to walk off the line without permission. The instructor will give you an opportunity to get more ammunition, hydrate or do whatever you need to do. It is hard enough for the instructor to observe and control everyone on the firing line as it is. Help him by staying in your assigned spot on the firing line until given permission to leave it.

2. Do not handle your firearm off the firing line. The instructor has to focus his attention on the firing line, so he should not have to watch out for people behind him with guns out. Your handgun should not be out of the holster unless you are on the firing line, facing the backstop and you have permission to do so.

3. Do not dangle your handgun by your side. Unless you are at the ready or on target the gun should remain in the holster. If you blow a shot, don't throw up your hands or drop them by your side with a gun in your hand. Keep the gun under control and, again, if you don't want it in your hands put it back in holster.

4. Don't turn around with a gun in your hand and sweep the line, the instructors or observers. Always holster the gun before walking off the line, picking up any object or doing anything else not directly involved in firing.

5. On the firing line there should be no casual chatting. Wait until you are off-line to talk about your performance, or anything else with other students. When you are talking you cannot be listening to the instructor's comments, to range commands or to other important input. An exception would be when you are acting as a coach for another shooter, however, if the primary instructor begins talking you should stop talking and listen to him. You can resume your coaching when the primary instructor is finished.

6. Immediately obey any instruction or command from the instructor. Do what he says first, and you can question it later. There might be circumstances of which you are unaware.

7. Electronic hearing protection, which allows you to hear ambient sounds such as conversations yet blocks the load report of gun shots, is such an asset that it really should be mandatory equipment for a shooting class. With electronic earmuffs, you will pick up tidbits from the instructor you might have missed otherwise, including hearing coaching directed at other students. The same coaching may well apply to you.

If you will follow these guidelines you will be safer, your classmates will be safer, and just as importantly, you and they will derive the maximum benefit from class.

When multiple people are practicing from the same shooting line, at the same time, it is imperative that everyone knows, and follows, the same rules, both while shooting and while observing others who are shooting.

25

FUNCTIONING IN LOW LIGHT

Most of us conduct almost all of our training in broad daylight on an outdoor range, or in a well-lighted indoor range, largely due to convenience. We tend to overlook the fact that the majority of defensive confrontations take place under conditions of reduced lighting. Confronting an intruder in your home at night, or facing a stickup man on the restaurant parking lot, you will probably not have full daylight to shoot in. This is, however, grossly misunderstood by an awful lot of people.

Many times, over the years, I have heard or seen in print that 80 percent of gun fights occur in the dark. This statistic is tossed around in an effort to sell everything from night sights, to flashlights or laser aiming devices. Too bad it's not true. A much more accurate statement would be that 80 percent of pistol fights occur during the hours of darkness. For statistical purposes, the hours of darkness are 6 p.m. to 6 a.m. As you can see, in much of the country during much of the year it is not dark during a good bit of that time frame.

The second issue is that crime does not occur in a vacuum. If it's too dark to see, why the hell are you there and why would a criminal be there? Some years ago, someone coined the term "street crime" to describe violent interpersonal crime. The truth is, almost none of it occurs in the street. You'd get run over. The fact is, most violent crime occurs on parking lots, but "parking-lot crime" isn't as catchy as "street crime."

The parking lot of the convenience store, the grocery store, the apartment complex, the office building, the bank or the liquor store are where the vast majority of defensive shootings take place. Please note that these are not dark. Anyplace they are trying to sell you something the parking lot will be fairly well-lighted. In fact, I have seen my sights far better lighted and more clearly on the convenience store parking lot at 3 a.m., than on an overcast day at 3 p.m. The time of day is irrelevant. All we care about is the ambient light. At the kind of distances involved in interpersonal confrontations, and in the lighting conditions found on the typical parking lot, you will be able to do just fine.

In typical urban settings, true darkness is rare. Streetlights, vehicle headlights and storefront lighting, add to moonlight to form a fairly well-lighted environment. Under these conditions, at normal engagement distances, your frequent practice will pay off. By presenting your weapon consistently and using the sights every time, you have trained your hands and eyes to bring the gun up fairly well-aligned with the target.

"Dry practice, over and over, forms a sense of muscle memory that will suffice at close range."

The author has seen his sights far better lighted and more clearly on a convenience store parking lot at 3 a.m., than on an overcast day at 3 p.m. All we care about is the ambient light. At the kind of distances involved in interpersonal confrontations, and in the lighting conditions found on the typical parking lot, your frequent practice will pay off.

Dry practice, over and over, forms a sense of muscle memory that will suffice at close range. If you consistently present the weapon and look at the front sight, whether you can see it or not, you will get a hit. Your front sight is right there on the end of your pistol, so shift your focus to that point as the gun comes up in front of your face, just like you do every time when shooting in daylight. If you practice, this will result in your hands automatically aligning the gun with the target.

Tritium night sights are often proposed as the answer for this reduced-light environment, but the truth is they are not as valuable as you might believe. If you are in an environment that is well enough lighted to see who your opponent is and see what is in his hands, you will be able to see typical sights. If it is too dark to see your sights, it will be too dark to see

his hands or even be certain it's not a family member in front of you. Under those conditions you will need flashlight to illuminate, identify and justify your target. If you have to light them up with a flashlight, you will see non-tritium sights just fine. Night sights do not help you find the target, they do not help you identify, and they really only help you hit in fairly narrow circumstances. Frequent practice in sighted fire will serve you better if you have to use the gun under less than optimal lighting conditions.

A lot of shooting schools or instructors spend a fair bit of time working on flashlight techniques. This is another example of training taken

out of context. Those are critically important skills for military and law-enforcement personnel, who are tasked with going into dark areas to seek out and confront people. This is the opposite of the civilian paradigm where we wish to avoid armed confrontation if at all possible. Of our more than 60 civilian-student-involved shootings over the last few years, none used a flashlight and not one student indicated to me they felt like they needed a flashlight during their confrontation. This goes back to why a private citizen would need a handgun in the first place. If someone is trying to rob you on the parking lot you don't need a flashlight to see them, see who they are or see what they're doing. Flashlight skills are very low priority item for the private citizen.

About the only need for a private citizen to use a flashlight and a pistol at the same time would be in the home-defense scenario in which you are awakened in the dead of night by a suspicious noise, burglar alarm or the sound of breaking glass. Under those conditions it would

A lot of shooting schools or instructors spend a fair bit of time working on flashlight techniques. This is another example of training taken out of context. Those are critically important skills for military and law-enforcement personnel, who are tasked with going into dark areas to seek out and confront people. This is the opposite of the civilian paradigm, where we wish to avoid armed confrontation if at all possible. (File photos)

be wise to have a flashlight along with your handgun, primarily to avoid shooting a family member. If parts of your house are actually dark you would need to illuminate a potential target to be certain of its identity before engaging with your handgun. By the way, this means you need a handheld flashlight, not a weapon-mounted light. Again, the weapon-mounted light is intended for the military and police paradigm. In your case, if you use a weapon-mounted light in your home you are pointing your gun at an unknown person in order to light them up and see if you need to point a gun at them. Not good. Pointing your weapon-mounted light at a possible family member requires you to point a loaded firearm at a family member under highly stressful conditions. This is a recipe for disaster. With a handheld light, you can illuminate the shadowy figure without pointing your gun at it unless you make a decision to shoot. This all goes back to context.

The author demonstrates the proper way to do the Neck Index for using a flashlight in combination with a handgun when needed in low-light situations.

One thing I would suggest, is reducing the possibility of ever needing that flashlight in your home. How can we do that? Well, here's what I've done. First, all the exterior doors to my home are metal doors in metal frames. Wooden doors in wooden frames are ridiculously easy to kick open, even if they have a decent deadbolt. A powerful kick simply tears the deadbolt through the wooden frame and the door flies open. If one kicks a steel door correctly mounted in a steel frame all he accomplishes is making a loud noise. Next, I have a burglar-alarm system and I use it. Third, I have spiral florescent light bulbs installed in several lamps on both floors of my home. These cost only a few pennies a day if you just leave them on 24 hours a day. Turning them on and warming them up requires more energy than just leaving them on. There are two lamps downstairs and two lamps upstairs with these bulbs that remain on 24/7. This accomplishes two things. First from the outside, my home looks the same all the time. This keeps anyone casing the neighborhood guessing as to whether I'm home or not. Second, once I emerge from my bedroom I can see. Both floors are well-illuminated by these lamps that do not need to be turned on, since they are on all of the time. Consequently, my need for a flashlight is greatly diminished.

If we are going to use a flashlight and a handgun at same time, we need a technique that allows us to check an area or a person without pointing the pistol at them prematurely. We also need a position that enhances our ability to retain the pistol, since it will be in one hand. In our context, our flashlight technique should allow for:

• The ability to illuminate objects with a flashlight without pointing the pistol;

• The ability to retain the pistol and use a flashlight to defend it;

• The ability to see the sights, illuminated by the flashlight, if shooting becomes necessary.

The technique I have found that meets all these criteria better than others is the Neck Index. As far as I can tell, this was first taught on an organized basis by Ken Goode and Brian Puckett, independently. I have been teaching it for years as a simple, easy to use flashlight technique.

To use Neck Index properly, the pistol should be at Position Two of your presentation stroke. The gun is in your dominant hand, trigger finger straight and in register, thumb of the gun hand touching your pectoral muscle, and the muzzle pointed at the ground a few feet in front of you. The flashlight is held in the support hand. You need a flashlight with the tail switch. The head of the flashlight should protrude from the bottom of your palm and your thumb rests on the switch. The flashlight is indexed against the angle of your jawbone, the bottom of your cheekbone, or your earlobe. This gives you a repeatable index for the flashlight. You don't want to hold the light any higher than the bottom of your cheekbone so that you do not occlude your peripheral vision to your support side.

With very little practice it's easy to swivel at the waist and keep your flashlight, eyes and handgun all oriented in the same direction. When you detect something that needs to be illuminated, you simply press the tail cap to turn on the light. If shooting is required, the pistol is thrust forward into the light beam which illuminates the sights. As soon as firing stops, the flashlight is turned off, the pistol comes back to your pectoral index, and you take a couple of lateral steps so that you are no longer where the flashlight was. You will find this technique illuminates your sights very well while illuminating the target at the same time.

Use the light sparingly. I tend to think of the flashlight as runway lights for incoming fire. Anytime the light has been on for a couple of seconds, turn it off and take a couple lateral steps. Avoid painting your way to something you want to light up. Use the technique described above to orient the flashlight on the object you wish to illuminate, and only then is the switch activated. When you have seen what you need to see is not a threat, turn off the light and move.

> **"Use the light sparingly. I tend to think of the flashlight as runway lights for incoming fire. Anytime the light has been on for a couple of seconds, turn it off and take a couple lateral steps."**

Should you need to use your hands to reload the pistol, fix a malfunction or something else, tuck the flashlight into the armpit of your gun arm, clamping the flashlight between your arm and chest. This leaves your hands fully free to manipulate the weapon, turn doorknobs or light switches, work a cellphone or whatever else you might need to do with your support hand. This is better than putting the flashlight between your legs, since if you have to move you would lose the flashlight. With the flashlight clamped under your arm you can step without dropping the flashlight.

Leaving lights on in your house all night can reduce the chances you'll need to use a flashlight in conjunction with a pistol in your home.

26

REALISTIC, RELEVANT PRACTICE

When you have acquired the basic gun-handling and marksmanship skills, you must practice periodically to maintain and polish them. Pistol shooting is a combination of motor skills and hand-eye coordination that degenerates rapidly without structured practice. It makes little sense to work hard to achieve a life-saving skill, then let that skill dissipate over a period of months from lack of practice.

Proper practice also ingrains the correct responses to the point they become automatic responses to threatening stimuli.

"You play the way you practice," as coaches are fond of saying. Sports psychology research indicates it takes around 2,500 repetitions of any complex motor skill for that skill to become automated. An automatic response is one that occurs in response to an outside stimulus, without conscious thought, controlled by your subconscious mind. This is our goal with gun handling and basic marksmanship practice. If we find ourselves in an evolving tactical situation on the street, we want to be able to focus our conscious thoughts and reasoning on recognizing danger cues, evaluating the situation and formulating a tactical plan. We do not want to have to tie up the conscious brain trying to remember how our pistol works.

Fortunately, much of gun handling, including the presentation, reloading, etc., can be practiced dry at home. This sort of practice is invaluable, and 15 minutes two or three days a week can go a long way toward building and keeping fighting skills.

Some skills, however, require live fire for the most effective learning experience. Besides, shooting is an enjoyable and challenging sport,

"It makes little sense to work hard to achieve a life-saving skill, then let that skill dissipate over a period of months from lack of practice."

To be of value to you, your range practice sessions must be realistic and goal oriented. In setting up practice drills or scenarios, use a term called combat logic. This means, set up target placements and distances you might actually encounter in your real-world activities.

and your practice sessions can be a good way of relaxing and relieving stress. Recoil control and smoothly switching among multiple targets are two skills that require live fire, and seeing your bullets impacting in the vital zone of the target rewards and reinforces your dry fire home practice regimen.

To be of value to you, your range practice sessions must be realistic and goal oriented. In setting up practice drills or scenarios, use a term called combat logic. This means, set up target placements and distances you might actually encounter in your real-world activities. If "That would never happen in real life" can be said about a scenario, don't waste time on it. Let's look at two examples:

First, if you work behind the counter in a jewelry store in a high-crime area, holdups are a prime concern to you. The following skills would be of value to you:

1. 3 yards – one target straight ahead – draw and quickly fire two to three shots. Repeat this drill several times.

2. 5 yards – one target – start facing 90 degrees to the left or right, pivot, draw and fire two to four shots at the target. Do this three times facing to the left, and three times facing to the right.

3. 3 yards and 5 yards – two targets, one at 3 yards, one at 5 yards – draw and fire two or three shots at one, immediately fire two or three shots at the other. Do this two or three times.

4. 3 yards and 5 yards – two targets, as above – draw and fire two or three body shots at each, then one headshot on each. Do this a couple of times.

The drills described above can be completed as described in about 75 rounds of ammunition. This would be more beneficial than just standing there drawing and shooting pairs on a stationary silhouette over and over again. The drills described above are relevant to your employment and the physical environment in which you work.

Conversely, I once shot with an IPSC club that had gotten bored with realistic exercises, because they always involve a small number of targets and close ranges. The last match of theirs I observed involved swinging from a tree in a parachute harness, shooting at targets on the ground. This might be great fun, but it is a sort of ballistic masturbation, having very little application in most people's real life.

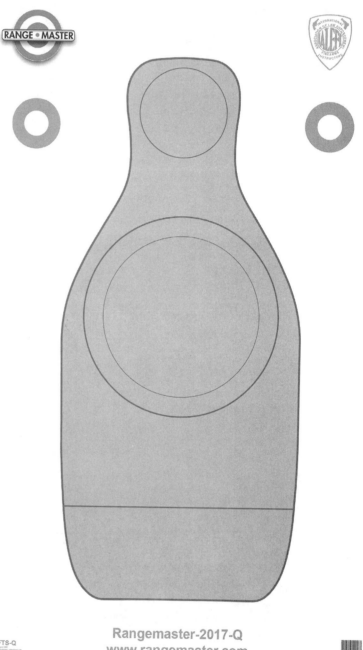

RFTS-Q

Rangemaster-2017-Q
www.rangemaster.com

Targets fall into two general categories: basic marksmanship targets and graphic targets. Basic marksmanship targets are used early in our training to help program us to shoot the right part of the target and allow us to see our progress. Author Tom Givens designed this target. (Photo courtesy Action Target)

With the simple scenarios you should concentrate on in practice, your goal is always to get good, solid center hits, but as quickly as possible. You should always shoot just as fast as you can get good hits, but no faster. If you start to spray, slow down a bit. You cannot miss fast enough to catch up. If you are getting well-centered hits quickly, stretch the distance a little at a time, or throw in additional difficulties, like shooting while seated, shooting with one hand disabled, etc. Remember combat logic, and keep it simple, straightforward and realistic.

Another concern is the selection of realistic practice targets. The target you fire on should:

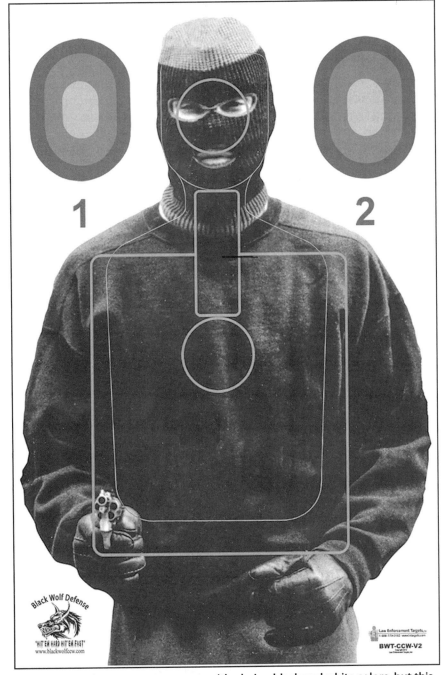

The author prefers not to use targets with glaring black and white colors, but this one has highly visible scoring areas and could be a good option for a new shooter transitioning from basic marksmanship targets to graphic targets. (Photo courtesy Action Target)

> ## "With the simple scenarios you should concentrate on in practice, your goal is always to get good, solid center hits, but as quickly as possible."

1. Be approximately the size and shape of an adult human, not larger;

2. Preferably not be of glaring black and white, but gray, tan or other neutral shade;

4. Not have clearly defined scoring rings that can be seen at distance and;

5. Have anatomically correct vital zones/scoring areas.

These considerations are important because you are programming your subconscious to perform under life-threatening stress. You must be accustomed to shooting at humanoid figures, and you must be conditioned to shooting at the correct part for maximum incapacitation. The vital zone/max scoring area on your target must correspond to the same area on a live human being, or you are teaching yourself to shoot at the wrong place on a real assailant. It is also an excellent idea to vary your targets, even during the same training session. This keeps you from getting locked into only one mental image for shooting.

Targets fall into two general categories: basic marksmanship targets and graphic targets. Basic marksmanship targets are used early in our training to help program us to shoot the right part of the target and allow us to see our progress. Generally, they will have more visible scoring areas for this purpose. One good example is the IALEFI-QP silhouette, designed by the International Association of Law-Enforcement Firearms Instructors (IALEFI). The milk bottle shaped torso and head are a realistic size. The chest contains an 8-inch circle surrounded by a 10-inch circle that are properly located, anatomically speaking. The top of the circle is right at collarbone level, the bottom is at diaphragm level, and the sides are about where the nipples would be on an actual person. In the head there is a circle to represent the ocular window. Across the lower torso of the target is a dark stripe representing the belt or waistline. This helps us visualize what we need to be able to see when at the ready. The IDPA cardboard

silhouette is a pretty good target as long as you only count the zero down ring and the area immediately around it as a hit. Action Target (shop.actiontarget.com) makes literally hundreds of target designs. Take a look at the website and you will find the targets such as described and a number of others that would be useful.

The other type targets are graphic targets. These are usually photographic illustrations of an actual human being threatening you with some type of weapon. The best of these have subdued scoring rings in the correct anatomical locations, but you typically can't see them while firing. These help in a couple ways. First, shooting a target that actually looks like a real person menacing you with a weapon helps create the correct response at the subconscious level. Second, we need to be used to hitting people in the upper center chest without obvious scoring rings to guide us. The IALEFI target series has several different versions of a man with a gun pointed at

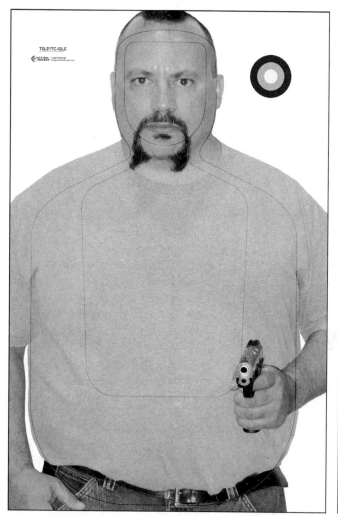 

Graphic targets are usually photographic illustrations of an actual human being threatening you with some type of weapon. The best of these have subdued scoring rings in the correct anatomical locations, but you typically can't see them while firing. (Photos courtesy Action Target)

you with the same scoring rings found on the basic IALEFI-QP target. These come in different races and ethnicities so we can vary our mental programming.

If at all possible, practice with a friend of similar skill level. This has several advantages, including:

1. It's more fun. If it's more fun, you're more likely to do it.

2. You can time, coach and score the each other.

3. It is safer than if you have the range to yourself.

The friendly spirit of competition will make you want to do better than your buddy, to gratify your ego. Strangely, this seems to be more of a motivator for most people than the thought of getting killed by a thug.

Concentrate on basic skills and on doing it right every time. Speed will come with practice, as smoothness and familiarity build.

As you practice and begin to acquire skill with your sidearm, you will naturally want to know how you are progressing. Reasonable, realistic goals allow you to structure your training and identify areas of weakness, so you can concentrate effort in areas where it is needed.

Earlier in this chapter we looked at a series of practice drills for a hypothetical jeweler to assist him in preparing for the likelihood of a holdup. These drills involved close ranges and one or two targets. The jeweler was instructed to shoot as quickly as he could and still get good hits. Remember, only hits count. How, then, will we know if our shooting is fast enough?

First, let's examine some real-life facts that impact on our need for speed. According to the FBI, which annually examines 100 or so killings of peace officers in the line of duty, the average gun fight is finished in 2.5 to 3 seconds once the shooting starts. Extensive testing by several researchers indicate the average man can take off and cover 7 yards in 1.5 seconds from a standing start. This means a man standing 21 feet away can be at your throat with a knife in 1.5 seconds. Finally, as stated before in this text, civilian armed encounters normally take place at conversational distances, due to the very nature of crimes against persons. All this means that a close-in, armed assailant has to be neutralized quickly, or you might be killed or injured.

Your basic defensive stroke consists of drawing your weapon from its normal place of concealment and delivering two to four well-centered hits to the vital zone. In practice, your goal should be to deliver these hits in the time frames noted below, including reaction time:

1. 5 to 7 yards, 2 seconds

2. 8 to 10 yards, 2.5 seconds

3. 15 yards, 3 to 3.5 seconds

These times serve simply as guidelines, to force you to push to make an efficient presentation, get a flash sight picture, and cleanly press off two to four shots quickly. You will not be able to meet these goals at first. This takes practice. Start slowly, concentrate on smoothness and precision. Speed will come with practice.

"Reasonable, realistic goals allow you to structure your training and identify areas of weakness, so you can concentrate effort in areas where it is needed."

27

BASIC TACTICS

An in-depth look at tactics for personal combat would take an entire book. Instead, I'm going to point out some basic concepts, and give you some things to think about.

Building searches are among the most difficult and dangerous tasks one can undertake. Moving through a building in which an armed adversary might be hiding is akin to walk-ing through a minefield. If you misstep, it might be all over.

Look over the list of building-clearing tips that follow and think about your own home or place of business in relation to searching it for an intruder. I urge you to conduct some dry rehearsals, moving through your building just as you would if you thought an intruder were there. Do it from different starting points, in different directions. Do it a couple of times with the lights on, then do it in the dark with a flashlight. One thing this will accomplish is reveal to you the staggering number of corners, doorways and blind spots a typical building contains. You don't want your first search of the place to be the time the Bad Guy is really there.

The next tactical issue concerns being limited in your thinking. We tend to compartmentalize ourselves, thus limiting ourselves. Many people who get into shooting and firearms training think of themselves as gunfighters, when to be truly secure in today's world, one needs to be a fighter. Not every conflict calls for gunfire. There will be circumstances in which the gun might not be the best tactical answer. To the man who only owns a hammer, everything looks like a nail.

Seek out some competent basic hand-to-hand training. You need to be able to fall without being injured; to be able to block basic blows and kicks; to strike without damaging yourself; and to break out of common grabs and holds. You don't need a black belt, but little hands-on exposure to these techniques could be a lifesaver. Explore alternatives to the gun, such as a fighting knife. I often carry two folding knives, one accessible to either hand, primarily as an aid to firearm retention. They can also be used for cutting seatbelts in a vehicle extraction, and other less glamorous uses. Investigate OC (pepper spray) as a defensive option between empty hands and deadly force. You should have some basic exposure to all of these major forms of fighting in self-defense so you will have options in the tactical situation.

> **"Not every conflict calls for gunfire. There will be circumstances in which the gun might not be the best tactical answer. To the man who only owns a hammer, everything looks like a nail."**

Building searches are among the most difficult and dangerous tasks one can undertake. Moving through a building in which an armed adversary might be hiding is akin to walking through a minefield. If you misstep, it might be all over. People who might find themselves in these situations, are advised to seek training from a qualified instructor.

TACTICAL TIPS

Tactics, "the use of skillful means to achieve a desired result." Anything we do to give ourselves an advantage and take the advantage away from the bad guys constitutes tactics.

Remember the survival chain and the TEAM concept: Tactics. Equipment. Attitude. Marksmanship.

Shooting skills alone will not suffice. You must cultivate your awareness skills and your determination not to be a victim. You must actually carry effective equipment on your person. You must think tactically, "If he does this, I will do that."

Maintain Distance

The closer you are to a potential threat, the more danger you are in. The purpose of your sidearm is to create distance. Get farther away. Use your skills to your advantage.

Watch Their Hands

Hands kill. Whether it's a gun, knife, screwdriver, broken beer bottle, golf club, hammer or tire iron, he has to hold it in his hands in order to hurt you.

Stay out of Doorways

Doorways are the picture frame of your death. Stay out of the picture.

Stay Away From Corners

Corners are death traps. Approach them from as far back as possible, always slicing the pie, checking small angular bites of a room before approaching the doorway.

Move Tactically

Maintain your balance at all times. If your weapon is out, have it at the ready, not dangling. When searching, look from near to far, gradually moving

Proper use of cover and concealment is an essential skill for the defensive shooter. Cover, such as a large tree trunk, will stop, deflect or break up incoming bullets.

the search pattern laterally. This is referred to as searching in rays, as opposed to bands. It will help you pick up on the danger from farther away, which is always our goal.

Maintain Light and Noise Discipline

Do not drag your feet, or allow keys, equipment, etc., to jangle. Do not drag clothing or your back along walls. Use a flashlight sparingly, in small bursts of light.

Do Not Relax Too Soon

Avoid assuming it's another false alarm. If you use your weapon, come to a hard ready and assess the scene thoroughly before you holster. If you have fired, ask yourself these questions: "Did I hit him? Is he down? "If he is out of the fight, does he have friends?"

Always know what is behind you. If practicable, keep a wall behind you. Use storefront glass, mirrors, etc., to watch your back trail. Make it hard to surprise you.

Avoid Complacency

It's easy to say, "I'm only going to the store for bread and milk," or "Things like that don't happen in my part of town," or "Why would anyone want to hurt me?" It happens to somebody every few minutes, in every conceivable environment. It can happen to you. Be prepared.

Movement

Move out of the way of incoming fire
Off the line of attack
Vector angle, not straight back
Evade incoming blows or blades
Make it hard to hit you
Exit the kill zone quickly
Neutralize the threat
Take cover and assess for further threats

Use of Cover and Concealment

Proper use of cover and concealment is an essential skill for the defensive shooter. There is an awful lot of misinformation in this area, however, and we need to get some basic concepts straight on the front end.

First, we need to define our terms. Cover will stop, deflect or break up incoming bullets. Concealment merely hides you from an assailant's view. Examples of good cover include large trees, brick walls, soft drink vending machines, fire hydrants and the engine compartment of a car. Examples of concealment may include shrubbery, darkness, deep shadows, interior drywall and automobile sheet-metal. Some-

Concealment, such as shrubbery, merely hides you from an assailant's view.

times your opponent's weapon defines the distinction between cover and concealment. A postal collection box, for instance, will stop most handgun and shotgun ammunition, but rifle bullets zing right through.

Bear in mind that while cover is always preferable to concealment, concealment might be better than nothing. Many people have a strong reluctance to shoot at something they cannot see. If you're hidden behind an obstacle your assailant might hesitate to fire at you. Don't fall victim to this phenomenon yourself, if you can see that you are justified in shooting an attacker who is behind a bush or similar obstacle, shoot.

When should you seek cover? The ideal time to seek cover is before the incident escalates to gunfire.

Trying to move to cover in a close-range encounter after the shooting starts is a good way to get hit. Better to already be there. Certainly, move to a position of cover before challenging an intruder, so that if he elects to attack rather than surrender, you are in a commanding position.

Stay well back from cover, at least arm's length away from it. This is important for a number of reasons, including: If you extend your weapon past the cover, an unseen assailant might grab it; your visibility is limited when you crowd cover; if a bullet impacts your cover, it might skip into you or splash fragments and other debris into your face and eyes. Keep your feet planted inside a line extending back from the edge of the cover. Roll out at the waist and

When shooting from a defensive position behind cover, stay well back from the cover, at least arm's length away from it. This is important for a number of reasons, including: If you extend your weapon past the cover, an unseen assailant might grab it; your visibility is limited when you crowd cover; and if a bullet impacts your cover, it might skip into you or splash fragments and other debris into your face and eyes.

expose only part of your gun hand and part of your face to shoot just past the edge of the barrier. Be sure your muzzle clears the edge of the barrier, to prevent peppering yourself with splash.

Whenever possible, it is preferable to shoot around the side of cover, rather than over the top. If you must shoot over the top of the barrier, be certain to stay back at least arm's length and shoot just over the top edge of the cover. Crowding the cover while shooting over it exposes your upper torso and neck and head to incoming fire.

When shooting around the weak side of cover (the left edge of the barrier, for a right-handed shooter), should you keep your gun in your dominant hand or switch it to your weak hand? There are two schools of thought on this issue.

Some schools, like the FBI Academy, promote using the weak hand to shoot around the weak side of cover, to minimize the target you present to a downrange adversary. Done properly, only part of your hands and a small part of the weak side of your face will be exposed. The only problem is, human beings have a deep-seated, instinctive reluctance to take a weapon out of their dominant hand under stress. In the NYPD SOP-9 study, for instance, researchers pored over written reports covering 6,000 gunfights and found not one single instance of an officer firing with his weak hand. I have never been able to find a documented case of a participant in a gunfight voluntarily switching his gun to his weak hand. Why waste training time and ammo on a skill you will not use?

The method I prefer involves using your normal grip on the gun, but bending at the waist, canting the gun, and shooting just past the edge of the cover. Done correctly, I doubt that any more of the shooter is exposed, and it takes advantage of your more familiar grip and dominant-hand trigger control. Canting the sights does not affect bullet impact at the distances involved in typical gunfights.

One tactical aspect that causes a lot of controversy is that of movement. In the civil self-defense context, shooting while actually moving is probably not a good idea. It is a lot easier for you to stand still and hit an adversary who is moving than it is for you to move at even a moderate pace and hit a stationary target. I find people frequently who tell me they can hit a stationary target while on an almost dead run. Usually, when I have them demonstrate this for me, they fire 10 or 12 rounds and get one or two hits on the target. Since they are on the range with a berm behind the targets, they think they're doing just great. The problem is, on the supermarket parking lot there is no berm behind the target and each of those rounds that did not hit the intended target will hit an unintended target.

One way to think of this is in the real world there are no misses, only unintended hits. The rounds that miss your adversary will continue across the parking lot until they strike something solid enough to stop them. That might be a child or other innocent party. If you have to move to try to keep from being shot, run flat out as fast as you can to get to cover, to an exit or just get as far away as possible. If you need to shoot, stop, get stable and deliver hits. Then, if necessary, run again.

One type of movement that might actually be a real benefit, especially at very close range, is a large sidestep as you present the pistol. First, this gets us out from in front of our attacker's muzzle. To hit us he will have to move the gun to get it back on us, which takes a little time. Secondly, everything in his life experience as a thug makes him expect you to comply when he points a gun at you and makes a demand. The

"If you have to move to try to keep from being shot, run flat out as fast as you can to get to cover, to an exit or just get as far away as possible."

last thing he expects from you is sudden lateral movement and a gun. This creates mental lag time on his part, again buying us some time (see the previous information on Col. Boyd's OODA Cycle). The closer we are to our attacker the more important the sidestep becomes.

To do this correctly, always lead with the foot on the same side as the direction of travel. In other words, if you're going to move to the left, step off with the left foot. Never cross your feet. That's a great way to fall down as you add the upper body motions involved in drawing your gun. We want to wind up in a stable shooting platform, so take a large step with the lead foot and then just bring the other foot under your shoulder. If you take big step, big step, you wind up with both feet next to each other in an unstable platform. If you take big step, half-step, you wind up with the feet under your shoulders in a stable shooting platform. Fortunately, this is a skill we can work on in our dry practice at home.

WHAT ARE S.M.A.R.T. GOALS?

A critical step in increasing your defensive shooting skill is to be able to set up S.M.A.R.T. training goals. Think of it as driving your vehicle from your home to a destination you are not familiar with. You could drive around aimlessly and hope you eventually arrive at the address you seek. A better solution would be to get directions, plot them on a map and follow those directions directly to your destination. That is our goal in S.M.A.R.T. training.

I've been teaching people professionally for more than 40 years, for 18 years I owned a range where people often came to practice, and I teach almost every weekend somewhere in the U.S. On my range, I frequently saw people come and practice with no plan, no goal and little or no organization. When they left, they were not one bit better than when

they arrived, and they could have accomplished every bit as much with dry practice at home.

In our classes, no matter what part of the country we are in, I see the same errors by shooters who have had a fair bit of prior training. The problem is, after the training their practice is unorganized, haphazard and without real goals. Since they practiced so inefficiently, they come to class shooting no better than when they came to the last class. We basically start over with these folks every time we get them in class.

For your practice regimen to be of any real value you have to set goals and attain them. You can't just say your goal is to be a better shot, or to be "really good." That is so vague as to be meaningless. We need a standard to achieve and roadmap to get there.

For a goal to be effective and useful to you, it should be S.M.A.R.T.: S (Specific), M (Measurable),

A (Attainable), R (Realistic) and T (Timely). Broadly general goals, generally speaking, will not be achieved. So, let's look at each of these criteria and see how they apply to the defensive shooter.

SPECIFIC

Each range trip or dry-practice session should be planned around working on and improving one or two specific skills. The skill should be identified in advance so you can have the correct supplies, targets and any other equipment you need to work on those specific skill sets. Trying to work on everything at once leads to improving nothing significantly. It is far better to concentrate your attention on one or two skills in each session. In advance of your range trip or dry-practice session, identify the skill set you want to work on and then identify the drills that would help polish those particular skills. For instance, if you want to work on accuracy, a bull's-eye course of fire might be in order, or perhaps one of the small-dot drills.

MEASURABLE

Time and accuracy standards give you a metric for seeing if you are actually getting better or not. Never just blow rounds down range. Every drill fired, and practice string, should be critiqued and/or scored, and targets taped or replaced before shooting again so you can see exactly where hits are going. Never rely on your subjective idea of how fast you're working, you will just about always be wrong. You

> **"Each range trip or dry-practice session should be planned around working on and improving one or two specific skills...Trying to work on everything at once leads to improving nothing significantly."**

The author practices a rapid-fire drill (note the two spent cartridge casings in the air in the center of the photo, just above the hill in the background). Using time and accuracy standards when you practice gives you a metric for seeing if you are actually getting better or not.

can have a training partner with a stopwatch, or if you practice alone you can use an electronic timer to verify your progress. Many smart phones now have timer apps available, so there's really no excuse for not using a timing device in your range trips. To measure your progress accurately, you can use standardized drills, exercises and courses of fire. By scoring your targets and noting your time it's pretty easy to track progress or the lack of it. There are a lot of standardized drills that emphasize discrete skills with well-known time/accuracy requirements. The FAST drill devised by Todd Green is just one example. You either get your hits into the 3x5 card and the 8-inch circle or you don't, and you either make the time specified or you don't. It's a great idea to use a small notebook as a log and note the date and time of practice, the individual drills worked on, and your scores/times. Tracking your progress in this manner gives you an accurate idea of how you are progressing.

Running timed drills in a scored competition lets you measure your improvement when working on individual skills.

ATTAINABLE

Be realistic when setting your goals to avoid frustration and burnout. If you're just starting out as a defensive shooter, a 1.2-second draw from concealment to a hit at 7 yards is probably beyond your reach. Find your current baseline by shooting scored drills, record your score or time and set a reasonable goal for improvement. For instance, if a slide-lock reload currently takes you four seconds, make your goal cutting your time to three seconds. Once you achieve that goal, make your next goal cutting the time to two and a half seconds. Each time you have a major improvement, it is going to be harder to make the next improvement, so work in increments that you can manage. Trying to go from that four-second reload to a two-second reload in one jump is a lot to ask. If you shot the current FBI pistol qualification course at 75 percent today, make your next goal shooting 85 percent, rather than 100 percent. How do you eat an elephant? One bite at a time.

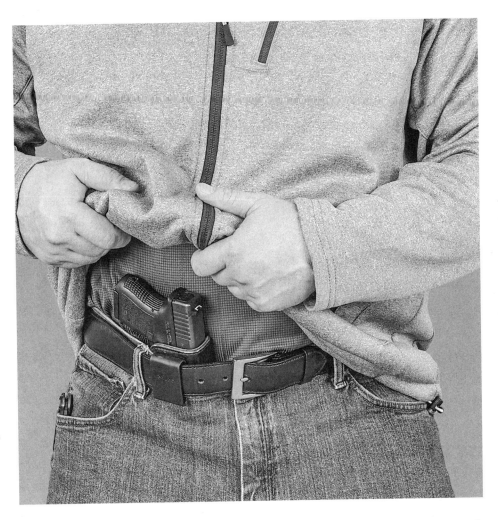

It is counterproductive to set goals built around what Grand Master USPSA shooters do with match gear worn openly if you are wearing a compact pistol concealed under clothing in an IWB holster. (Photo courtesy Galco)

REALISTIC

When setting goals take into account your physical attributes, your training resources (time, ammunition and money), your equipment limitations and the context for which you are training. For instance, it is counterproductive to set goals built around what Grand Master USPSA shooters do with match gear worn openly if you are wearing a compact pistol concealed under clothing in an IWB holster. If you are older or have physical limitations, take those into account realistically in your training plan.

TIMELY

Set a real-time goal for your desired improvement. This helps you stay on track by putting in the work. If you want to improve one specific skill, such as the slide-lock reload mentioned above, you might set a goal of shaving the time from four seconds to three seconds in three months of combined range work and dry practice. If your goal is to reach a certain score on a broad course of fire that covers a lot of different skills, you might set a time limit of six months. As mentioned before, use a logbook to record your efforts and your achievements as you work toward your goal.

Using the S.M.A.R.T. approach you can make the most of your training resources and I assure you, you will progress faster and get a lot more out of your limited training time.

29

CONTINUING EDUCATION AND FURTHER TRAINING

THE ANNUAL TACTICAL CONFERENCE

The Tactical Conference is an annual event hosted by Rangemaster at different locations each spring, usually in March. At this writing, this event has been held every year for 21 years and has become the premier training gathering in the U.S. each year.

The venue is usually a large training complex in a somewhat central U.S. location, which have included: the Memphis Police Department Training Academy in Memphis, Tennessee; the United States Shooting Academy in Tulsa, Oklahoma; the Direct Action Resource Center (DARC) in Arkansas; and the Dallas Pistol Club in Texas. This allows us to involve 35 to 40 nationally known trainers from all over the United States, who conduct two-hour to four-hour blocks of instruction continually over a three-day period, Friday through Sunday. Courses include classroom lectures, hands-on defensive exercises, live-fire classes and more. In 2019, the trainers who participated included John Farnam, Massad Ayoob, Southnarc, John Holschen, William Aprill, Chuck Haggard, Marty Hayes, Claude Werner, Wayne Dobbs, Darryl Bolke, Tatiana Whitlock, Cecil Burch, Karl Rehn, Gabe White, Tom and Lynn Givens and two dozen others.

Attendees may participate in as many training blocks as time will allow. This event always fills up four or five months in advance. Information can be found on our website www.Rangemaster.com.

In this book, I can give you a fair education on a lot of the background topics, give you some guidance on equipment selection and explain to you the basics of defensive shooting technique.

You need to understand, however, that teaching yourself to shoot from a book or a DVD is somewhat akin to teaching yourself to play the piano the same way. Is it possible? Of course it is, with enough hard work and time. It is hardly the most efficient or productive way, though.

There simply is no substitute for an in-person, hands-on class to learn how to shoot. A competent instructor will not only be able to explain and demonstrate the techniques in more depth in person, he will also be able to observe you, identify errors or weaknesses in your technique, and correct them.

My wife, Lynn, and I conduct classes literally all over the United States every year. These are normally two- or three-day courses in which we can give you a very good start in defensive skills and teach you how to practice and continue to learn after class. You can see our website at www.Rangemaster.com for course details and schedules.

There are also several other training organizations I would like to point out to you for more specialized pieces of the puzzle. The following are people I have trained with personally and in whom I have a great deal of confidence. I suggest training with these people to give you a more well-rounded skill set as a defensive shooter.

MASSAD AYOOB, LEGAL ISSUES

Massad Ayoob has been handgun editor of Guns magazine and law-enforcement editor of American Handgunner since the 1970s, and has published thousands of articles in gun magazines, martial arts publications and law enforcement journals. He is the author of more than a dozen books on firearms, self-defense and related topics, including In the Gravest Extreme, widely considered to be the authoritative text on the topic of the use of lethal force.

The winner of the Outstanding American Handgunner of the Year Award in 1998, Mas has won several state and regional handgun-shooting championships. Ayoob is one of approximately 10 Five-Gun Masters among the 10,000-member International

There simply is no substitute for an in-person, hands-on class to learn how to shoot. A competent instructor will not only be able to explain and demonstrate the techniques in more depth in person, he will also be able to observe you, identify errors or weaknesses in your technique, and correct them.

Defensive Pistol Association and was the first to earn that title. He served 19 years as chair of the Firearms Committee of the American Society of Law Enforcement Trainers, and several years as a member of the Advisory Board of the International Law Enforcement Educators and Trainers Association. In addition to teaching for those groups, he has also taught for the International Association of Law Enforcement Firearms Instructors and the International Homicide Investigators seminars.

Mas has received judicial recognition as an expert witness for the courts in weapons and shooting cases since 1979, and has been a fully sworn and empowered, part-time police officer for more than three decades. Ayoob founded the Lethal Force Institute in 1981 and served as its director until 2009, and now trains through Massad Ayoob Group. He has appeared on CLE-TV delivering continuing legal education for attorneys, through the American Law Institute and American Bar Association, and has been retained to train attorneys to handle deadly force cases through the Armed Citizens Legal Defense Network. Ayoob served for two years as co-vice chair of the Forensic Evidence Committee of the National Association of Criminal Defense Lawyers. He also appears in each episode of Personal Defense TV (Sportsman's Channel).

See www.massaday-oobgroup.com for more information.

ANDREW BRANCA, LEGAL ISSUES

Andrew F. Branca, Esq., is one of the foremost experts in U.S. self-defense law across all 50 states, whose expertise has been used by the The Wall Street Journal, the Chicago Tribune, NPR, numerous other media organizations, as well as many private,

state and federal agencies. He is a Massachusetts lawyer, life member of the National Rifle Association (NRA), and adjunct instructor on the Law of Self Defense at the SIG-SAUER Academy in Epping, New Hampshire. He regularly lectures and speaks throughout the country on how to protect yourself against both an attack and the legal machine after.

Andrew is a multi-division Master-Class competitor in IDPA and an NRA-certified firearms instructor. He holds or has held concealed-carry permits for Massachusetts, Connecticut, Rhode Island, New Hampshire, Maine, Pennsylvania, Florida, Utah, Virginia and other states.

Andrew conducts live in-person seminars and also has web-based seminars you can take at your own convenience at very low cost.
See www.lawofselfdefense.com for more information.

CRAIG DOUGLAS, "SOUTHNARC," SHIVWORKS

Craig is a recently retired police captain who commanded a regional SWAT team and Drug Task Force for many years. Prior to that, he engaged in undercover narcotics investigations. Craig has done more to study and advance the art of defense at zero to five feet than any other single person. His training centers around teaching concepts, then having the students apply those concepts in live force-on-force training with marking cartridges. Pre-fight positioning and decision making are combined with empty-hand skills, in-fight weapon access, and contact-distance shooting techniques to maximize a student's chances of success in an entangled fight.

His Managing Unknown Contacts (MUC) course is a must-have for anyone serious about self-defense, and Extreme Close Quarter Concepts (ECQC) is also highly recommended. Here is a description, from Craig's website:

EXTREME CLOSE QUARTER CONCEPTS (ECQC)

The ShivWorks Extreme Close Quarter Concepts (ECQC) course is a two and a half day (20 hours) block of instruction which focuses on a multi-disciplinary approach to building functional, combative handgun skills at zero to five feet. The course is designed to instill core concepts of seamless integration and provide the platform for aggressive problem solving during a life-or-death struggle. A heavy emphasis is placed upon commonality of body mechanics between skill subsets, which means all combative software is reinforcing. Once the student's skill sets are initially ingrained, the participant will be stress inoculated with force-on-force drills utilizing marking cartridges and protective equipment.

Topics covered include:

Day One (4 hours):
• Criminal Assault Paradigm
• Unequal Initiative Events
• Managing Unknown Contacts
• Practical Unarmed Combat

Day Two (8 hours):
• Introduction to the components of the Combative Draw stroke
• Building the No. 2 position in live-fire
• Firing throughout the horizontal line of presentation

Noted gun writer, competitive shooter and firearms instructor Massad Ayoob shoots in an International Defensive Pistol Association (IDPA) competition. He was the first person to earn the IDPA's Five-Gun Master title.

- Off-hand fending positions
- Default position
- Basic empty-hand blows
- Theory of in-fight weapon access
- Grounded basics

Day Three (8 hours):
- Challenging the potential attacker
- Pre-emptive weapon access
- Multiple attackers
- Negotiating the F.U.T.
- ECQ handgun retention in holster
- ECQ handgun retention out of holster
- Handgun recovery
- Handgun striking

Weapon and Gear Class Requirements:
- Reliable handgun
- Minimum two magazines
- Quality holster and magazine pouches
- 500 rounds of ammunition
- Heavy sweatshirt or soft body armor
- Mouthpiece and cup
- Seasonal weather gear
- Ballistic eye protection
- Ear protection
- Weapon lubrication and cleaning supplies.
- Good attitude

See www.shivworks.com for more information.

WILLIAM APRILL, APRILL RISK CONSULTING

William Aprill brings a unique background and perspective to his teaching. For some years now William has been a licensed psychologist, but before that he worked as a deputy sheriff and a deputy U.S. marshal. He has extensive training in martial arts and with firearms. He holds an instructor and advanced-instructor rating from Rangemaster and has attended training with numerous top-tier instructors. He holds an advanced rating at the prestigious Rogers Shooting School in Georgia and is an accomplished competitive shooter.

William has done extensive study in criminal psychology and his academic training combined with this field experience has given him a unique insight into how the criminal mind works regarding victim selection and offender motivation. His lectures on the topic will educate you on the threat you face and how to be mentally prepared to deal with it.

CALEB CAUSEY, LONE STAR MEDICS

Every person, whether they carry a gun or not, should have some basic life-saving immediate trauma care training. In live-fire training and practice there is always the possibility of a gunshot wound. Such training and practice is absolutely necessary to obtain and retain and meaningful level of skill, so you should know how to treat a gunshot wound until qualified medical help arrives. Off the range, you are probably more likely to encounter serious injuries to yourself or others as a result of traffic accidents, industrial accidents and other mishaps. I can highly recommend Caleb Causey at Lone Star Medics for such training. I can also recommend Hugh Coffey's Ditch Medicine program and Dr. Sherman House's programs, as well.

MORE INFORMATION

There is an awful lot of information available on the Internet. Unfortunately, an awful lot of it is misleading, incorrect or just laughably wrong. There are, however, some good sources of solid information that are absolutely free and offer reliable, sensible input.

The first is The Tactical Wire, which is posted each week on Tuesday and Thursday. This is actually a subscription newsletter which is free for the asking. The first part of this has press releases from gun and accessory manufacturers, trainers/schools and other suppliers of stuff you would be interested in. This is a good way to keep up with new products and services. Following those releases, there are one or two short articles on self-defense firearms, accessories or training in their use. These articles are usually written by Rich Grassi or Chuck Haggard, recently retired law-enforcement officers and trainers with an immense amount of experience, or by well-known trainer and friend of ours, Tiger McKee. There are articles from time to time by Dave Spaulding, Darryl Bolke and other well-known trainers, as well. To subscribe, go to http://www.thetacticalwire.com/subscription.html

Another source I can recommend is The Tactical Professor, a blog by our old friend and associate, Claude Werner. Claude served in the U.S. Army in both Ranger and Special Forces units and served for several years as the chief instructor at the famed Rogers School in Georgia. Claude is well known as a deep thinker in the tactical community and he sometimes takes somewhat unorthodox positions on matters. His writings are always insightful and thought-provoking. See http://tacticalprofessor.wordpress.com/

Finally, there is the Front Sight Press, by our own Tiffany Johnson. Tiffany is our webmistress and the editor of our newsletter. She is a Rangemaster certified instructor and advanced firearms instructor, an NRA certified instructor and she has trained with everyone from John Farnam, to Southnarc, to TDSA in Oklahoma. She is also an attorney and all-around

> **"My wife, Lynn, and I conduct classes literally all over the United States every year. These are normally two- or three-day courses in which we can give you a very good start in defensive skills and teach you how to practice and continue to learn after class."**
> — Author Tom Givens

great person. As an African-American woman with both a law degree and passion for firearms training, she has a pretty unique perspective. See http://frontsightpress.com/ for details.

There are also a few discussion forums that actually have useful information. Here are two I find particularly useful.

The first is www.totalprotectioninteractive.com, which is usually referred to as TPI. This discussion form was founded by Craig Douglas and is frequented by other trainers like Claude Werner, William Aprill and many others. There is a wealth of information here about a number of topics concerning personal self-defense.

The other is pistol-forum.com, founded by our late friend Todd L Green. Todd was a well-known trainer and competitive shooter and this forum attracts a lot of highly skilled shooters. If you want technical information about high-level shooting technique or the best equipment for self-defense shooting, this forum has a great deal to offer.

Additional Training Resources by Tom Givens

Rangemaster has several professionally produced educational DVDs. These can be purchased directly from Rangemaster:

Concealed Carry for Self Defense, 2 hours and 15 minutes.

Defensive Shotgun, 2 hours.

Cooper's Color Codes, 1 hour and 10 minutes.

These DVDs are available for $24.95 each, plus $4 shipping per order. Mail checks to:

Rangemaster
1808 James L Redman Parkway
Suite 226
Plant City, FL, 33563

Author Tom Givens and his wife, Lynn, both participate in the training sessions at the annual Tactical Conference hosted by Rangemaster at various locations across the United States each year.

30

PRACTICE COURSES OF FIRE

T o have any real skill with a handgun you are going to have to practice. Practice, however, does not consist of just banging away, burning ammunition. Your practice sessions will benefit you the most if you have some structure and goals in mind when you get to the range. I never "just shoot." When I get an opportunity for a practice session, every round I fire will be in a timed/scored drill or course of fire, to help me gain skill and track progress.

A properly designed course of fire can accomplish several things:

1. It adds structure and accountability to your session;

2. It makes you cycle through all the skills you need to work on;

3. It provides an objective view of performance, rather than a subjective view, which is often not accurate;

4. It identifies weak areas, so you know what to work on;

5. It allows you to check your skill against a known standard;

6. It allows some stress inoculation; and

7. It provides documentation of work done and progress made.

The following pages list some standardized courses of fire I recommend for your use.

The author's wife, Lynn Givens, is shown here shooting in a timed drill. When the author gets an opportunity for a practice session, every round he fires will be in a timed/scored drill or course of fire, to help him gain skill and track progress. (Photo by Tamara Keel)

RANGEMASTER BULL'S-EYE COURSE

Fired on NRA B-8, scored as printed, except outside 7 ring counts zero.

FBI-IP-1 bull's-eye target, as printed

All strings begin at the Ready
• 25 yards, 5 rounds, 1 minute
• 15 yards, 5 rounds, 15 seconds
• 10 yards, 5 rounds, 10 seconds
• 7 yards, 10 rounds, 15 seconds:
Start with 5 rounds in the gun. Fire 5 rounds, reload, fire 5 more rounds, all in 15 seconds.
• 5 yards, 5 rounds, 5 seconds

30 rounds total, 300 points possible, 270 to pass at Instructor level

RANGEMASTER ADVANCED BULL'S-EYE COURSE

All fired on an NRA B-8 Repair center, scored as printed. Hits outside the 7 ring are counted as misses. Overtime shots deduct 10 points per shot fired over time limit.

5-Yard Stage: Time limit is 2.5 seconds for each drill (Note: This is Justin Dyal's excellent
5-Yard Round-Up Drill)
• Draw and fire 1 shot, 2.5 secs
• From Ready, 4 shots, 2.5 secs
• Dominant Hand Only, from Ready, 3 shots, 2.5 secs
• Non-Dominant Hand Only, from Ready, 2 shots, 2.5 secs

10-Yard Stage: Time limit is 5 seconds
• Start at Ready, 5 shots, 5 secs

25-Yard Stage: Time limit is one minute
• Start at Ready, 5 shots, one minute

Totals: 20 rounds, 200 points possible, 180 or higher to pass

FBI PISTOL QUALIFICATION COURSE, REVISED JANUARY 2019

QIT silhouette, scored 2 points per hit.

3 yards: Draw and fire 3 rounds, strong hand only
• Switch hands and fire 3 rounds, support hand only, all in 6 seconds

5 yards: Draw and fire 3 rounds in 3 seconds
• From the Ready, fire 3 rounds in 2 seconds
• From the Ready, fire 6 rounds in 4 seconds

7 yards: Draw and fire 5 rounds in 5 seconds
• From the Ready, fire 4 rounds, conduct an empty-gun reload, and fire 4 more rounds, all in 8 seconds
•From the Ready, fire 5 rounds in 4 seconds

15 yards: Draw and fire 3 rounds in 6 seconds
•From the Ready, fire 3 rounds in 5 seconds

25 yards: Draw and fire 4 rounds from Standing
• Drop to a Kneeling Position and fire 4 more rounds from Kneeling, all in 20 seconds.

Totals: 50 rounds, 100 points possible, 90 or above for instructor

RANGEMASTER FIREARMS INSTRUCTOR QUALIFICATION COURSE, 2017

Fired on RFTS-Q silhouette, scored 5, 4, 3.

3 yards: Sidestep, draw and fire 3 rounds in 3 seconds.
• Repeat, moving in the other direction.

3 yards: Start with gun in hand, at Ready, dominant hand only.
• On signal, sidestep and fire 3 rounds in 3 seconds.
• Repeat, moving in the other direction.

3 yards: Start with gun in hand, non-dominant hand only.
• On signal, sidestep and fire 3 rounds in 3 seconds, one time.

5 yards: Sidestep, draw and fire 4 rounds in 4 seconds.
• Repeat twice, for a total of 3 strings.

5 yards: Sidestep, draw and fire 3 rounds to the chest and 1 round to the head, all in 5 seconds.
• Repeat twice, for a total of three strings.

5 yards: Start at Ready. One head shot in 1.5 seconds. Repeat.

7 yards: Start with gun in hand, 3 rounds ONLY in gun.
• On signal, fire 3 rounds, conduct an emergency reload, and fire 3 more rounds, all in 8 seconds.

7 yards: Start with gun in hand, chamber empty, loaded magazine in place.
• On signal, attempt to fire, remedy the malfunction and fire 3 rounds, all in 6 seconds.

15 yards: On signal, draw and fire 3 rounds in 6 seconds. Repeat.

25 yards: On signal, draw and fire 2 rounds from Standing Position, drop to a Kneeling Position, and fire 2 more rounds, all in 14 seconds.

Totals: 60 rounds, 300 points possible, 270 or above required to pass.

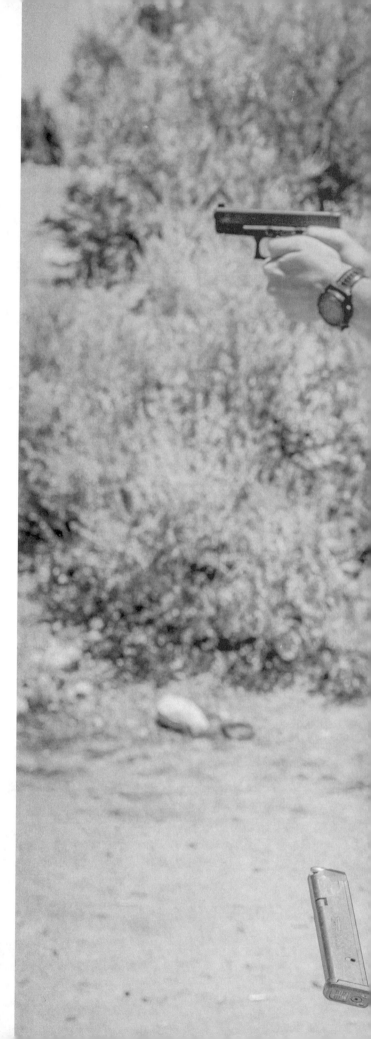

THE RANGEMASTER "CASINO DRILL"

In an actual defensive shooting, there will be skills involved besides shooting skills. The shooter will be tasked with target identification, target discrimination and target assessment, and these will all be changing and evolving continually throughout the incident. To help the shooter become accustomed to processing information at the same time he is running the motor program for shooting, we developed the "Casino Drill."

DT-2A target, available from Action Targets.

Three magazines.

21 rounds of ammunition.

This drill tests a rapid presentation from the concealed holster; fast, accurate shooting on multiple targets; two empty-gun reloads on the clock; target identification; and keeping up with changing circumstances; all under time pressure. Fired at 5 yards, starting with the pistol in the holster, concealed or in a secured police-duty rig.

Shooter begins with 7 rounds loaded in the handgun; handgun holstered concealed. Shooter will have two spare magazines, loaded with 7 rounds each.

On signal, the shooter will draw and engage target #1 with 1 round, target #2 with 2 rounds, target #3 with 3 rounds, target #4 with 4 rounds, target #5 with 5 rounds, and target #6 with 6 rds. Twice, the shooter will have to reload an empty gun and remember to finish up the required shots on the target before moving on to the next one.

Par time for this drill is 21 seconds, with ALL hits inside the numbered targets, and no procedural errors (right number of shots on each target, targets shot in numerical sequence).

Totals: 21 rounds in 21seconds, hence the name "The Casino Drill."

To run this as a scored competition, fastest total time wins. Add one second for EACH shot that misses a numbered target and one second for each procedural error.

THE 3M TEST (MARKSMANSHIP/ MOVEMENT/ MANIPULATIONS)

Pass/Fail or Modified for Comstock Count Scoring.

For many years, Larry Nichols was the rangemaster of the Burbank, California, police department. He devised the original, simpler version of this drill. He showed it to John Farnam probably 30 years ago, and John modified it to fit his curriculum. John showed his version to me 20 years ago, and I made changes to fit my curriculum. This is the version we currently use.

One silhouette target, at 5 yards. For our purposes, we will use an RFTS-Q, scored 5/3 or a VSRT, scored 5/4/3 or an IDPA target, scored 5/3/0 for the Comstock Count version. If pass/fail scoring, only the highest value hit zone counts.

Shooter starts with handgun loaded with 6 live rounds (1 in chamber, 5 in magazine) and one dummy round in the magazine. Dummy is not the top round nor the bottom round in the maga-

zine. Someone else should load the magazine so the shooter does not know where in the magazine the dummy round lies.

Shooter starts holstered, hands in interview stance. On signal, sidestep, draw and fire until a malfunction occurs. On the malfunction, sidestep, fix it and continue to fire. When the gun runs empty, sidestep, perform an emergency reload, and fire 3 additional shots to the chest, then 1 shot to the head.

Shooter must move on the draw, move on the malfunction, and move on the reload. There will be a 10-point penalty for any shot that misses the target, on Comstock. If Pass/Fail, any round outside the highest value zone is a failure.

COMSTOCK COUNT SCORING

Possible score = 45 points. Points divided by time = Index. Index X 30 = Score.

Example: 42 points, fired in 12.15 seconds = 3.46; 3.46 X 30 = 103.8; Score = 103.8

Par Score = 100

Anything over 100 is very good work. Anything over 125 is extremely high skill.

On Pass/Fail scoring, shooter fails if he:

1. Does not move on the draw, the malfunction and the reload

2. Does not tap the magazine before running the slide on the malfunction.

3. Places a single hit outside the highest scoring zone on the target.

Time limit is 15 seconds for a combative-pistol student, 12 seconds for instructors.

This drill tests movement off the line of force, a rapid presentation from concealment, accurate placement of multiple fast shots, a malfunction remedy, a precise head shot, and an empty gun reload, all under time pressure. It only requires 10 rounds, one target, and a timer or stopwatch to test/measure all of these skills.